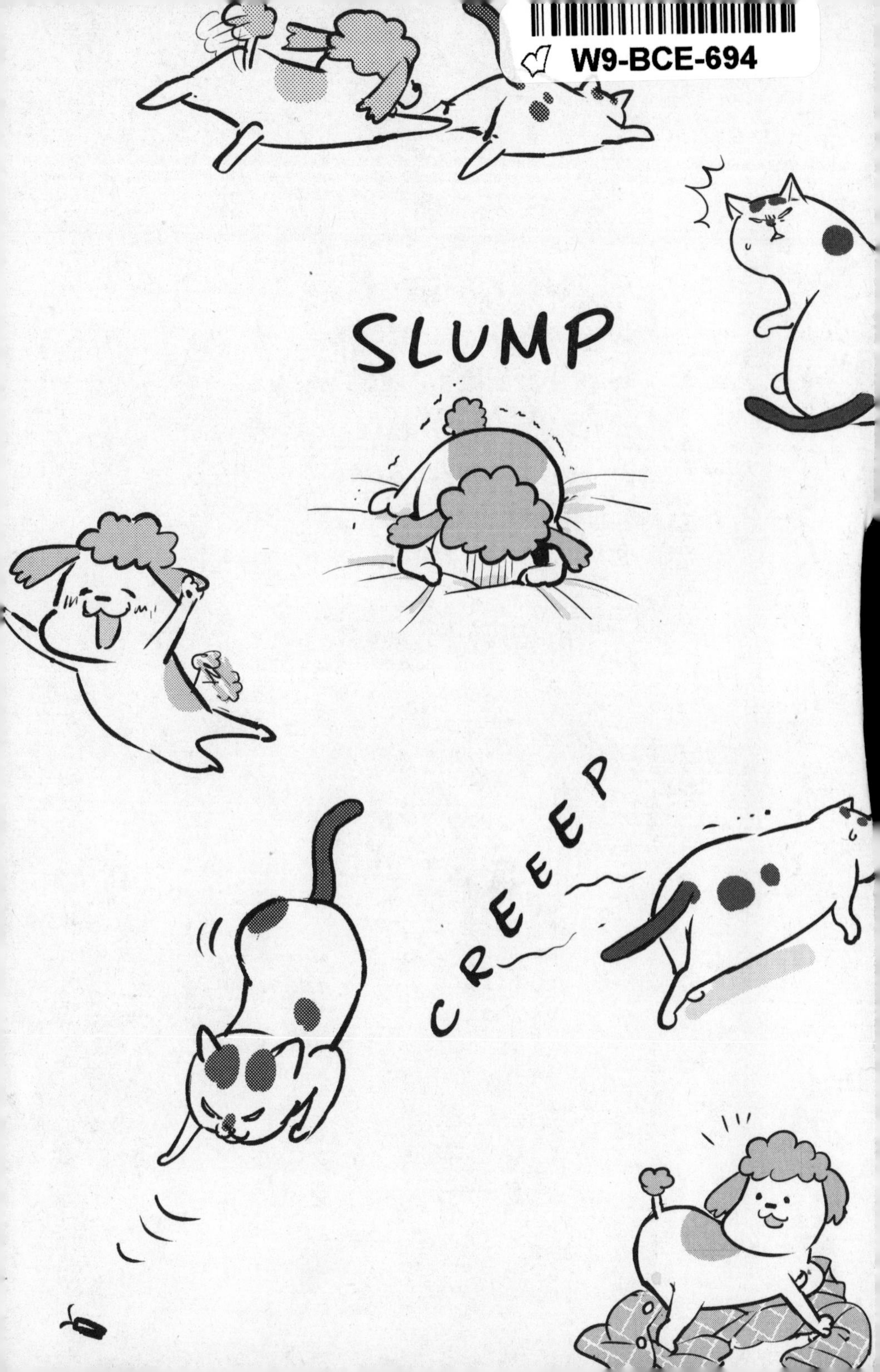
SLUMP
CREEEP

This is Volume 4.
As manga characters,
they have been getting
fatter and fatter,
but the real ones
haven't changed at all.

Hidekichi Matsumoto

With a Dog AND a Cat, Every Day is Fun

4

Hidekichi Matsumoto

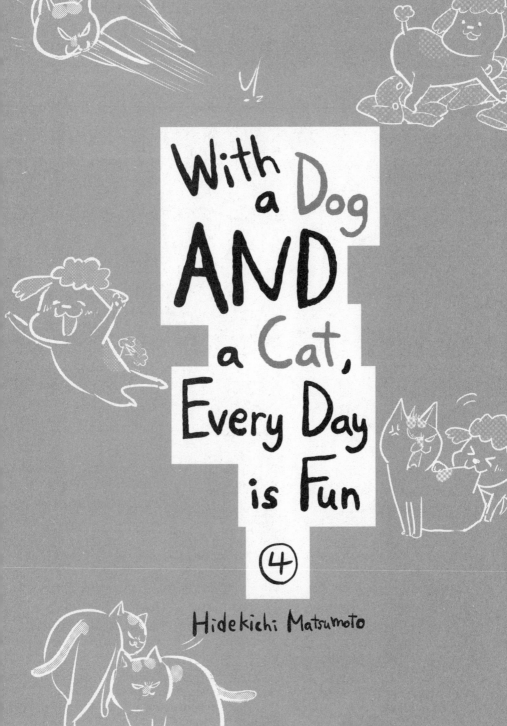

CAST

INU-KUN

Loves Neko. Even when he doesn't like something, if you sing and dance, he soon forgets about it.

NEKO-SAMA

A fearsome face. A cool customer. His passion for theft is staggering.

LEOPA

Nickname: Tokage-chan. A constant object of Neko's gaze. Has none of the cool composure you'd expect from reptiles.

HIDEKICHI MATSUMOTO

Manga artist. Loves animals.

MOM

Hidekichi's mother. Holds the #1 ranking in the Matsumoto household.

DAD

Hidekichi's father. A very kind man.

#97

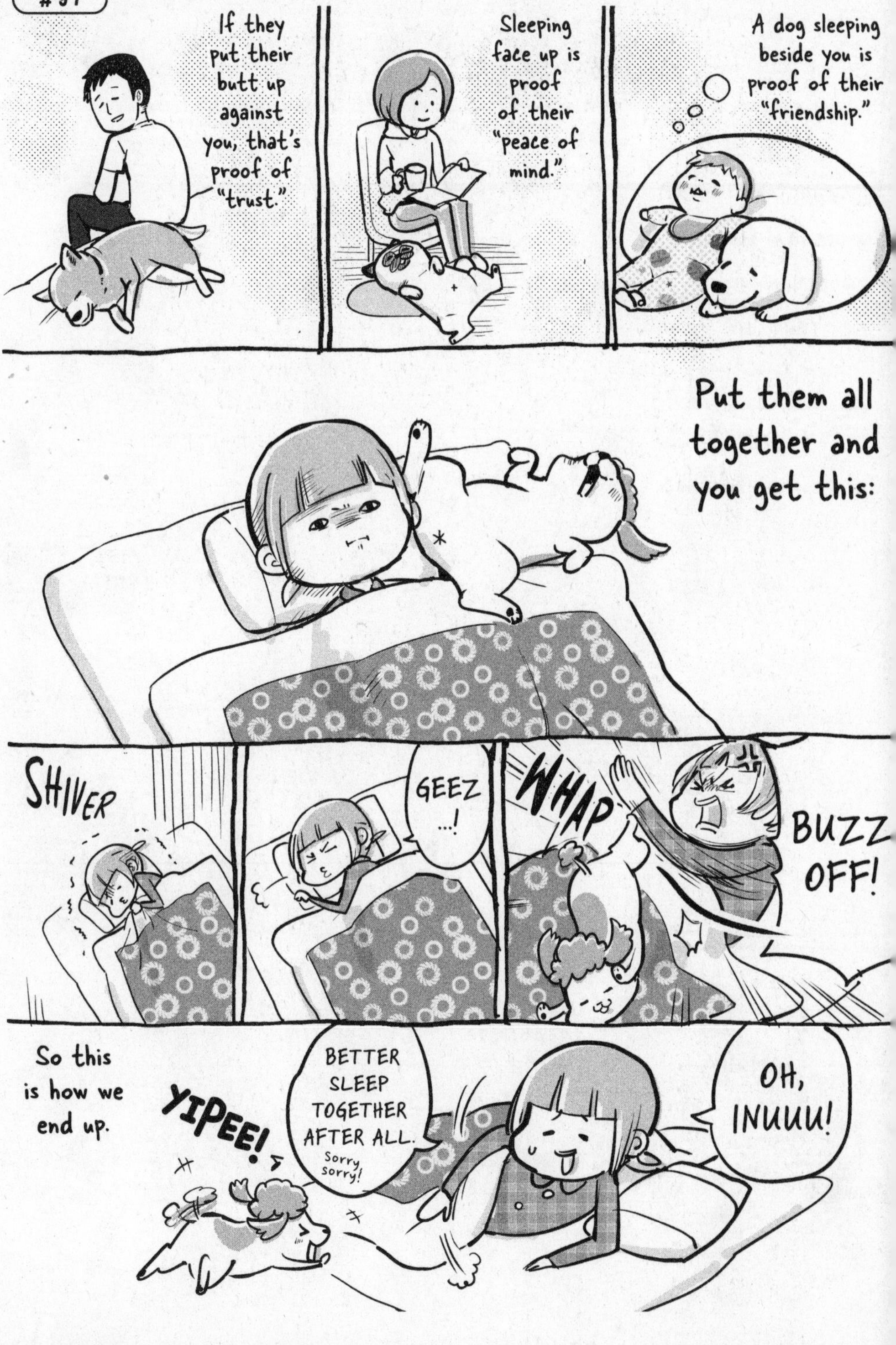
A dog sleeping beside you is proof of their "friendship."
Sleeping face up is proof of their "peace of mind."
If they put their butt up against you, that's proof of "trust."
Put them all together and you get this:
WHAP
BUZZ OFF!
GEEZ ...!
SHIVER
OH, INUUU!
BETTER SLEEP TOGETHER AFTER ALL.
Sorry sorry!
YIPEE!
So this is how we end up.

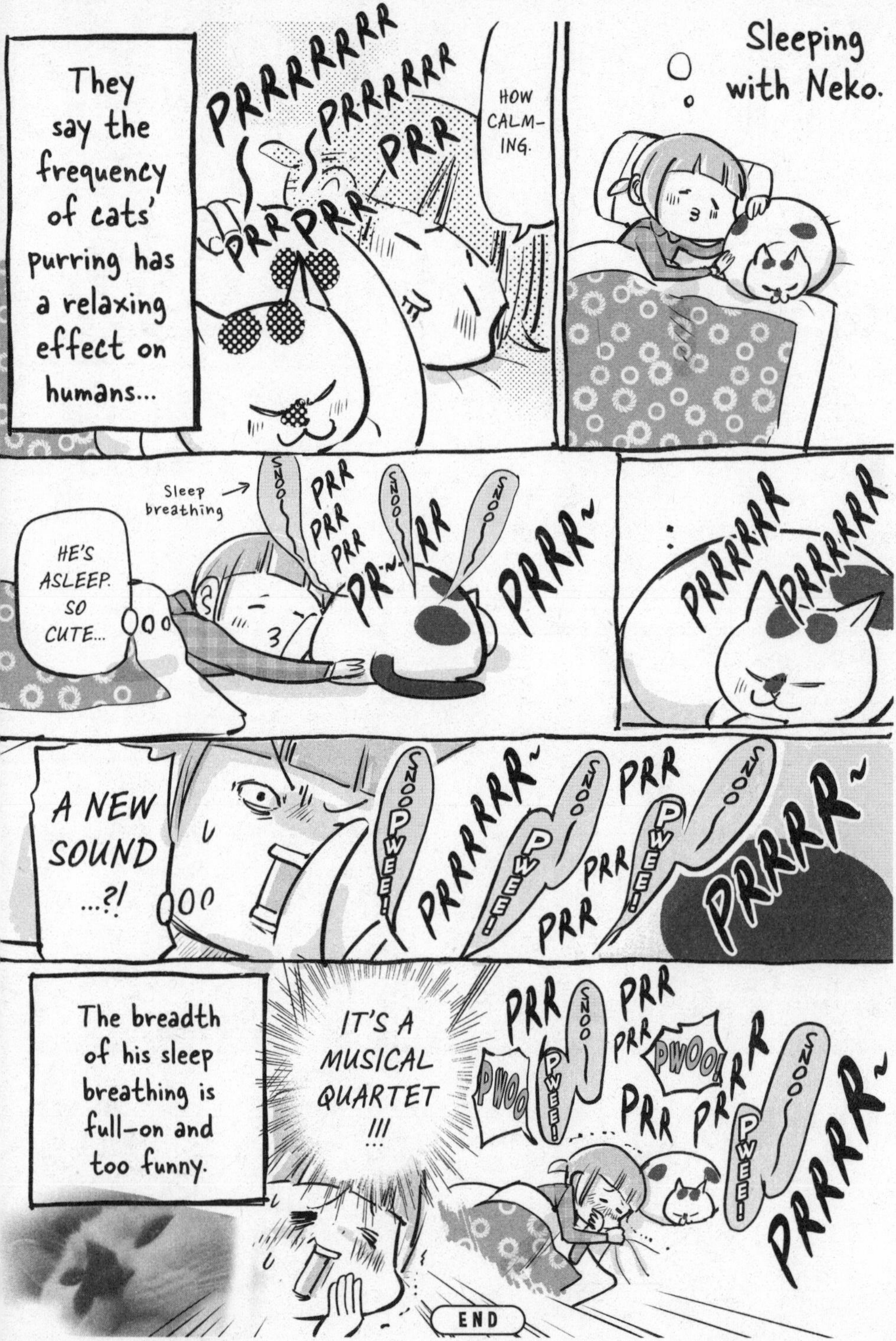

Sleeping with Neko.
HOW CALM-ING.
PRRRRRRR
PRRRRRRR
PRR
PRRPRR
They say the frequency of cats' purring has a relaxing effect on humans...
PRRRRRRR
PRRRRRRR
PRRR~
SNOO
PR~RR
SNOO
PRR PRR PRR
SNOO
Sleep breathing
HE'S ASLEEP. SO CUTE...
PRRRR~
SNOO
PWEE!
PRR
PRR PRR
SNOO
PWEE!
PRRRRRR~
SNOO
PWEE!
A NEW SOUND ...?!
PRRRR~
SNOO
PWEE!
PRRR
PRR PRR
PWOO!
PRR
PRR
SNOO
PWEE!
PWOO
IT'S A MUSICAL QUARTET !!!
The breadth of his sleep breathing is full-on and too funny.
END

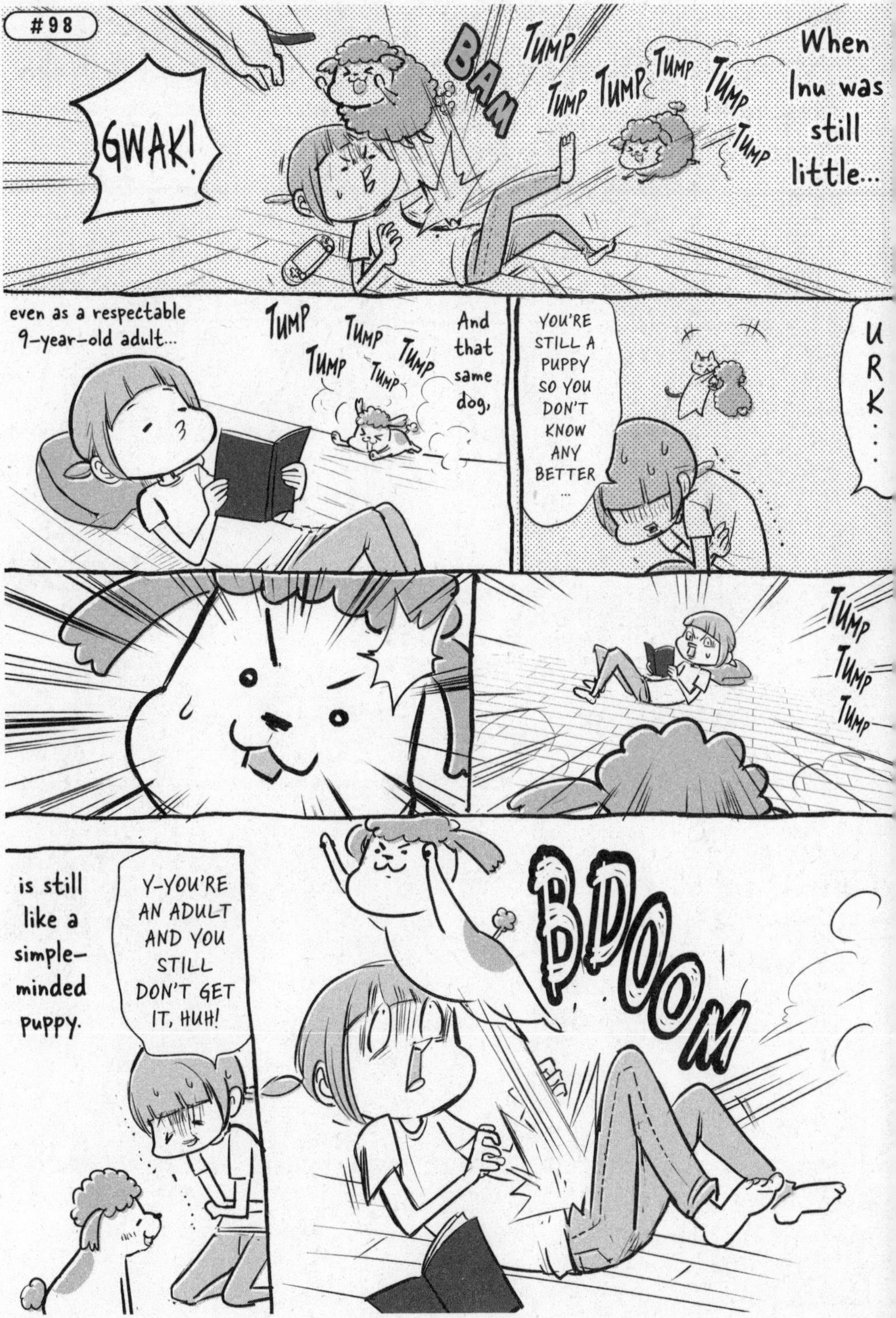
#98
When Inu was still little...
TUMP TUMP TUMP TUMP TUMP TUMP
BAM
GWAK!
URK...
YOU'RE STILL A PUPPY SO YOU DON'T KNOW ANY BETTER ...
And that same dog,
TUMP TUMP TUMP TUMP TUMP
even as a respectable 9-year-old adult...
TUMP TUMP TUMP
BDOOM
Y-YOU'RE AN ADULT AND YOU STILL DON'T GET IT, HUH!
is still like a simple-minded puppy.

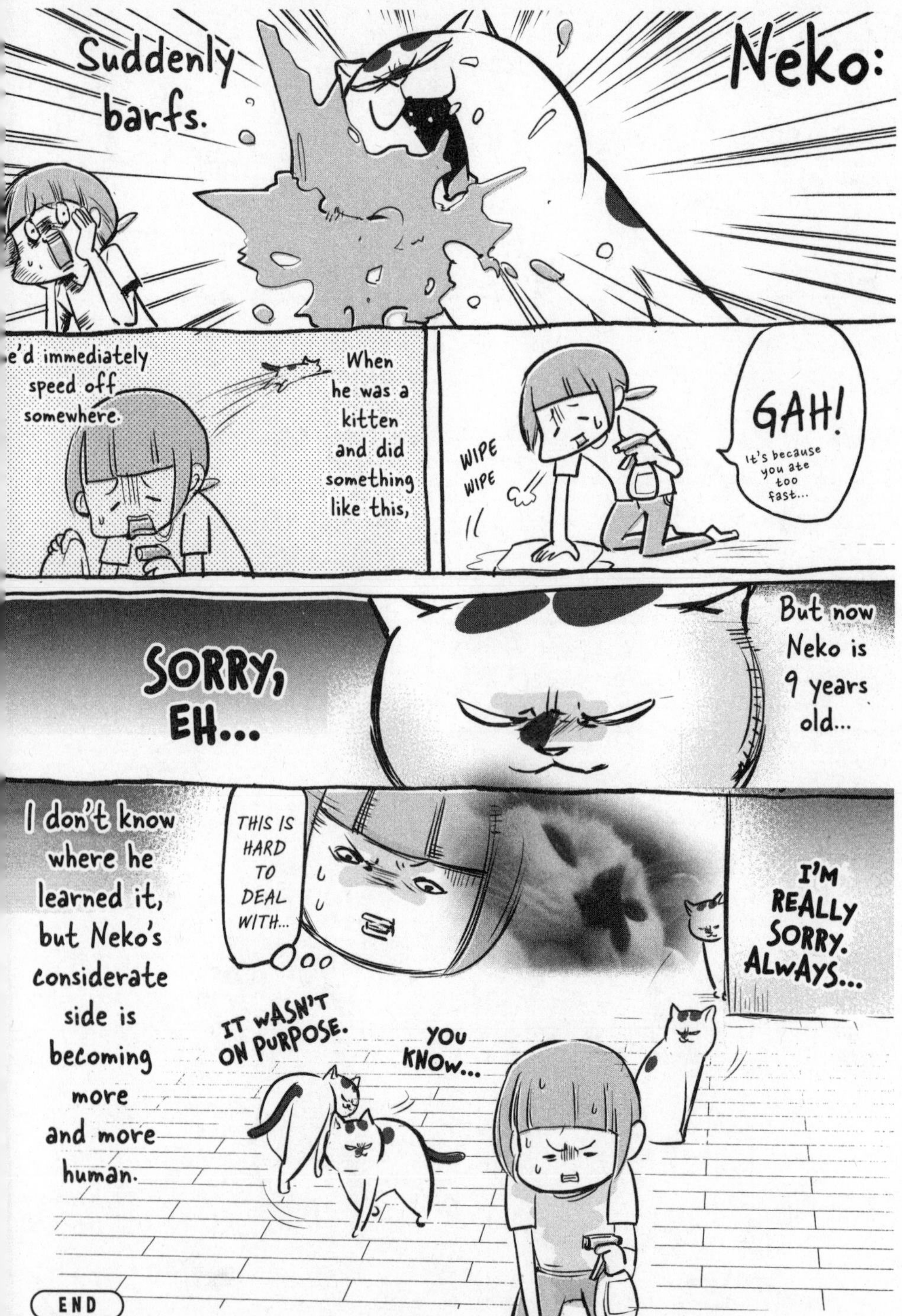
Neko:
Suddenly barfs.
GAH!
It's because you ate too fast...
WIPE WIPE
When he was a kitten and did something like this,
e'd immediately speed off somewhere.
But now Neko is 9 years old...
SORRY, EH...
I'M REALLY SORRY. ALWAYS...
THIS IS HARD TO DEAL WITH...
I don't know where he learned it, but Neko's considerate side is becoming more and more human.
YOU KNOW...
IT WASN'T ON PURPOSE.
END

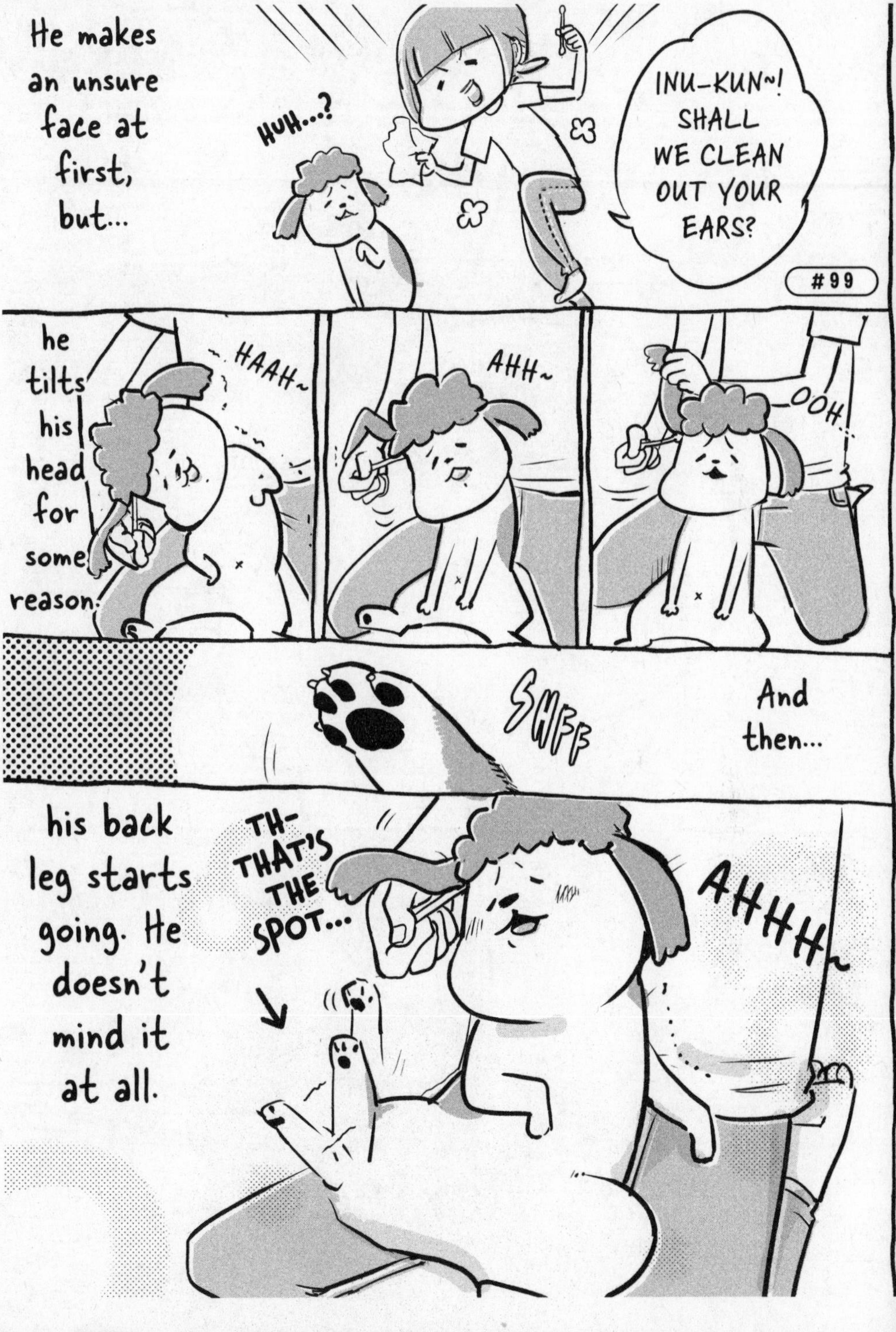
INU-KUN~! SHALL WE CLEAN OUT YOUR EARS?
He makes an unsure face at first, but...
HUH...?
#99
OOH...
AHH~
HAAAH~
he tilts his head for some reason.
And then...
SHFF
AHHHH~
TH- THAT'S THE SPOT...
his back leg starts going. He doesn't mind it at all.

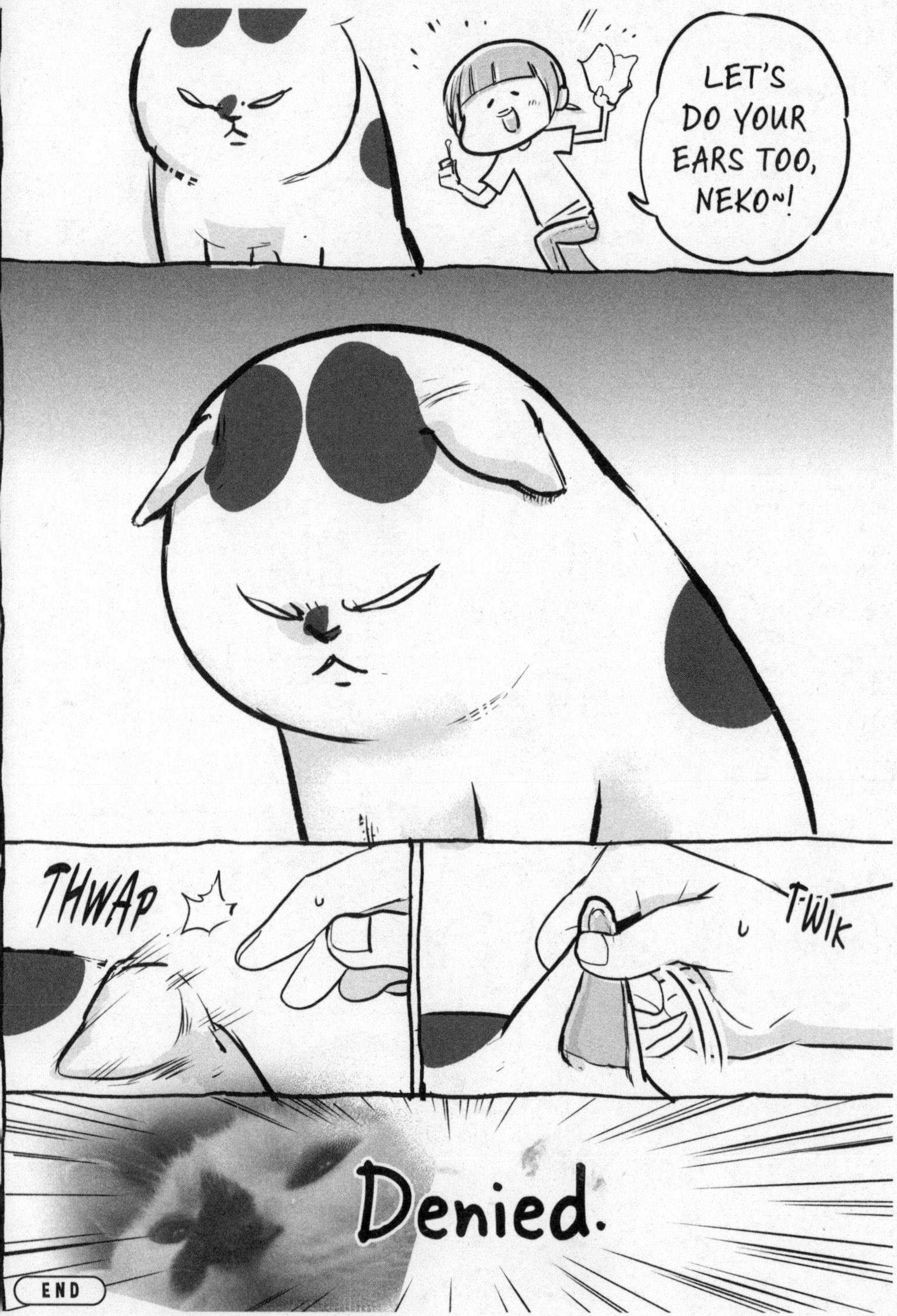
LET'S DO YOUR EARS TOO, NEKO~!
T-WIK
THWAP
Denied.
END

Not particularly angry or anything.

Newly-Drawn 4-Panel Strip

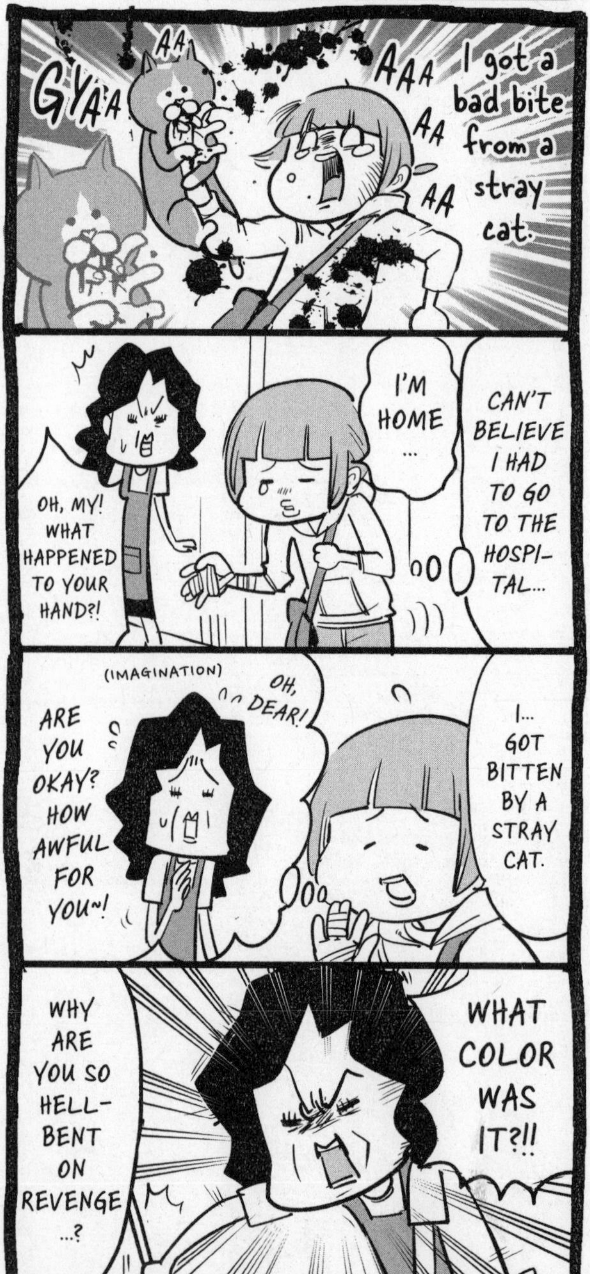
I got a bad bite from a stray cat.
AAA AA AA
AA
GYAAA
CAN'T BELIEVE I HAD TO GO TO THE HOSPITAL...
I'M HOME ...
OH, MY! WHAT HAPPENED TO YOUR HAND?!
I... GOT BITTEN BY A STRAY CAT.
OH, DEAR!
(IMAGINATION)
ARE YOU OKAY? HOW AWFUL FOR YOU~!
WHAT COLOR WAS IT?!!
WHY ARE YOU SO HELL-BENT ON REVENGE ...?

#100

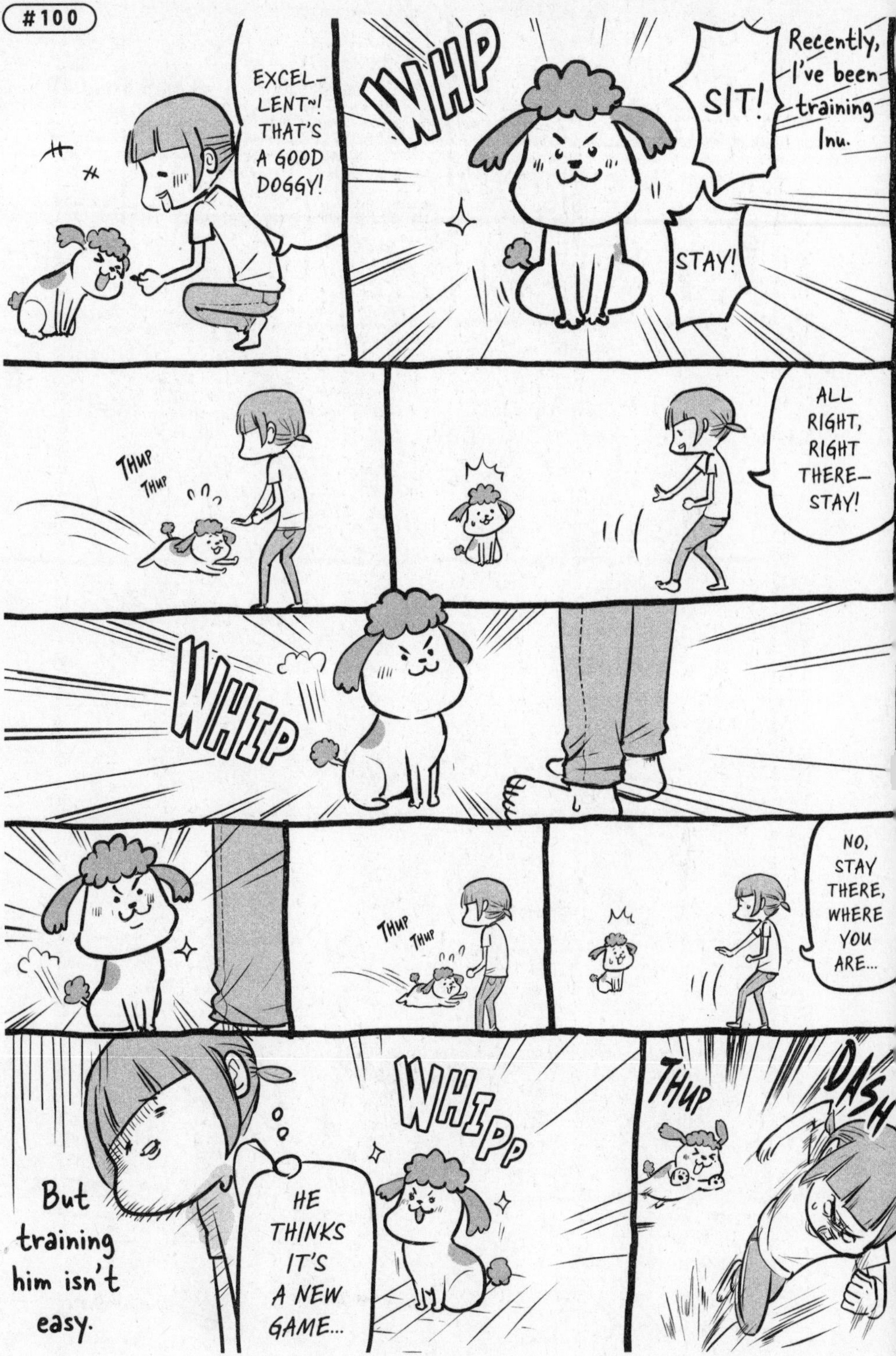
Recently, I've been training Inu.
SIT!
STAY!
WHP
EXCEL-LENT~! THAT'S A GOOD DOGGY!
ALL RIGHT, RIGHT THERE— STAY!
THUP THUP
WHIP
NO, STAY THERE, WHERE YOU ARE...
THUP THUP
THUP
DASH
WHIPP
HE THINKS IT'S A NEW GAME...
But training him isn't easy.

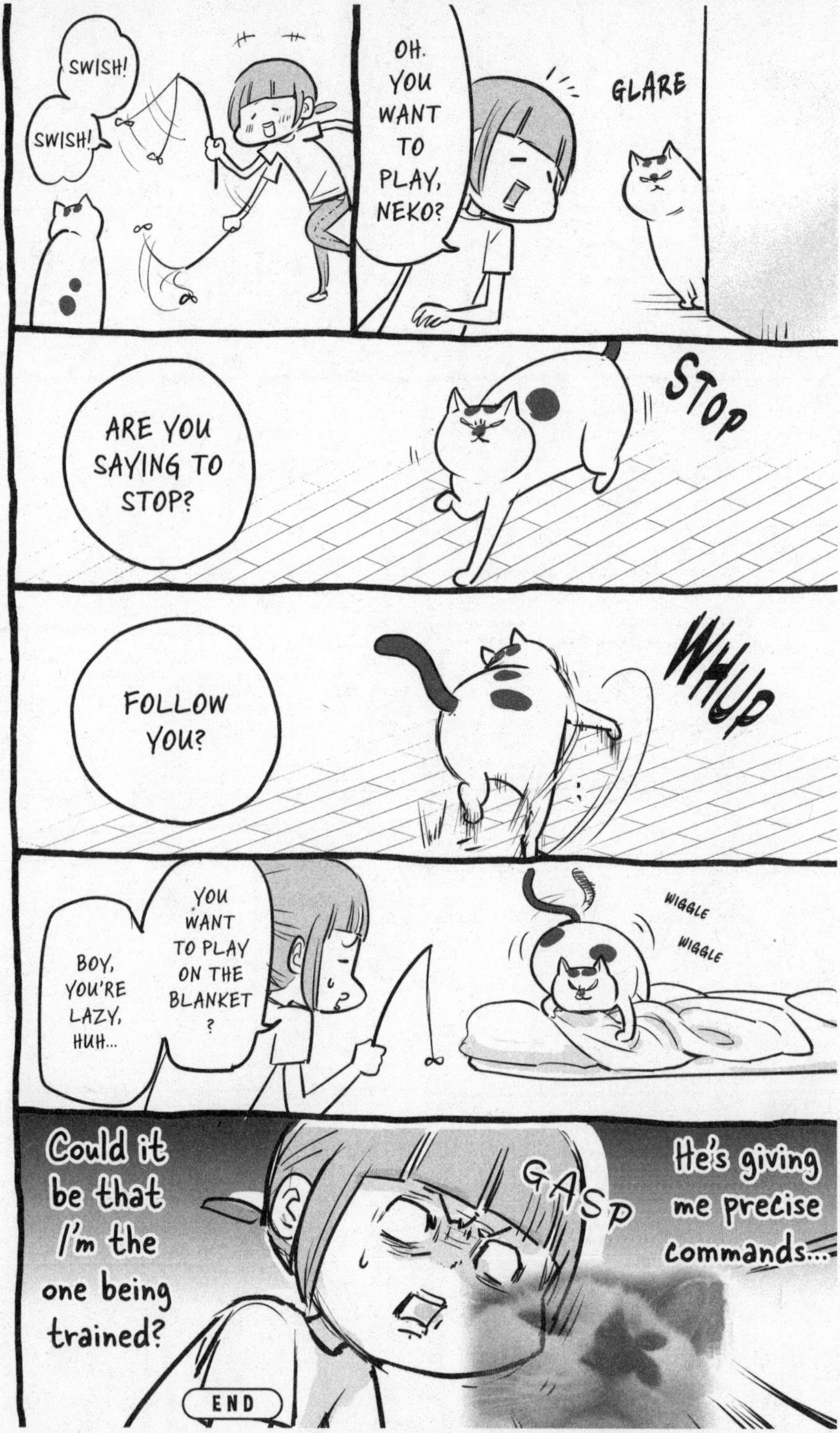

GLARE
OH. YOU WANT TO PLAY, NEKO?
SWISH!
SWISH!
STOP
ARE YOU SAYING TO STOP?
WHUP
FOLLOW YOU?
WIGGLE
WIGGLE
YOU WANT TO PLAY ON THE BLANKET?
BOY, YOU'RE LAZY, HUH...
He's giving me precise commands...
GASP
Could it be that I'm the one being trained?
END

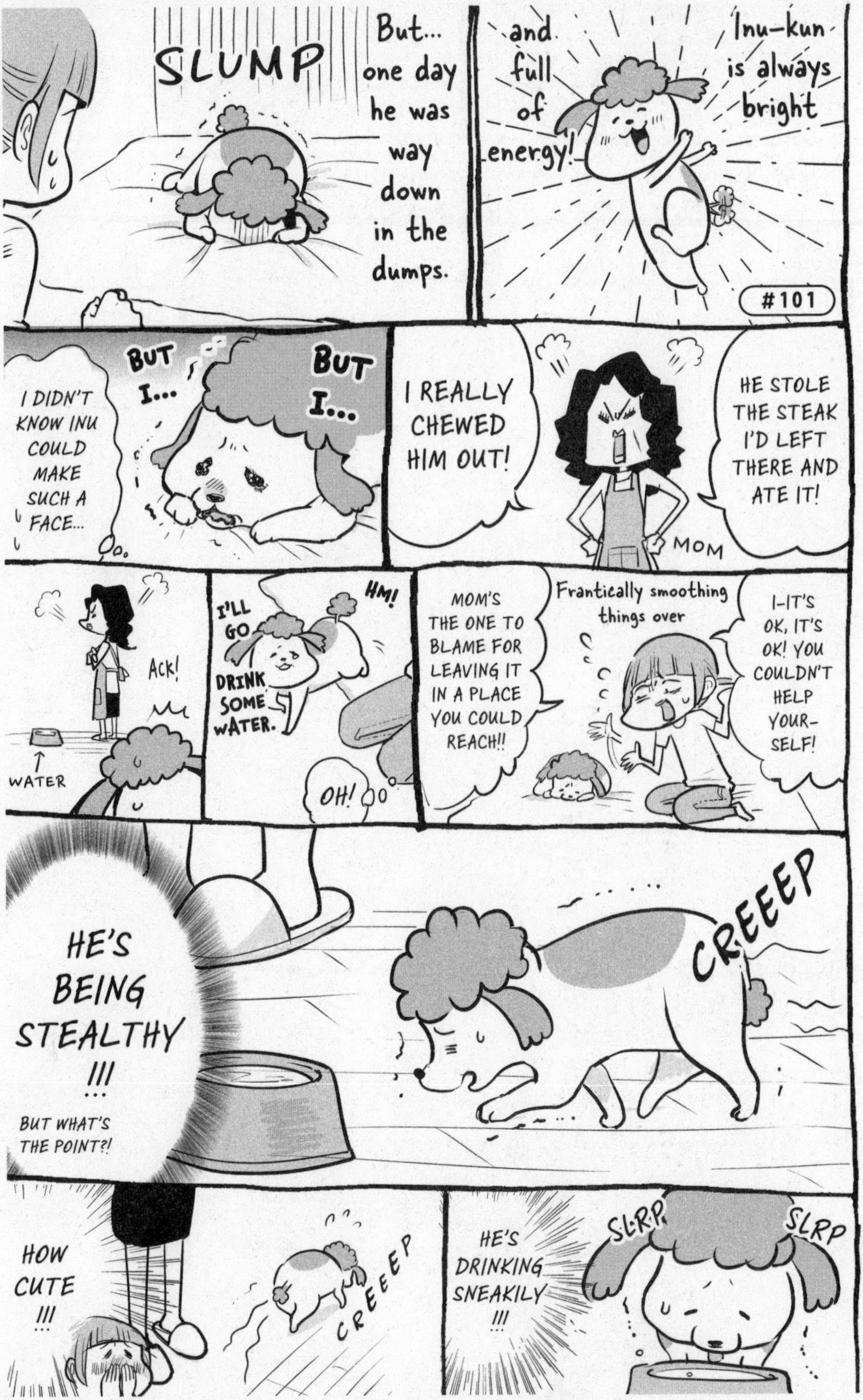
Inu-kun is always bright
and full of energy!
#101
But... one day he was way down in the dumps.
SLUMP
HE STOLE THE STEAK I'D LEFT THERE AND ATE IT!
I REALLY CHEWED HIM OUT!
MOM
BUT I...
BUT I...
I DIDN'T KNOW INU COULD MAKE SUCH A FACE...
I-IT'S OK, IT'S OK! YOU COULDN'T HELP YOUR-SELF!
Frantically smoothing things over
MOM'S THE ONE TO BLAME FOR LEAVING IT IN A PLACE YOU COULD REACH!!
HM!
I'LL GO DRINK SOME WATER.
OH!
ACK!
WATER
CREEEP
HE'S BEING STEALTHY!!!
...
BUT WHAT'S THE POINT?!
SLRP
SLRP
HE'S DRINKING SNEAKILY!!!
CREEEP
HOW CUTE!!!

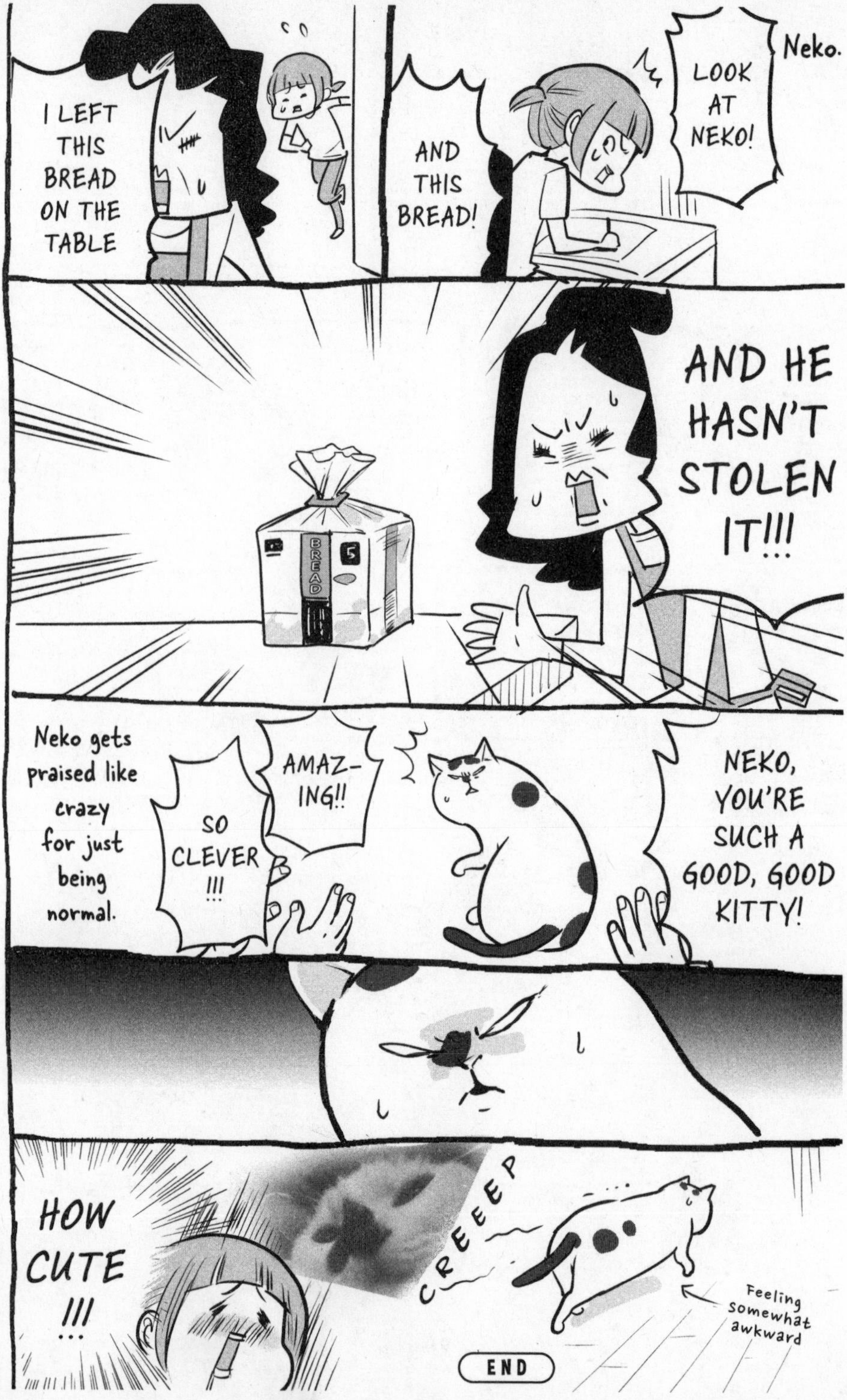

Neko.
LOOK AT NEKO!
AND THIS BREAD!
I LEFT THIS BREAD ON THE TABLE
AND HE HASN'T STOLEN IT!!!...
BREAD
5
NEKO, YOU'RE SUCH A GOOD, GOOD KITTY!
AMAZ-ING!!
SO CLEVER!!!
Neko gets praised like crazy for just being normal.
Feeling somewhat awkward
CREEEP
HOW CUTE!!!...
END

#102

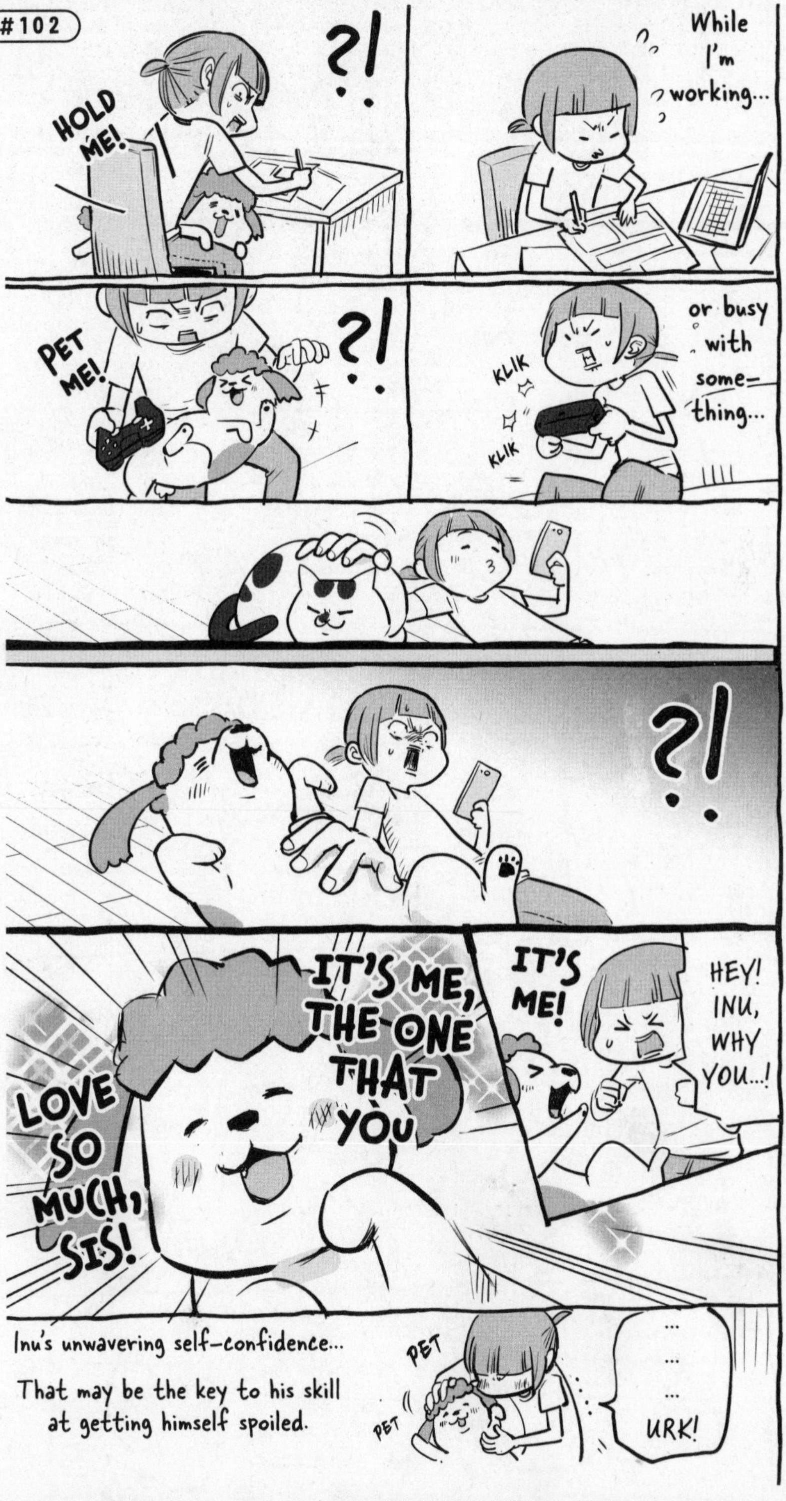
While I'm working...
?!
HOLD ME!
or busy with some-thing...
KLIK
KLIK
?!
PET ME!
?!
HEY! INU, WHY YOU...!
IT'S ME!
IT'S ME, THE ONE THAT YOU LOVE SO MUCH, SIS!
... ...
URK!
PET
PET
Inu's unwavering self-confidence...
That may be the key to his skill at getting himself spoiled.

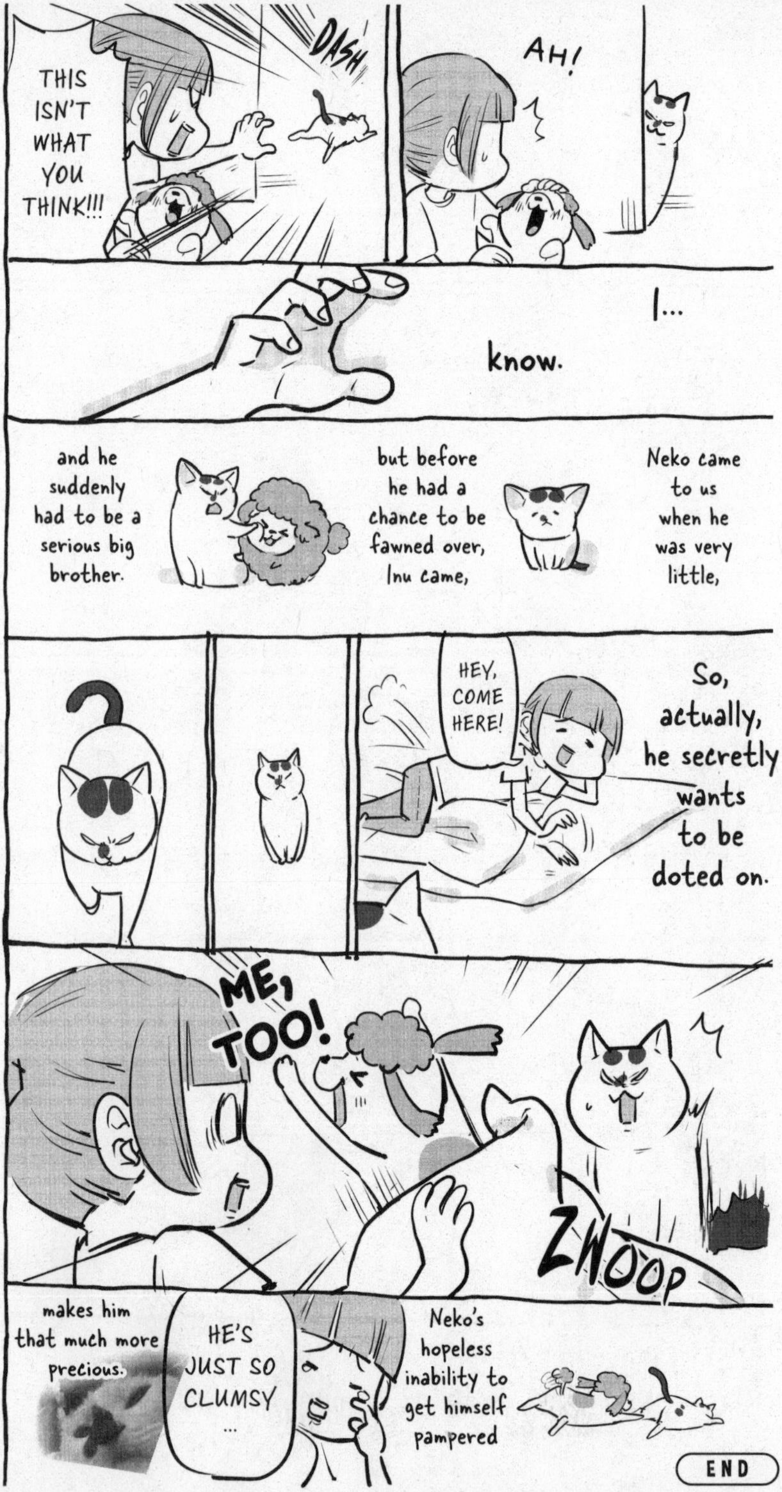
AH!
DASH
THIS ISN'T WHAT YOU THINK!!!
I...
know.
Neko came to us when he was very little,
but before he had a chance to be fawned over, Inu came,
and he suddenly had to be a serious big brother.
So, actually, he secretly wants to be doted on.
HEY, COME HERE!
ME, TOO!
ZWOOP
Neko's hopeless inability to get himself pampered
HE'S JUST SO CLUMSY ...
makes him that much more precious.
END

Smooch!

More About #102

I make sure to make some time that's just for the two of us and fawn over him.

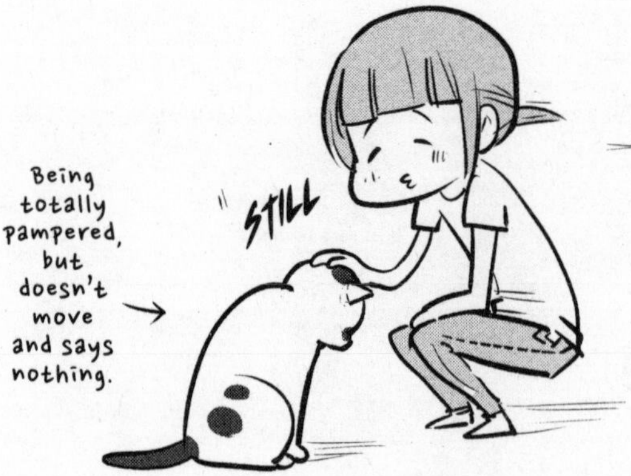
STILL
Being totally pampered, but doesn't move and says nothing.

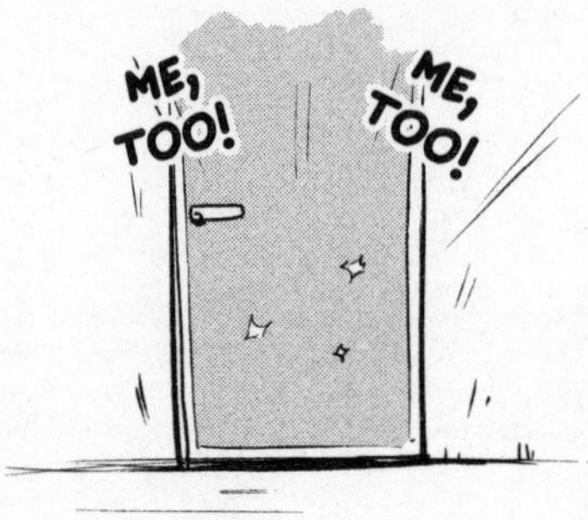
ME, TOO!
ME, TOO!

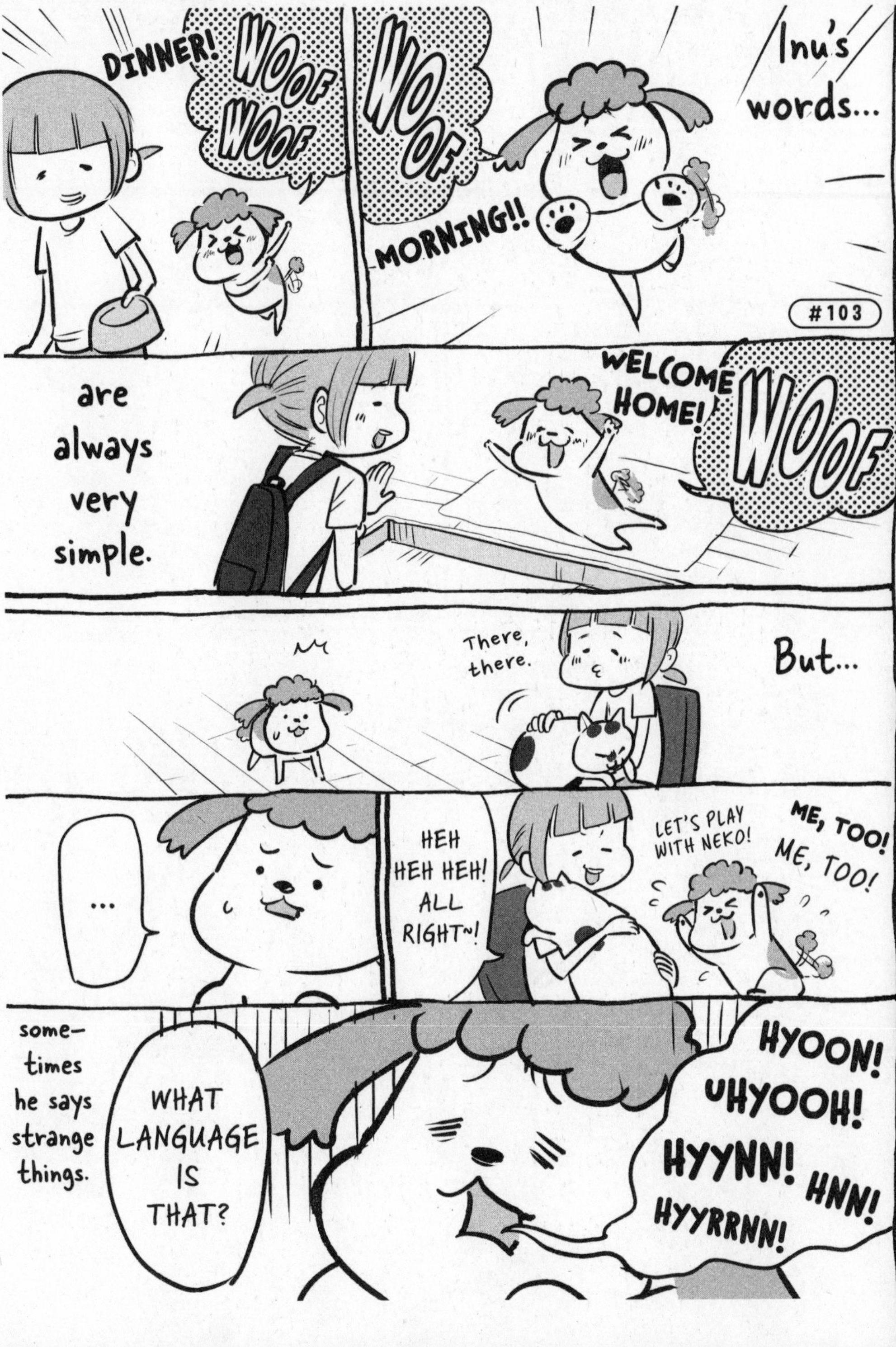
#103
Inu's words...
WOOF
MORNING!!
WOOF WOOF
DINNER!
WOOF
WELCOME HOME!
are always very simple.
But...
There, there.
ME, TOO! ME, TOO!
LET'S PLAY WITH NEKO!
HEH HEH HEH! ALL RIGHT~!
...
HYOON! UHYOOH! HYYNN! HNN! HYYRRNN!
WHAT LANGUAGE IS THAT?
some-times he says strange things.

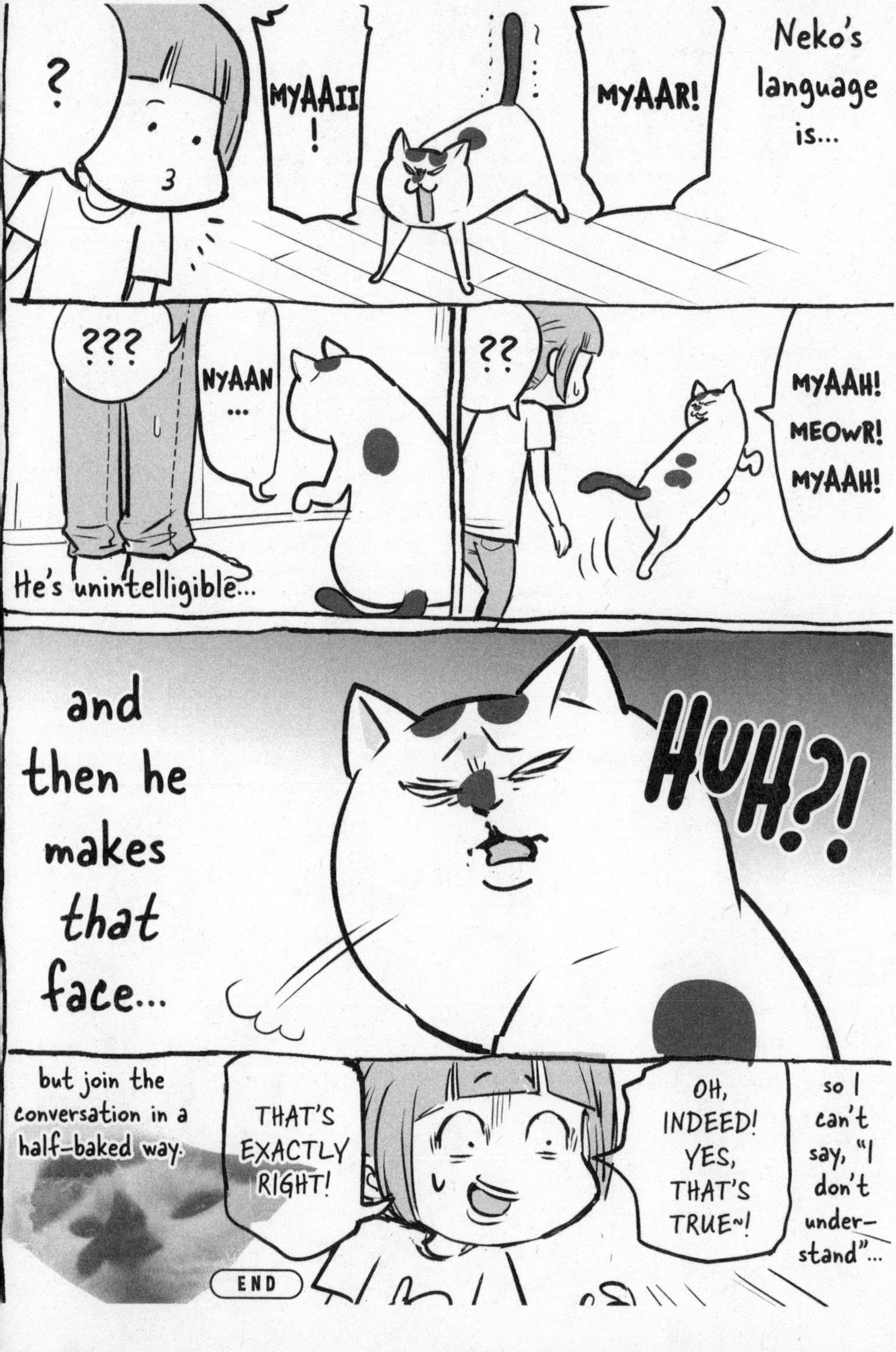

Neko's language is...
MYAAR!
MYAAII !
?
MYAAH! MEOWR! MYAAH!
??
NYAAN ...
???
He's unintelligible...
HUH?!
and then he makes *that* face...
so I can't say, "I don't under-stand"...
OH, INDEED! YES, THAT'S TRUE~!
THAT'S EXACTLY RIGHT!
but join the conversation in a half-baked way.
END

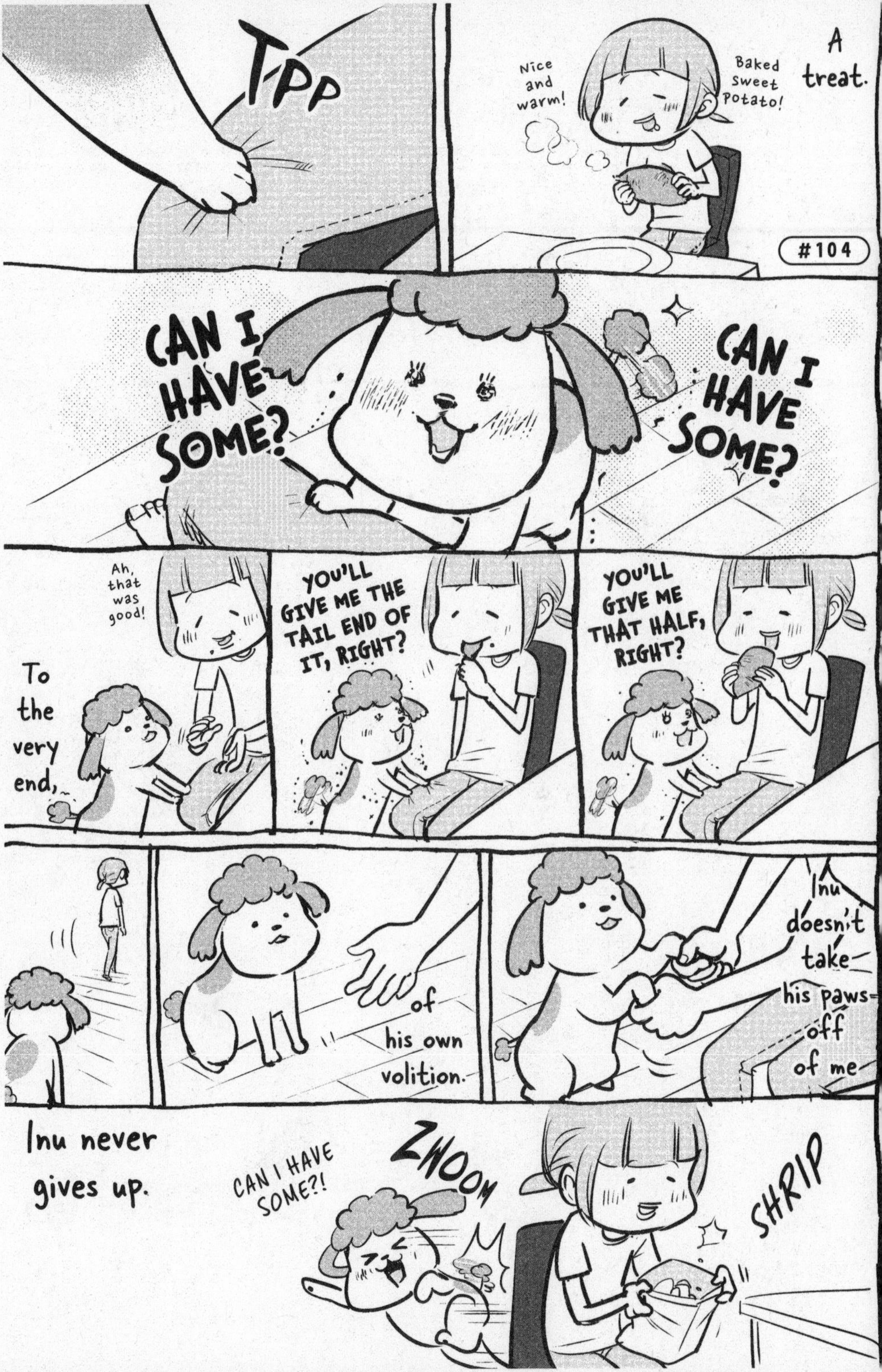
A treat.
#104
Baked Sweet Potato!
Nice and warm!
TPP
CAN I HAVE SOME?
CAN I HAVE SOME?
YOU'LL GIVE ME THAT HALF, RIGHT?
YOU'LL GIVE ME THE TAIL END OF IT, RIGHT?
Ah, that was good!
To the very end,
Inu doesn't take his paws off of me
of his own volition.
SHRIP
ZWOOM
CAN I HAVE SOME?!
Inu never gives up.

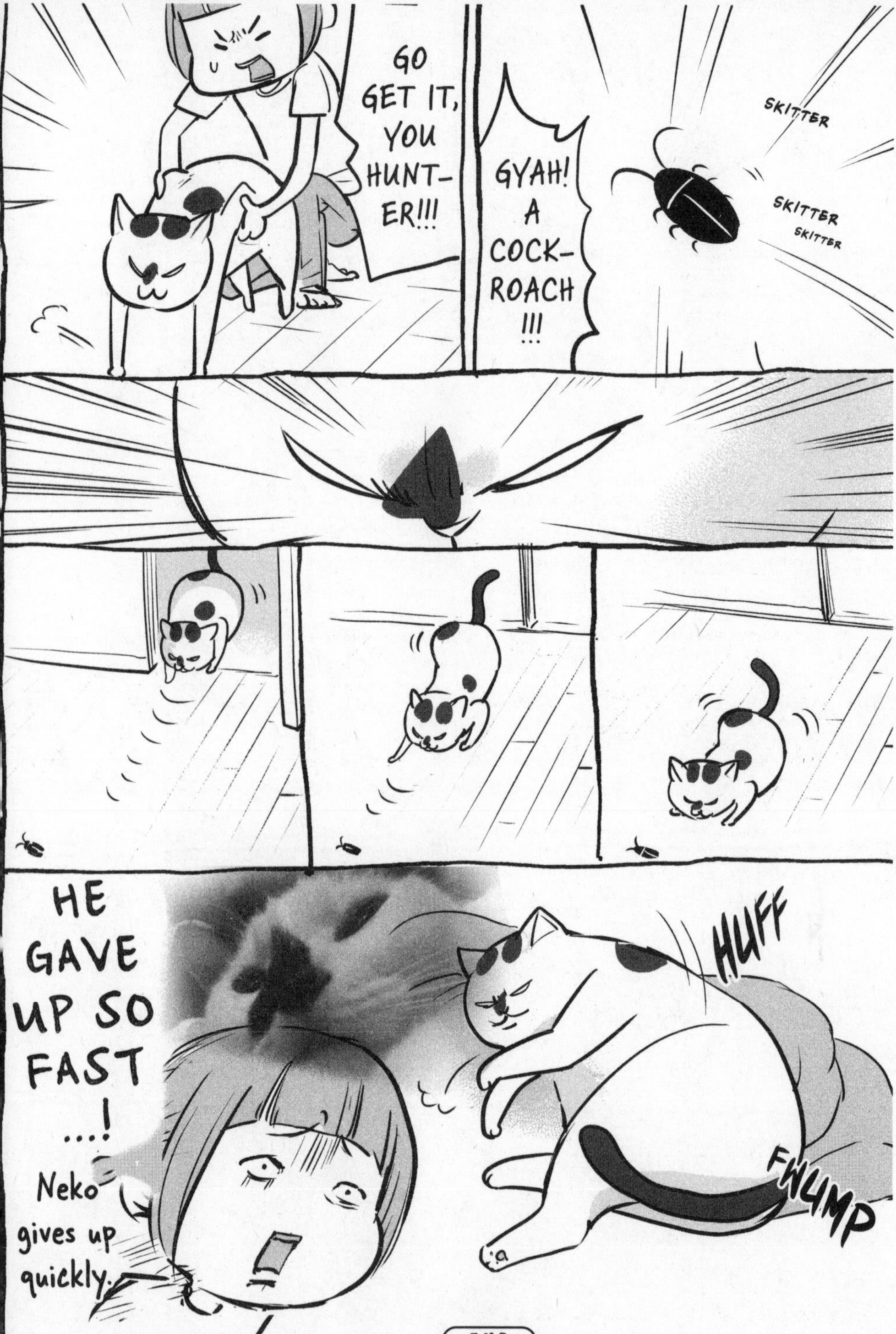
SKITTER
SKITTER
SKITTER
GYAH! A COCKROACH!!!
GO GET IT, YOU HUNTER!!!
HUFF
HE GAVE UP SO FAST...!
FWUMP
Neko gives up quickly.
END

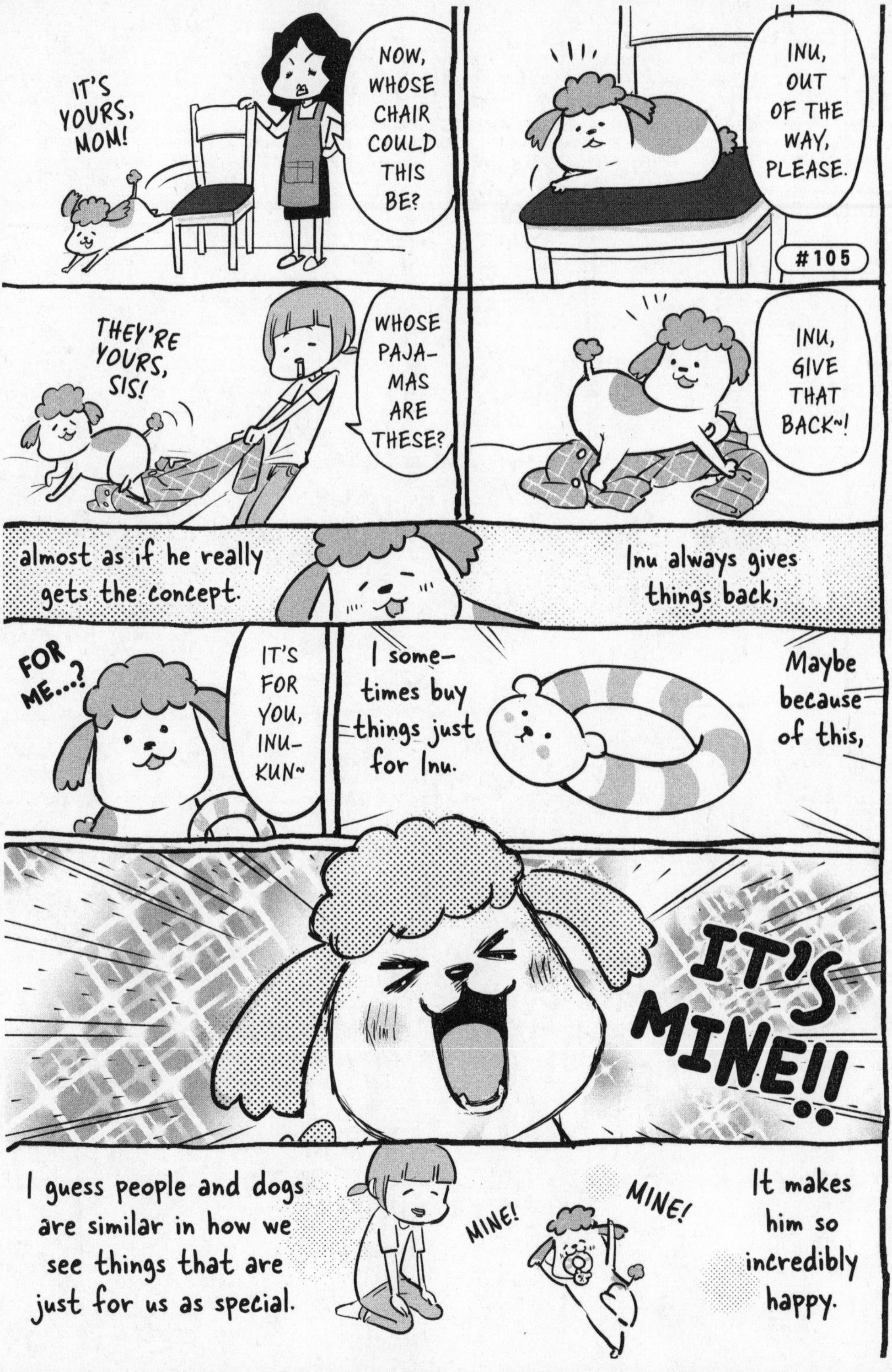
#105
INU, OUT OF THE WAY, PLEASE.
NOW, WHOSE CHAIR COULD THIS BE?
IT'S YOURS, MOM!
INU, GIVE THAT BACK~!
WHOSE PAJAMAS ARE THESE?
THEY'RE YOURS, SIS!
Inu always gives things back,
almost as if he really gets the concept.
Maybe because of this,
I sometimes buy things just for Inu.
IT'S FOR YOU, INU-KUN~
FOR ME...?
IT'S MINE!!
It makes him so incredibly happy.
MINE!
MINE!
I guess people and dogs are similar in how we see things that are just for us as special.

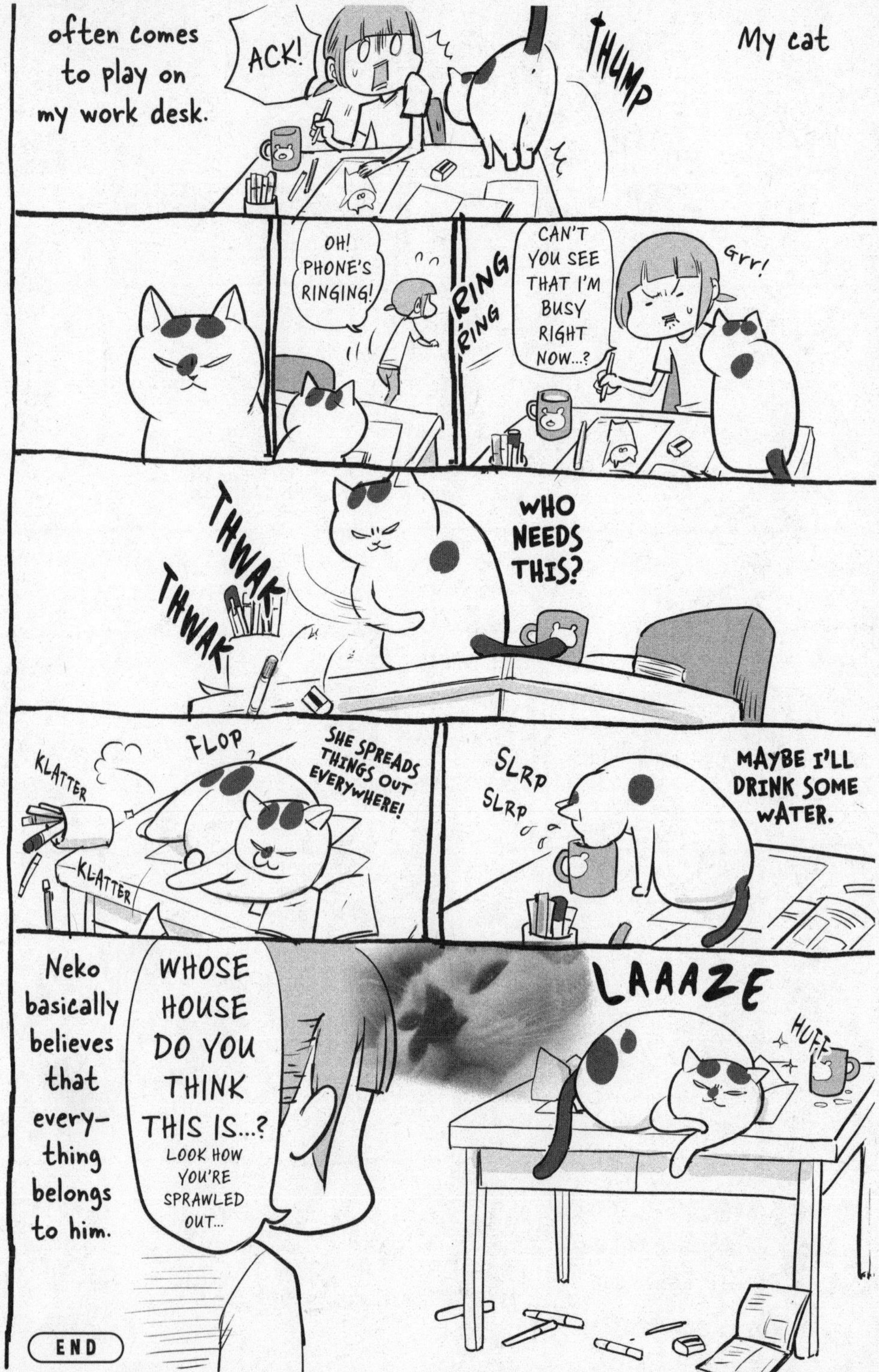
My cat
THUMP
ACK!
often comes to play on my work desk.
Grr!
CAN'T YOU SEE THAT I'M BUSY RIGHT NOW...?
RING RING
OH! PHONE'S RINGING!
WHO NEEDS THIS?
THWAK THWAK
MAYBE I'LL DRINK SOME WATER.
SLRP SLRP
SHE SPREADS THINGS OUT EVERYWHERE!
FLOP
KLATTER
KLATTER
LAAAZE
HUFF
WHOSE HOUSE DO YOU THINK THIS IS...?
LOOK HOW YOU'RE SPRAWLED OUT...
Neko basically believes that every-thing belongs to him.
END

It's a plush toy of me!

Newly-Drawn 4-Panel Strip

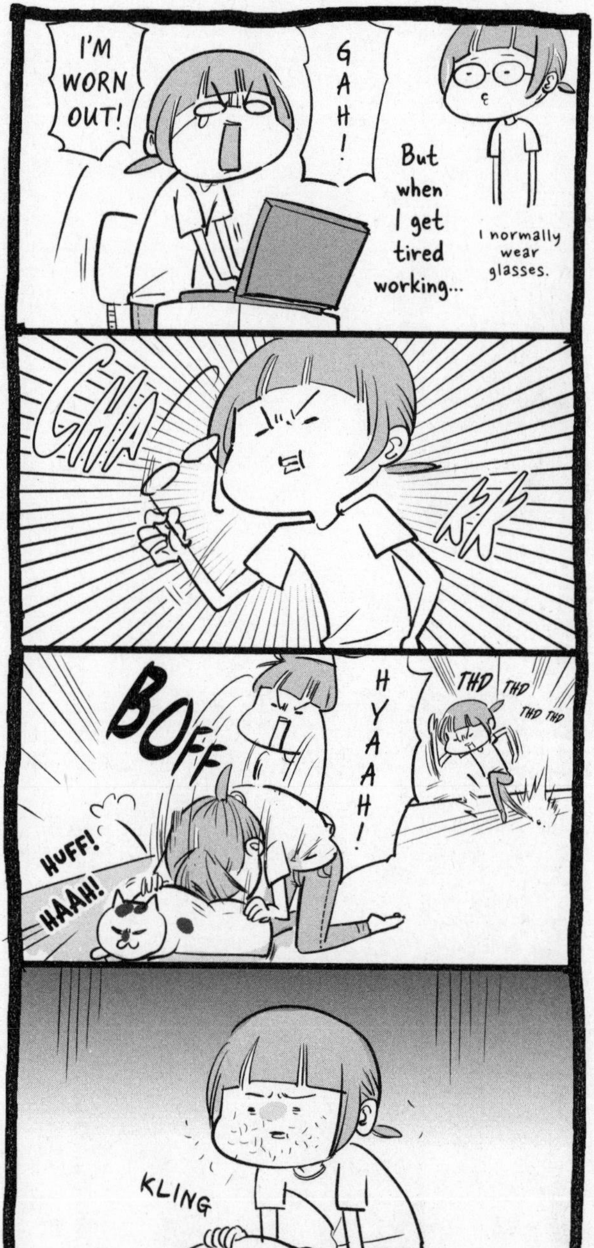
I normally wear glasses.
But when I get tired working...
GAH!
I'M WORN OUT!
CHA
KK
THD THD THD THD
HYAAAH!
BOFF
HUFF!
HAAH!
KLING

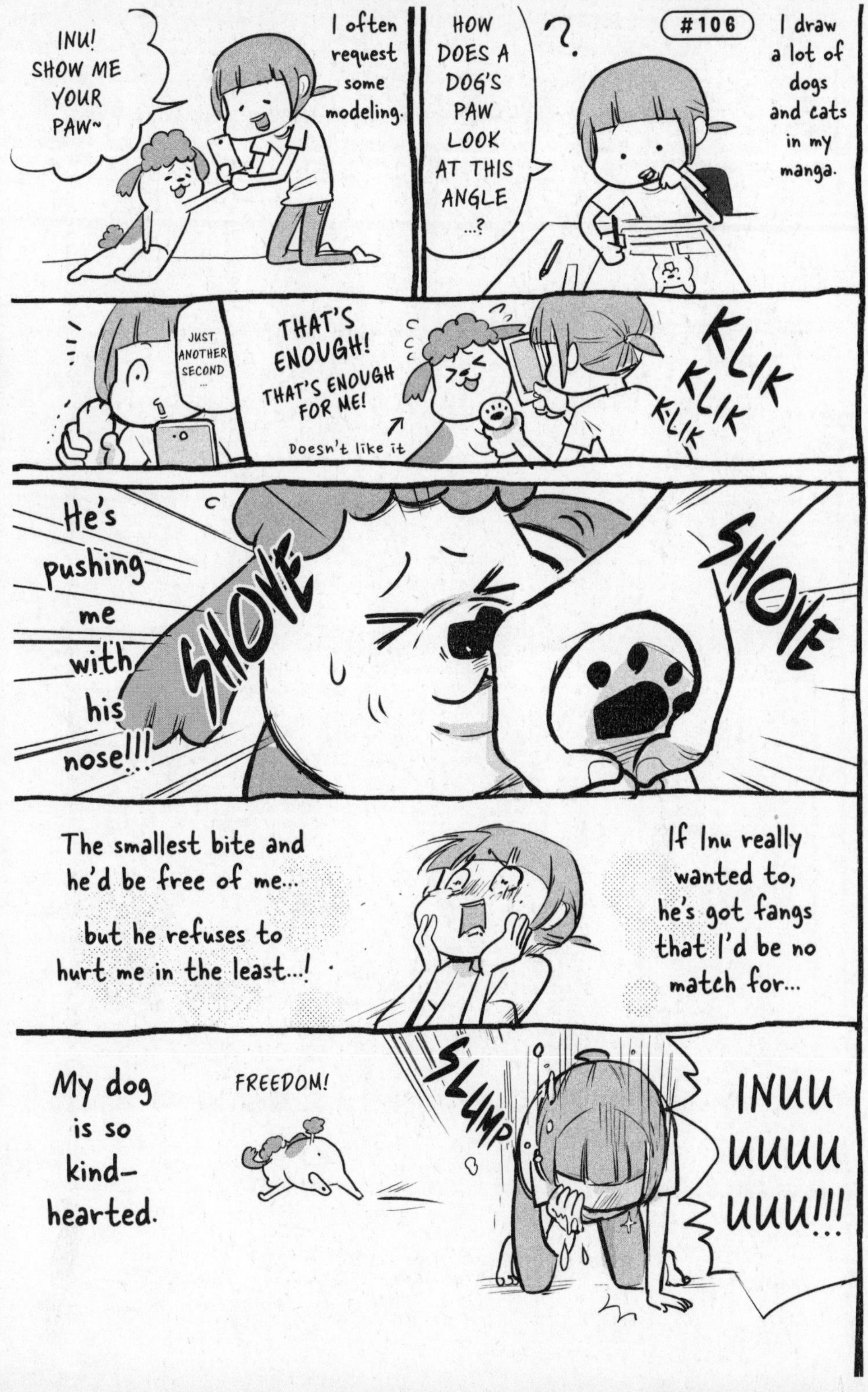
#106
I draw a lot of dogs and cats in my manga.
?
HOW DOES A DOG'S PAW LOOK AT THIS ANGLE ...?
I often request some modeling.
INU! SHOW ME YOUR PAW~
KLIK KLIK KLIK
THAT'S ENOUGH!
THAT'S ENOUGH FOR ME!
Doesn't like it
JUST ANOTHER SECOND ...
SHOVE
SHOVE
He's pushing me with his nose!!!...
If Inu really wanted to, he's got fangs that I'd be no match for...
The smallest bite and he'd be free of me...
but he refuses to hurt me in the least...!
INUU UUUU UUU!!!...
SLUMP
FREEDOM!
My dog is so kind-hearted.

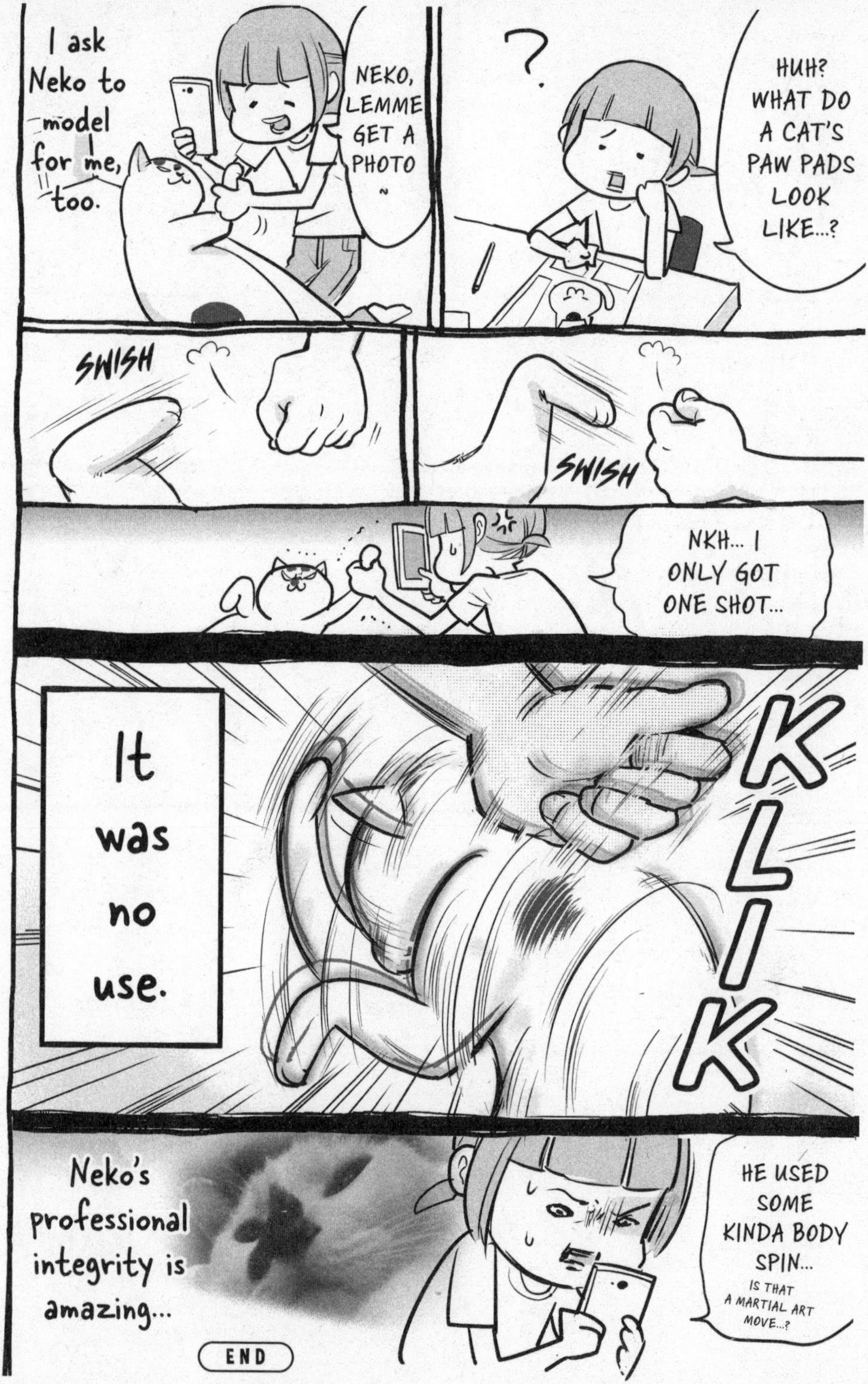
?
HUH? WHAT DO A CAT'S PAW PADS LOOK LIKE...?
NEKO, LEMME GET A PHOTO ~
I ask Neko to model for me, too.
SWISH
SWISH
NKH... I ONLY GOT ONE SHOT...
KLIK
It was no use.
HE USED SOME KINDA BODY SPIN...
IS THAT A MARTIAL ART MOVE...?
Neko's professional integrity is amazing...
END

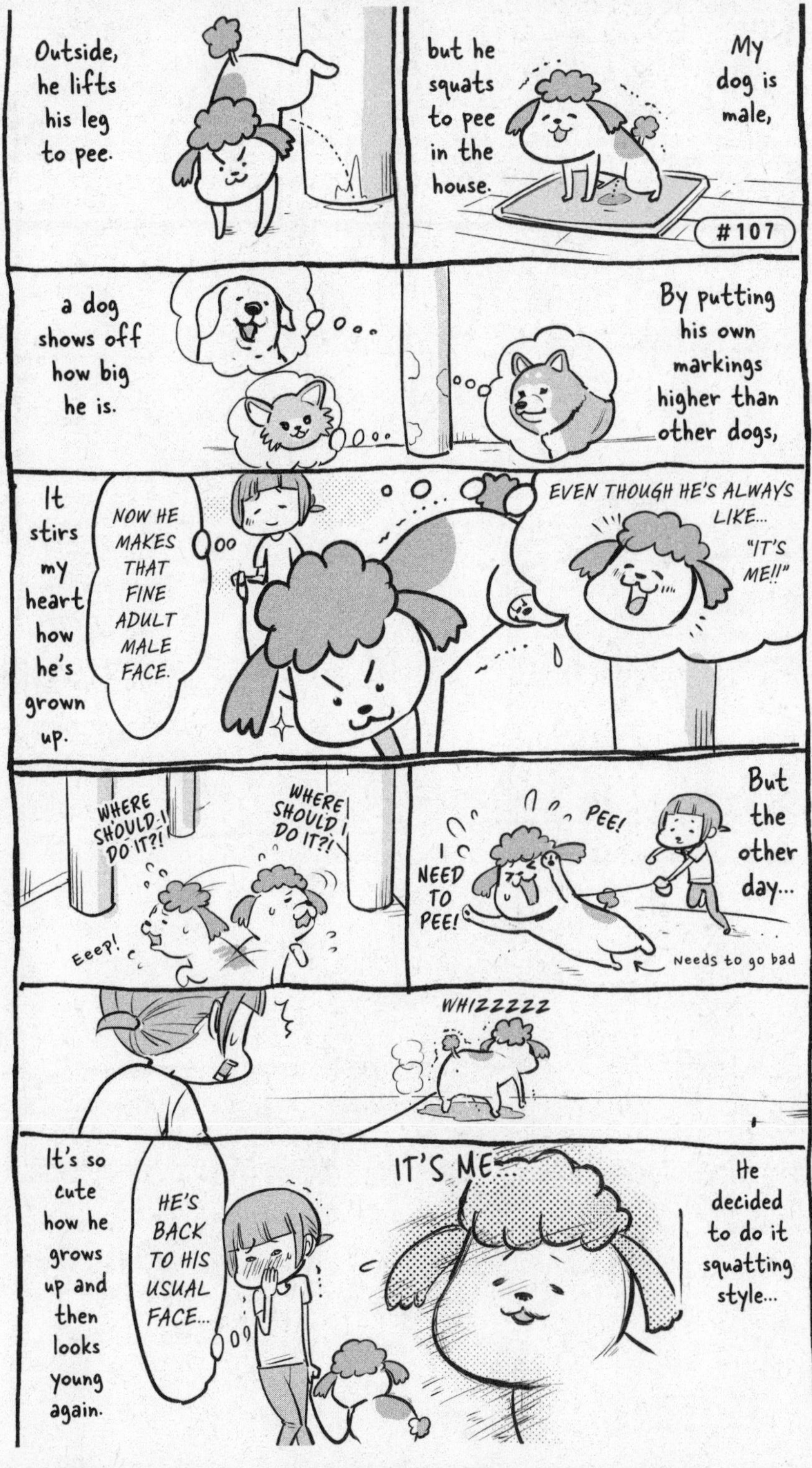
My dog is male,
but he squats to pee in the house.
#107
Outside, he lifts his leg to pee.
By putting his own markings higher than other dogs,
a dog shows off how big he is.
EVEN THOUGH HE'S ALWAYS LIKE...
"IT'S ME!!"
NOW HE MAKES THAT FINE ADULT MALE FACE.
It stirs my heart how he's grown up.
But the other day...
PEE!
I NEED TO PEE!
Needs to go bad
WHERE SHOULD I DO IT?!
WHERE SHOULD I DO IT?!
Eeep!
WHIZZZZZ
He decided to do it squatting style...
IT'S ME...
HE'S BACK TO HIS USUAL FACE...
It's so cute how he grows up and then looks young again.

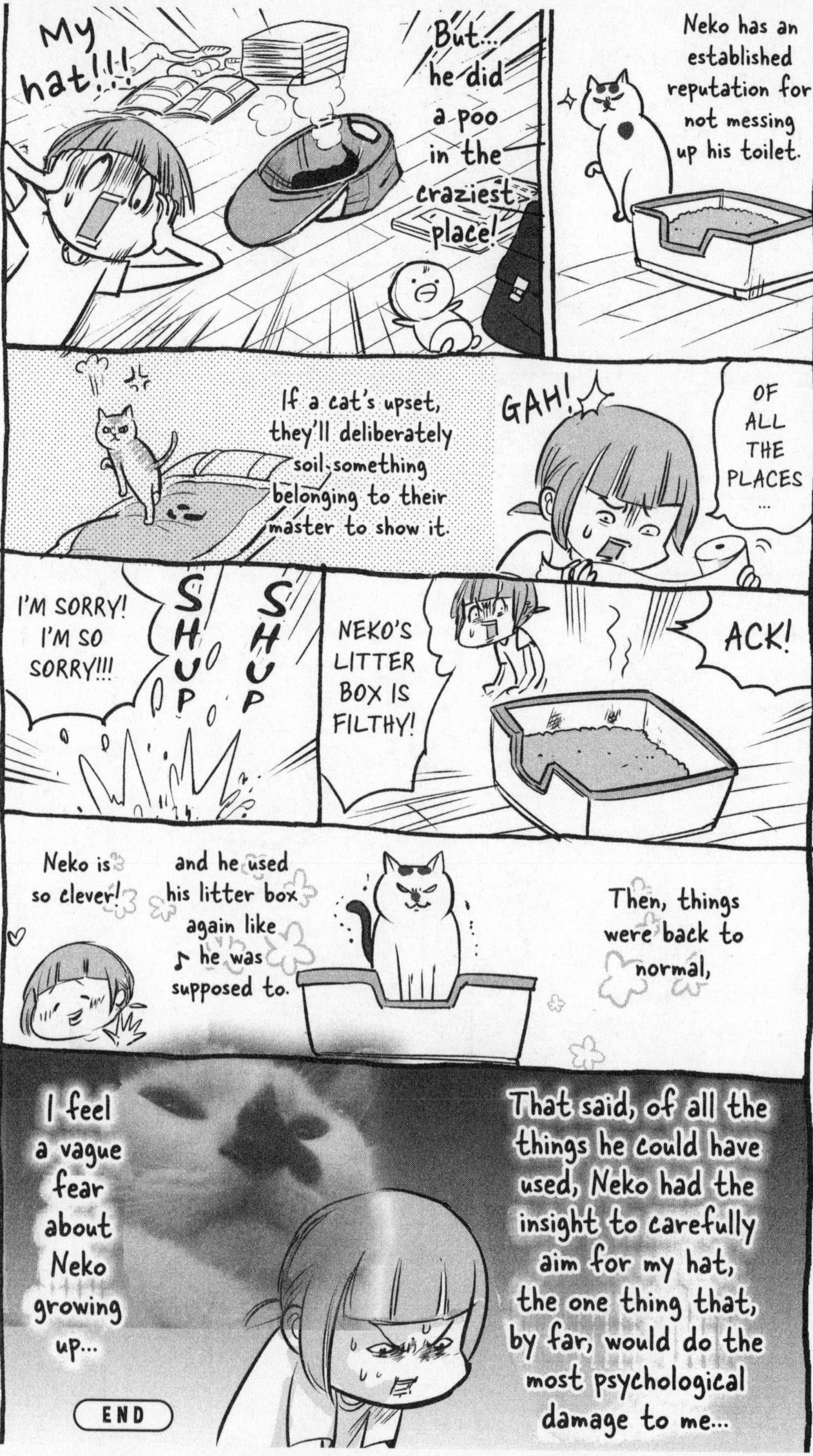
Neko has an established reputation for not messing up his toilet.
But... he did a poo in the craziest place!
My hat!!!
GAH!
OF ALL THE PLACES ...
If a cat's upset, they'll deliberately soil something belonging to their master to show it.
ACK!
NEKO'S LITTER BOX IS FILTHY!
SHUP SHUP
I'M SORRY! I'M SO SORRY!!!
Then, things were back to normal,
and he used his litter box again like he was supposed to.
Neko is so clever!
That said, of all the things he could have used, Neko had the insight to carefully aim for my hat, the one thing that, by far, would do the most psychological damage to me...
I feel a vague fear about Neko growing up...
END

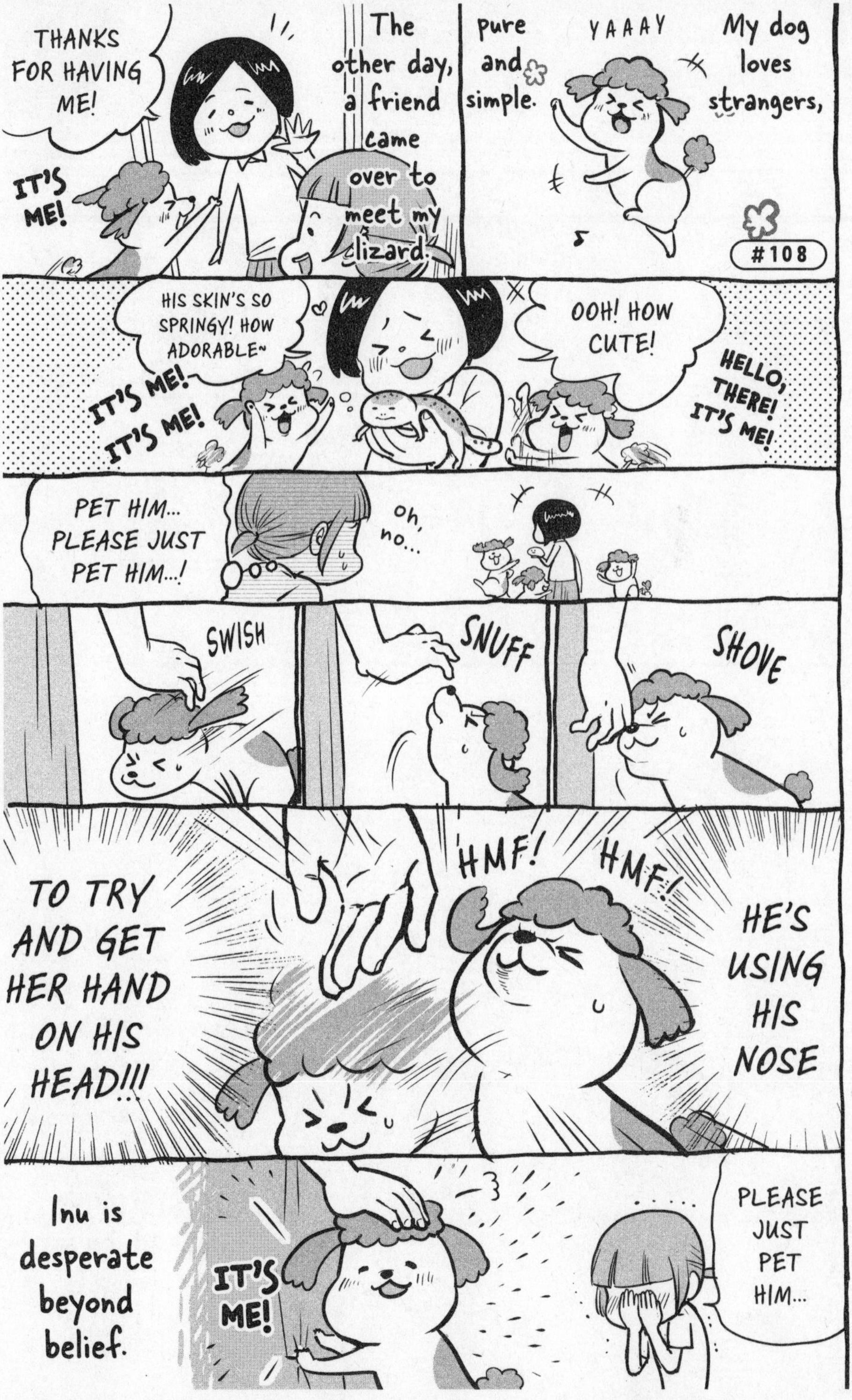
My dog loves strangers,
YAAAY
#108
pure and simple.
The other day, a friend came over to meet my lizard.
THANKS FOR HAVING ME!
IT'S ME!
HELLO, THERE! IT'S ME!
OOH! HOW CUTE!
HIS SKIN'S SO SPRINGY! HOW ADORABLE~
IT'S ME! IT'S ME!
oh, no...
PET HIM... PLEASE JUST PET HIM...!
SHOVE
SNUFF
SWISH
HE'S USING HIS NOSE
HMF!
HMF!
TO TRY AND GET HER HAND ON HIS HEAD!!!
PLEASE JUST PET HIM...
...
IT'S ME!
Inu is desperate beyond belief.

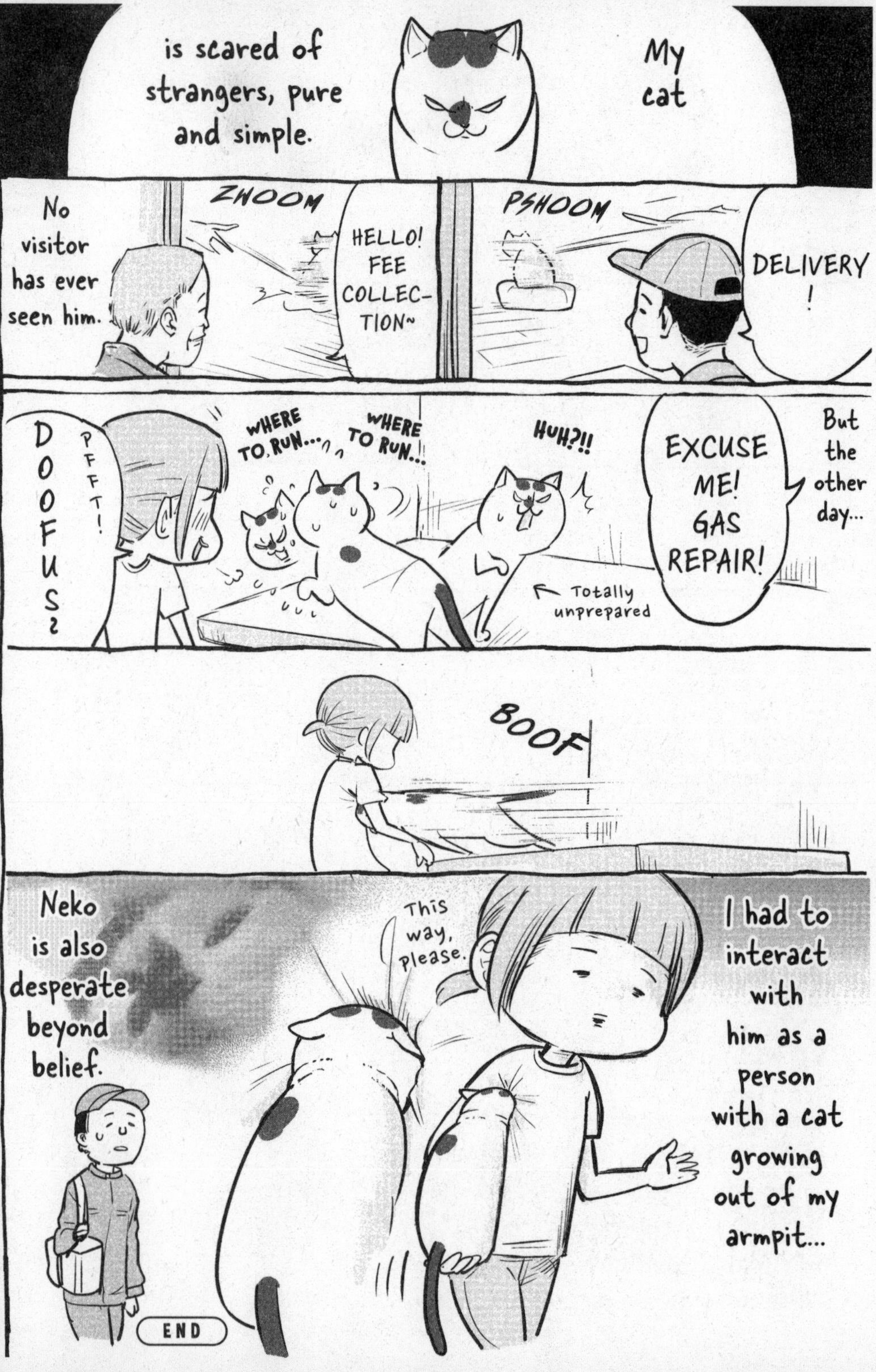
My cat
is scared of strangers, pure and simple.
DELIVERY!
PSHOOM
HELLO! FEE COLLECTION~
ZWOOM
No visitor has ever seen him.
But the other day...
EXCUSE ME! GAS REPAIR!
HUH?!!
Totally unprepared
WHERE TO RUN...
WHERE TO RUN...
PFFT!
DOOFUS?
BOOF
I had to interact with him as a person with a cat growing out of my armpit...
This way, please.
Neko is also desperate beyond belief.
END

This merchandise's likeness is unbelievably accurate.

Newly-Drawn 4-Panel Strip

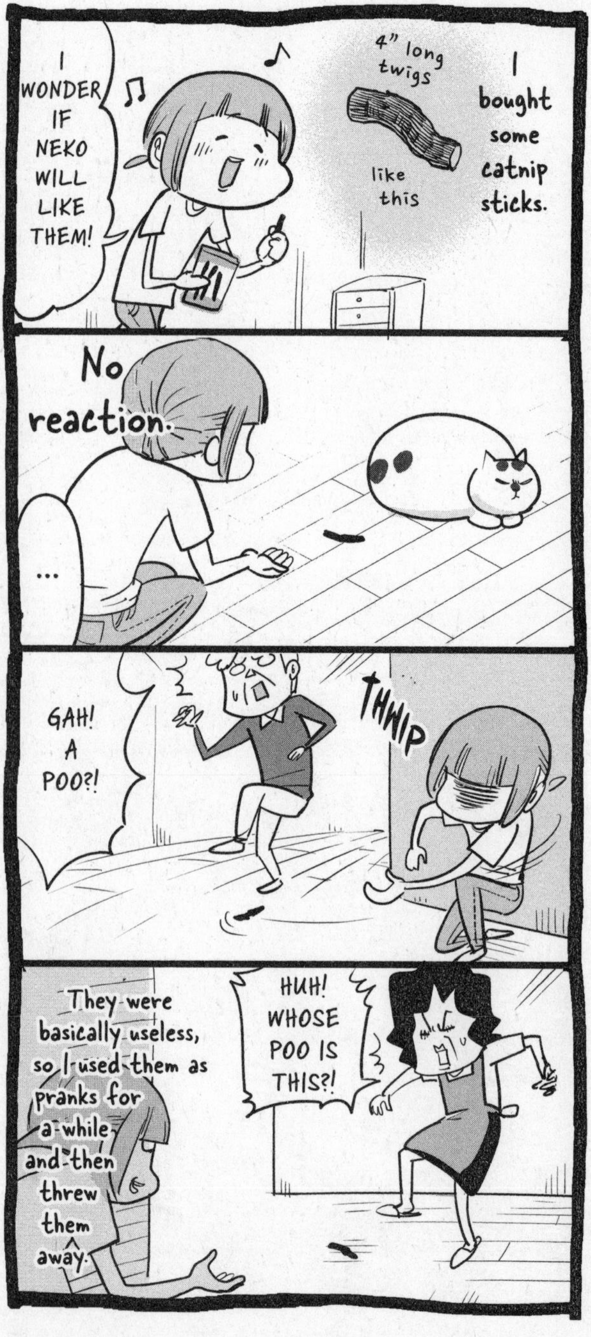
I bought some catnip sticks.
4" long twigs
like this
I WONDER IF NEKO WILL LIKE THEM!
No reaction.
...
THWIP
GAH! A POO?!
HUH! WHOSE POO IS THIS?!
They were basically useless, so I used them as pranks for a while and then threw them away.

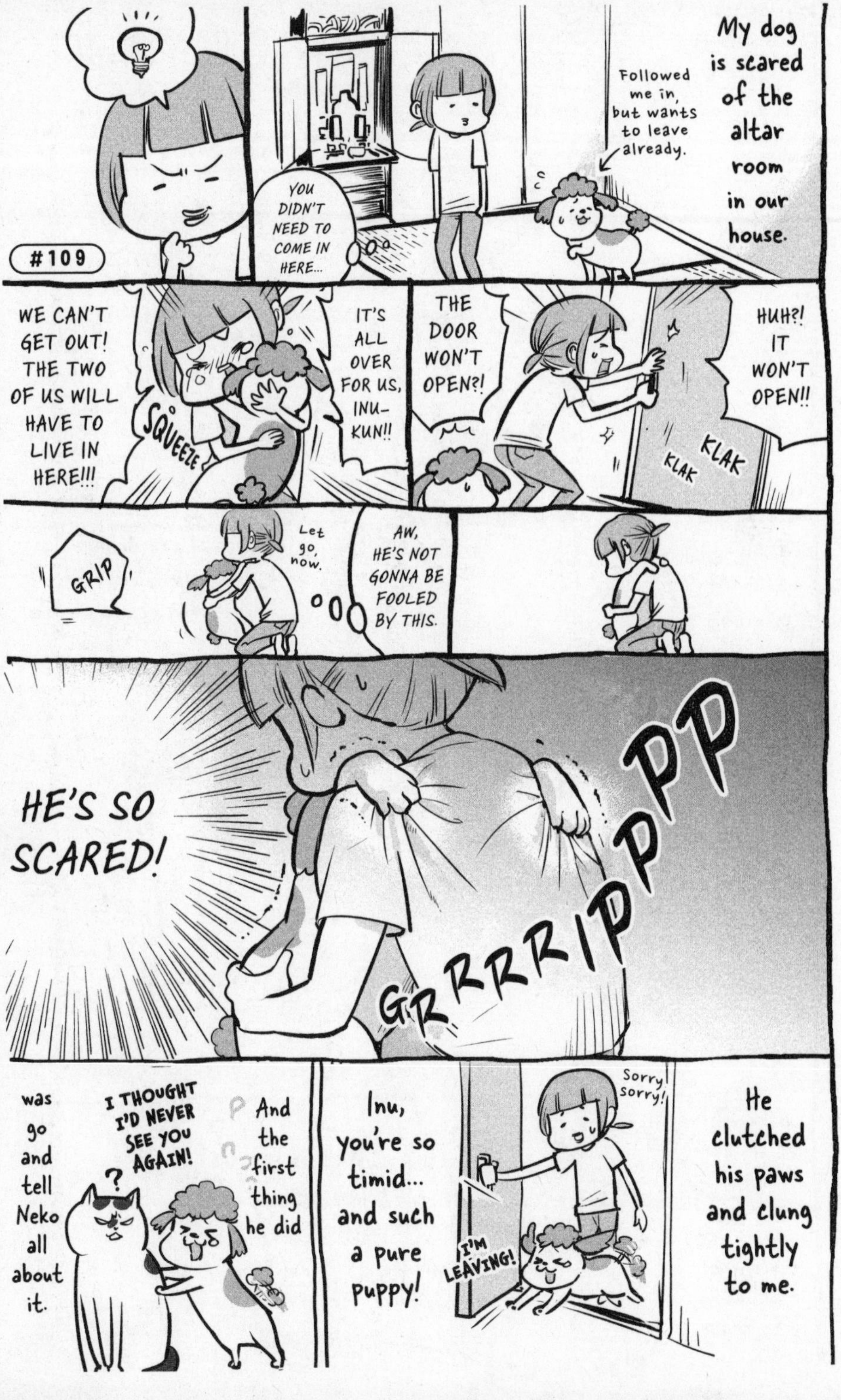

My dog is scared of the altar room in our house.
Followed me in, but wants to leave already.
YOU DIDN'T NEED TO COME IN HERE...
#109
HUH?! IT WON'T OPEN!!
KLAK
KLAK
THE DOOR WON'T OPEN?!
IT'S ALL OVER FOR US, INU-KUN!!
WE CAN'T GET OUT! THE TWO OF US WILL HAVE TO LIVE IN HERE!!!
SQUEEZE
AW, HE'S NOT GONNA BE FOOLED BY THIS.
Let go, now.
GRIP
GRRRIPPPPP
HE'S SO SCARED!
He clutched his paws and clung tightly to me.
Sorry sorry!
I'M LEAVING!
Inu, you're so timid... and such a pure puppy!
And the first thing he did
I THOUGHT I'D NEVER SEE YOU AGAIN!
was go and tell Neko all about it.

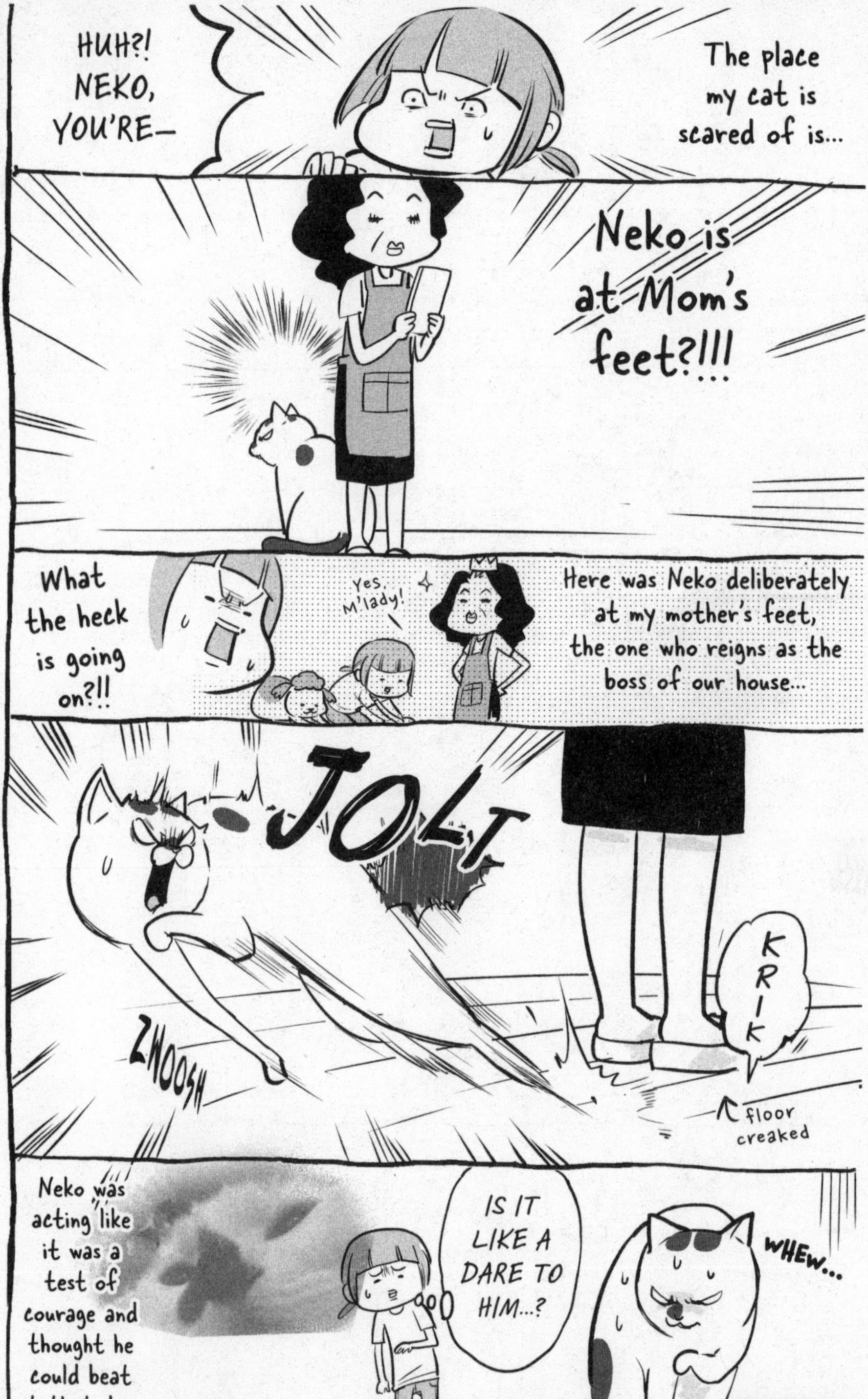
The place my cat is scared of is...
HUH?! NEKO, YOU'RE—
Neko is at Mom's feet?!!!...
Here was Neko deliberately at my mother's feet, the one who reigns as the boss of our house...
Yes, M'lady!
What the heck is going on?!!
JOLT
KRIK
floor creaked
ZHOOSH
WHEW...
IS IT LIKE A DARE TO HIM...?
Neko was acting like it was a test of courage and thought he could beat it that day.
END

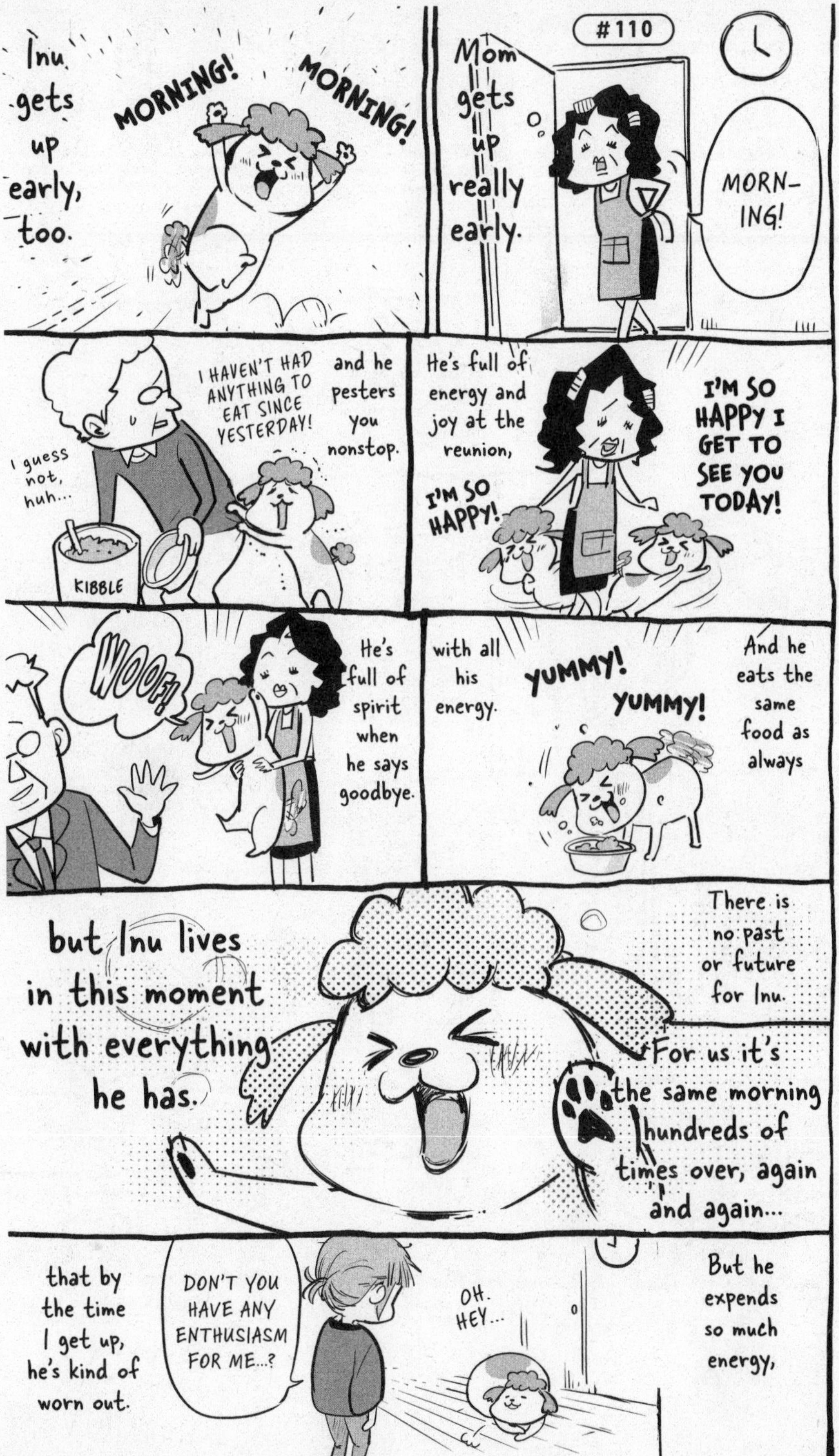
#110
Mom gets up really early.
MORN-ING!
Inu gets up early, too.
MORNING!
MORNING!
He's full of energy and joy at the reunion,
I'M SO HAPPY I GET TO SEE YOU TODAY!
I'M SO HAPPY!
and he pesters you nonstop.
I HAVEN'T HAD ANYTHING TO EAT SINCE YESTERDAY!
I guess not, huh...
KIBBLE
And he eats the same food as always
YUMMY!
YUMMY!
with all his energy.
He's full of spirit when he says goodbye.
WOOF!
There is no past or future for Inu.
For us it's the same morning hundreds of times over, again and again...
but Inu lives in this moment with everything he has.
But he expends so much energy,
OH. HEY...
DON'T YOU HAVE ANY ENTHUSIASM FOR ME...?
that by the time I get up, he's kind of worn out.

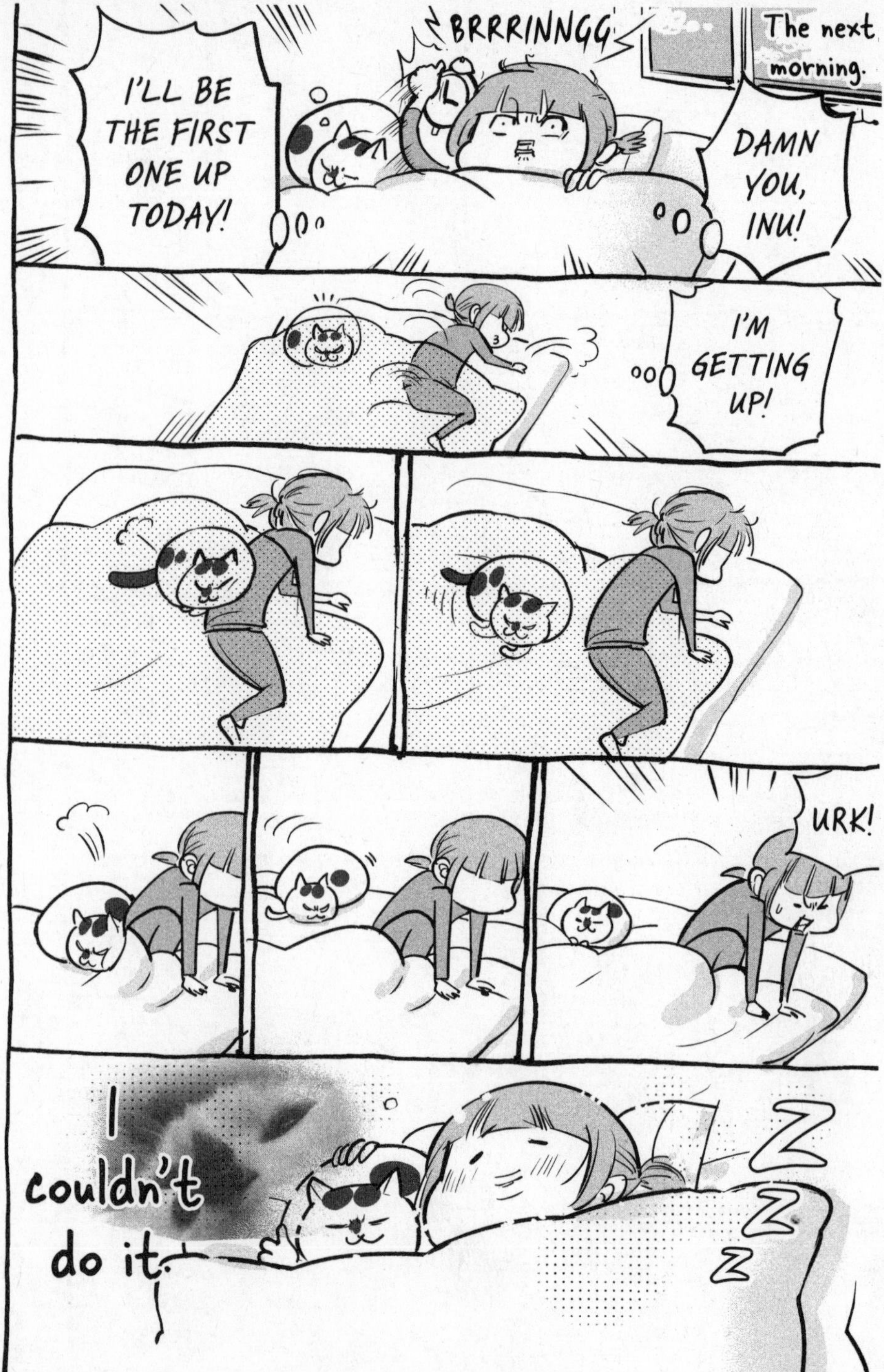
The next morning.
BRRRINNGG
DAMN YOU, INU!
I'LL BE THE FIRST ONE UP TODAY!
I'M GETTING UP!
URK!
Z Z Z
I couldn't do it.

END

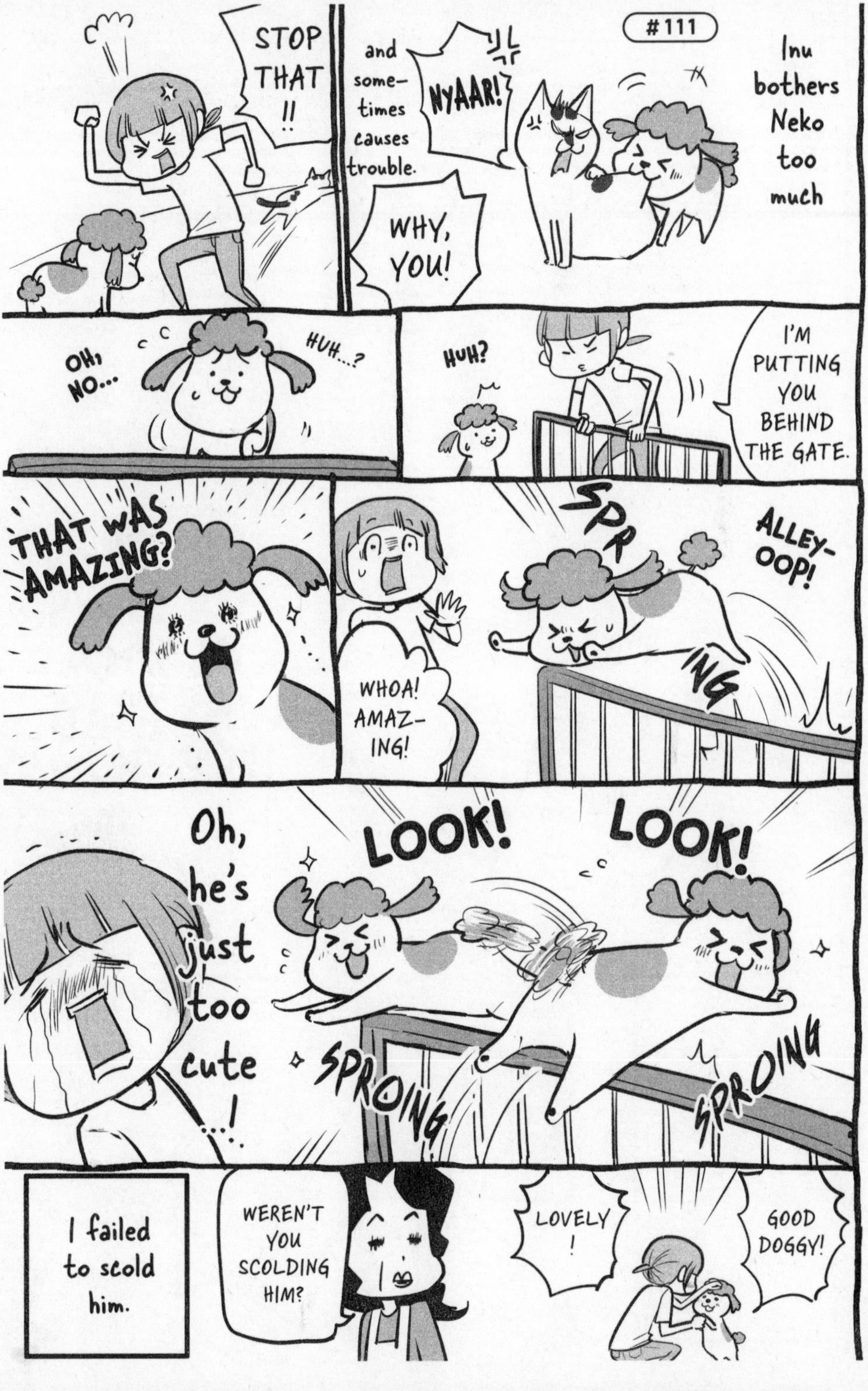
#111
Inu bothers Neko too much
and sometimes causes trouble.
NYAAR!
WHY, YOU!
STOP THAT !!
I'M PUTTING YOU BEHIND THE GATE.
HUH?
HUH...?
OH, NO...
SPRING
ALLEY-OOP!
WHOA! AMAZING!
THAT WAS AMAZING?
LOOK!
LOOK!
SPROING
SPROING
Oh, he's just too cute...!
GOOD DOGGY!
LOVELY!
WEREN'T YOU SCOLDING HIM?
I failed to scold him.

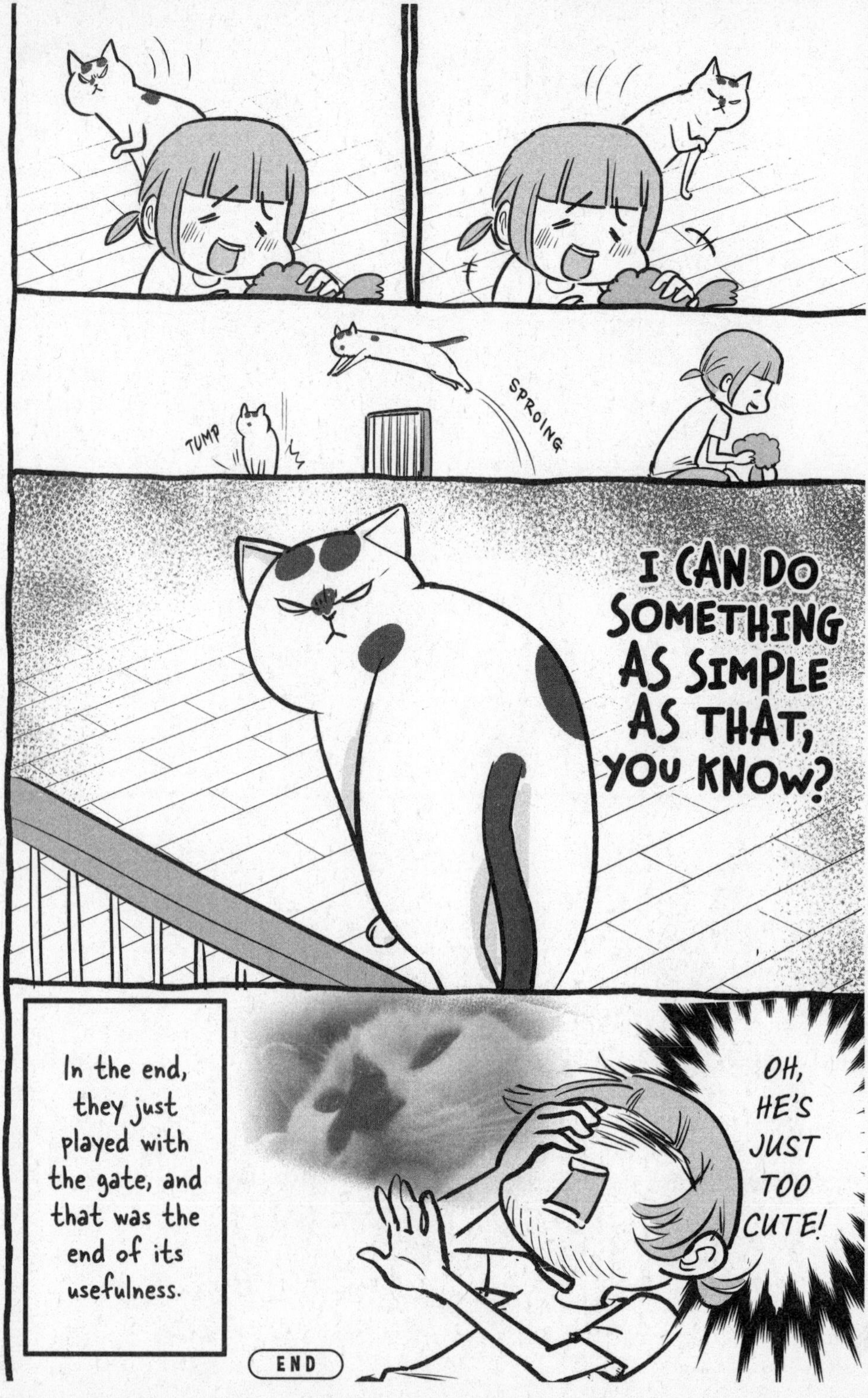
SPROING
TUMP
I CAN DO SOMETHING AS SIMPLE AS THAT, YOU KNOW?
OH, HE'S JUST TOO CUTE!
In the end, they just played with the gate, and that was the end of its usefulness.
END

Neko letting Inu smell just his paw since there's no helping it.

More About #111

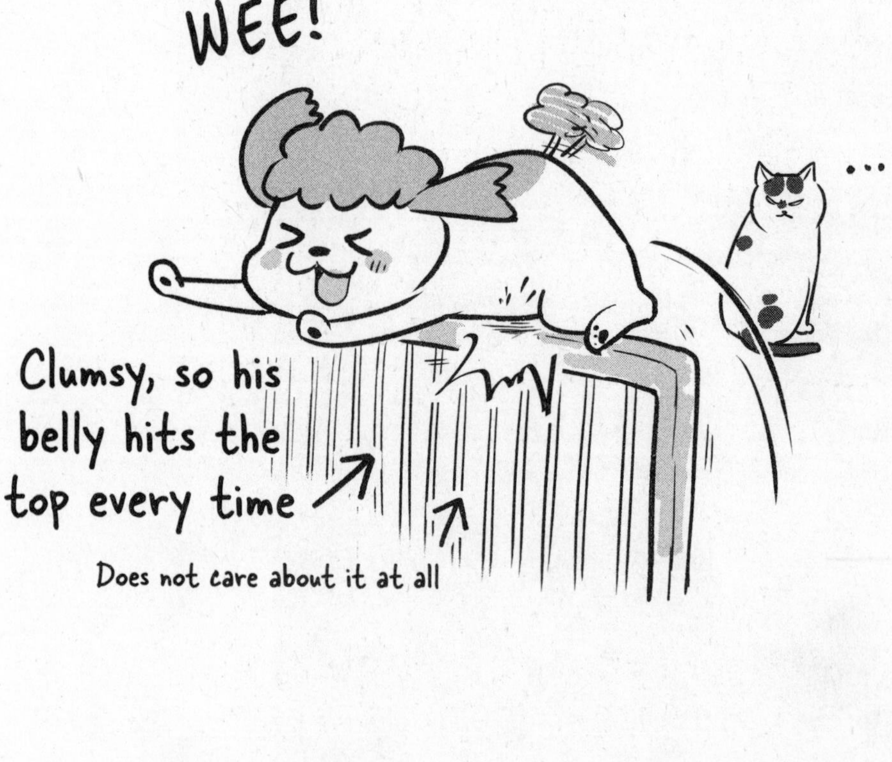
WEE!
...
Clumsy, so his belly hits the top every time
Does not care about it at all

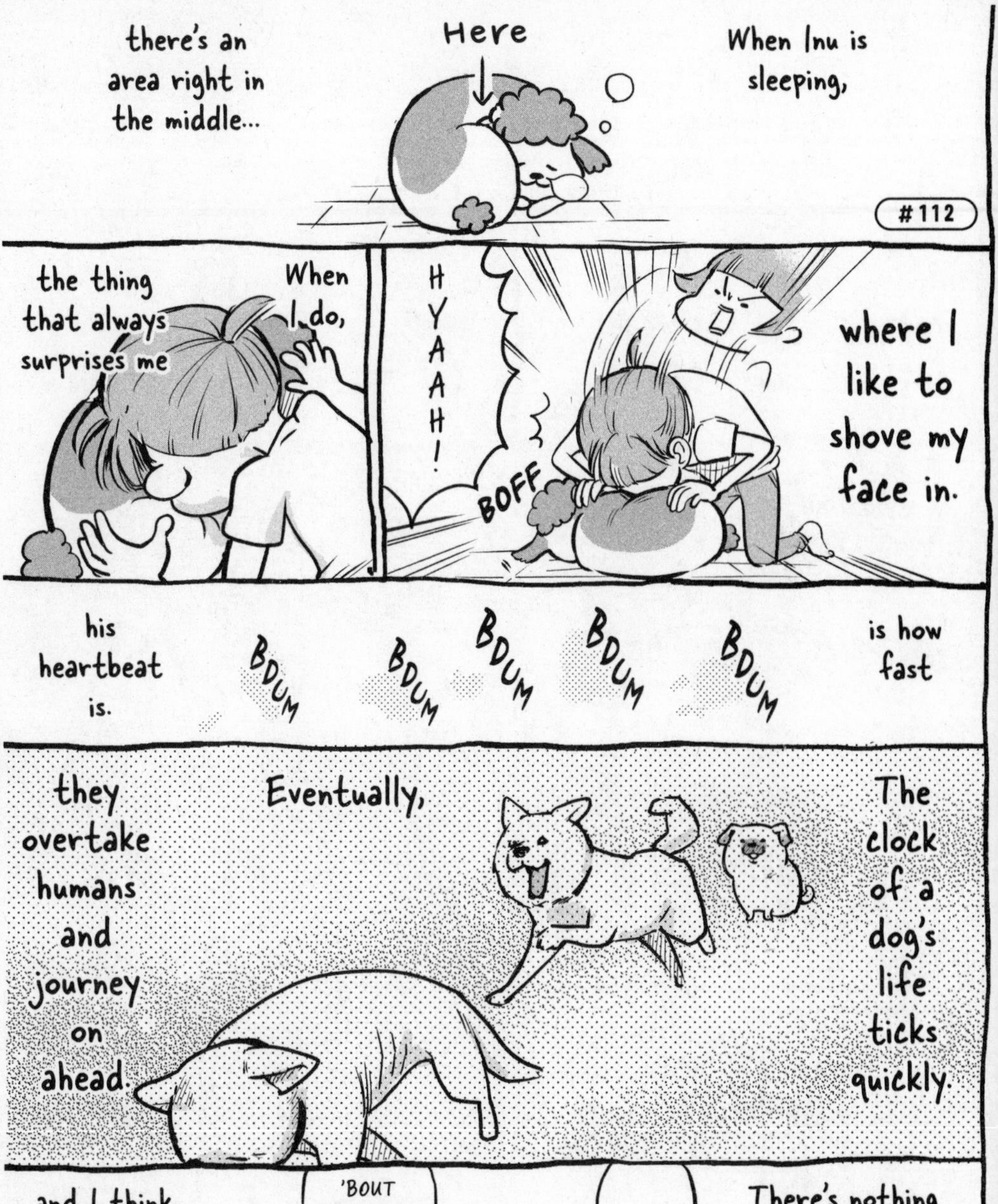
#112
When Inu is sleeping,
Here
there's an area right in the middle...
where I like to shove my face in.
HYAAAH!
BOFF
When I do,
the thing that always surprises me
is how fast
BDUM
BDUM
BDUM
BDUM
BDUM
his heartbeat is.
The clock of a dog's life ticks quickly.
Eventually,
they overtake humans and journey on ahead.
There's nothing special about this moment, but I'm extremely grateful for it,
...
'BOUT TIME YOU HAD A BATH. You smell.
HUH? NO, THANKS!
and I think, "Today is another happy day."

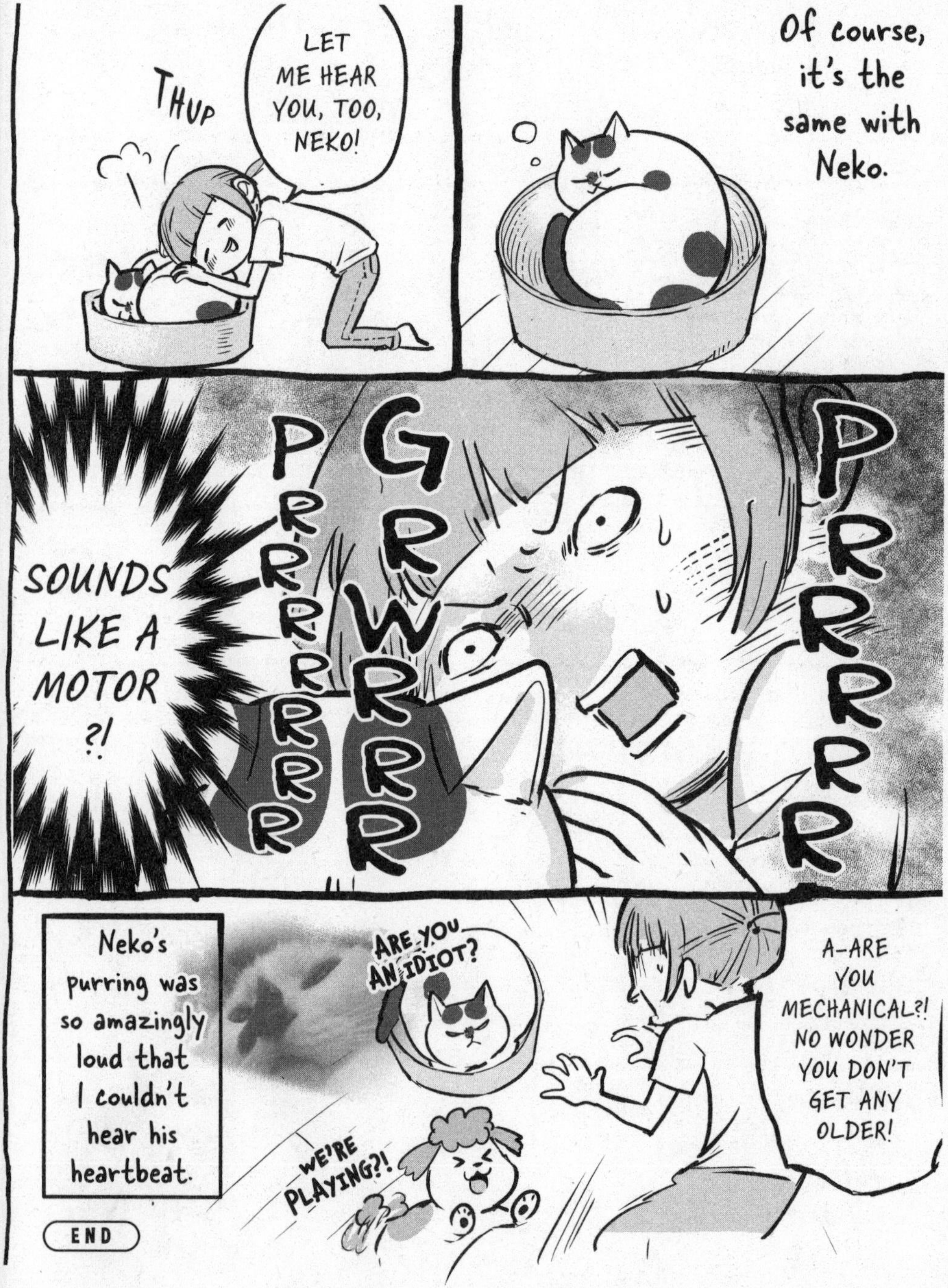
Of course, it's the same with Neko.
THUP
LET ME HEAR YOU, TOO, NEKO!
PRRRRR
GRWRRR
PRRRRRRR
SOUNDS LIKE A MOTOR ?!
A-ARE YOU MECHANICAL?! NO WONDER YOU DON'T GET ANY OLDER!
ARE YOU AN IDIOT?
WE'RE PLAYING?!
Neko's purring was so amazingly loud that I couldn't hear his heartbeat.
END

#113

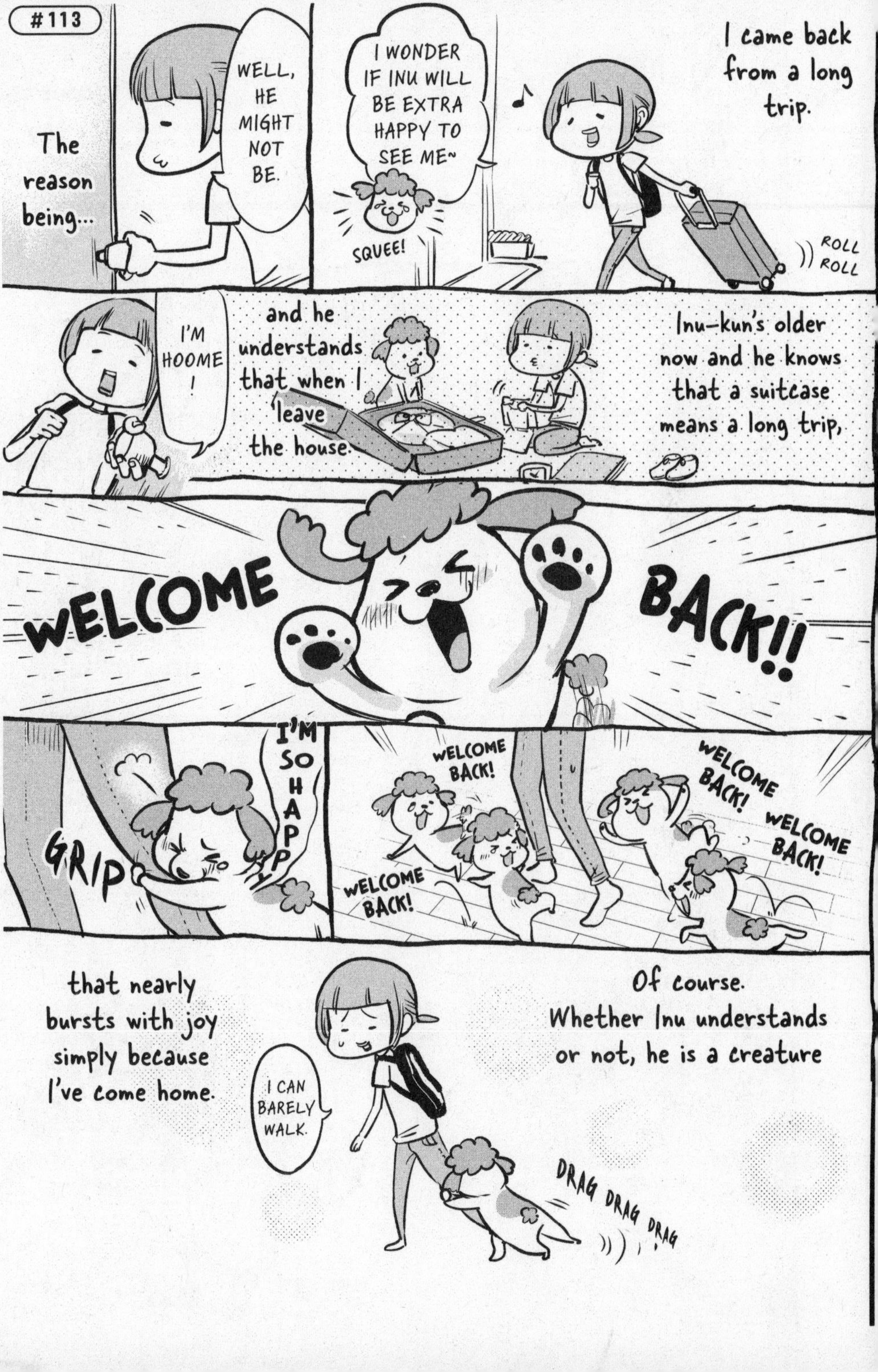
I came back from a long trip.
ROLL ROLL
I WONDER IF INU WILL BE EXTRA HAPPY TO SEE ME~
SQUEE!
WELL, HE MIGHT NOT BE.
The reason being...
Inu-kun's older now and he knows that a suitcase means a long trip,
and he understands that when I leave the house.
I'M HOOME!
WELCOME BACK!!
WELCOME BACK!
WELCOME BACK!
WELCOME BACK!
WELCOME BACK!
I'M SO HAPP
GRIP
Of course. Whether Inu understands or not, he is a creature
that nearly bursts with joy simply because I've come home.
I CAN BARELY WALK.
DRAG DRAG DRAG

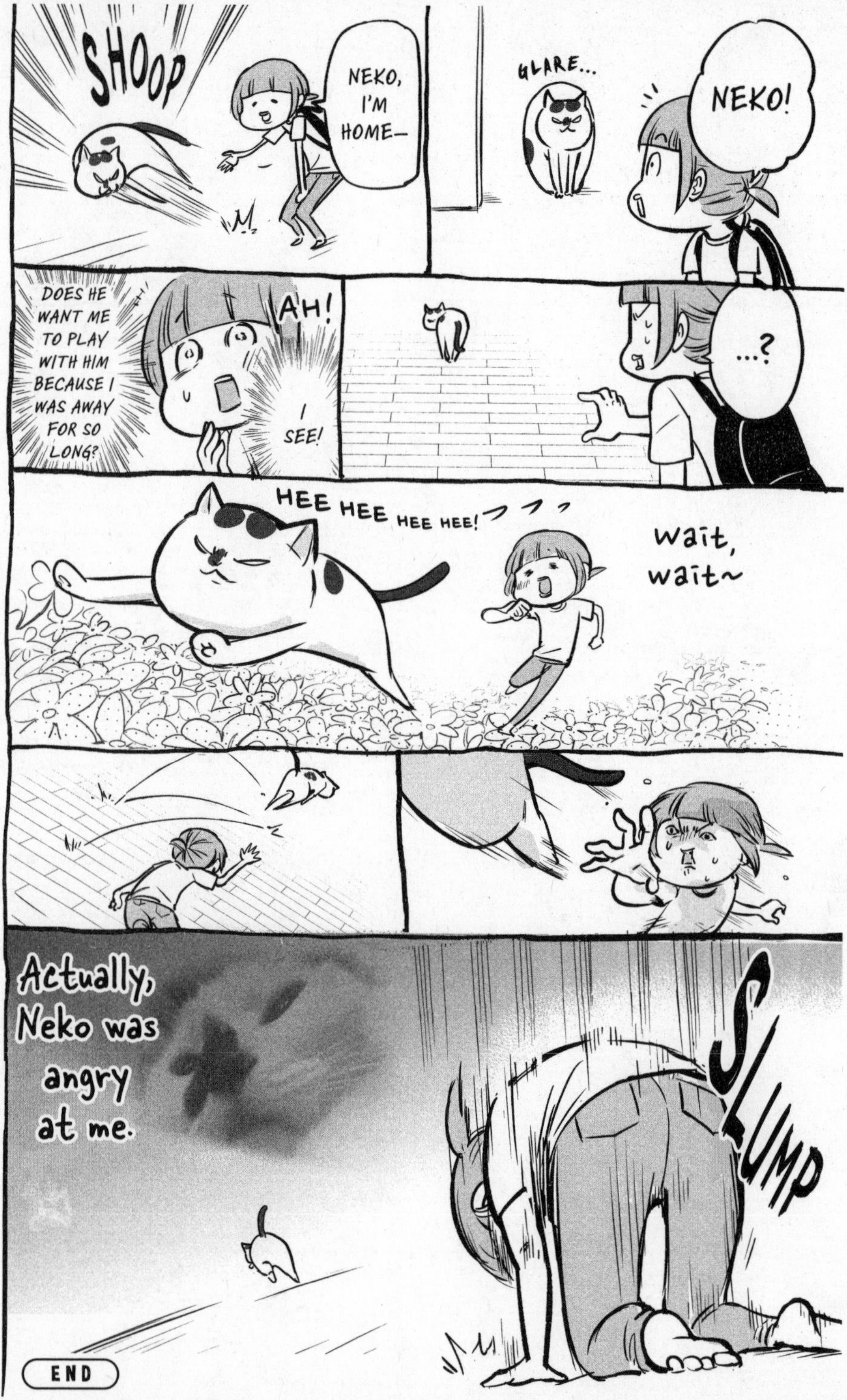
GLARE...
NEKO!
SHOOP
NEKO, I'M HOME—
...?
AH!
I SEE!
DOES HE WANT ME TO PLAY WITH HIM BECAUSE I WAS AWAY FOR SO LONG?
wait, wait~
HEE HEE HEE HEE!
SLUMP
Actually, Neko was angry at me.
END

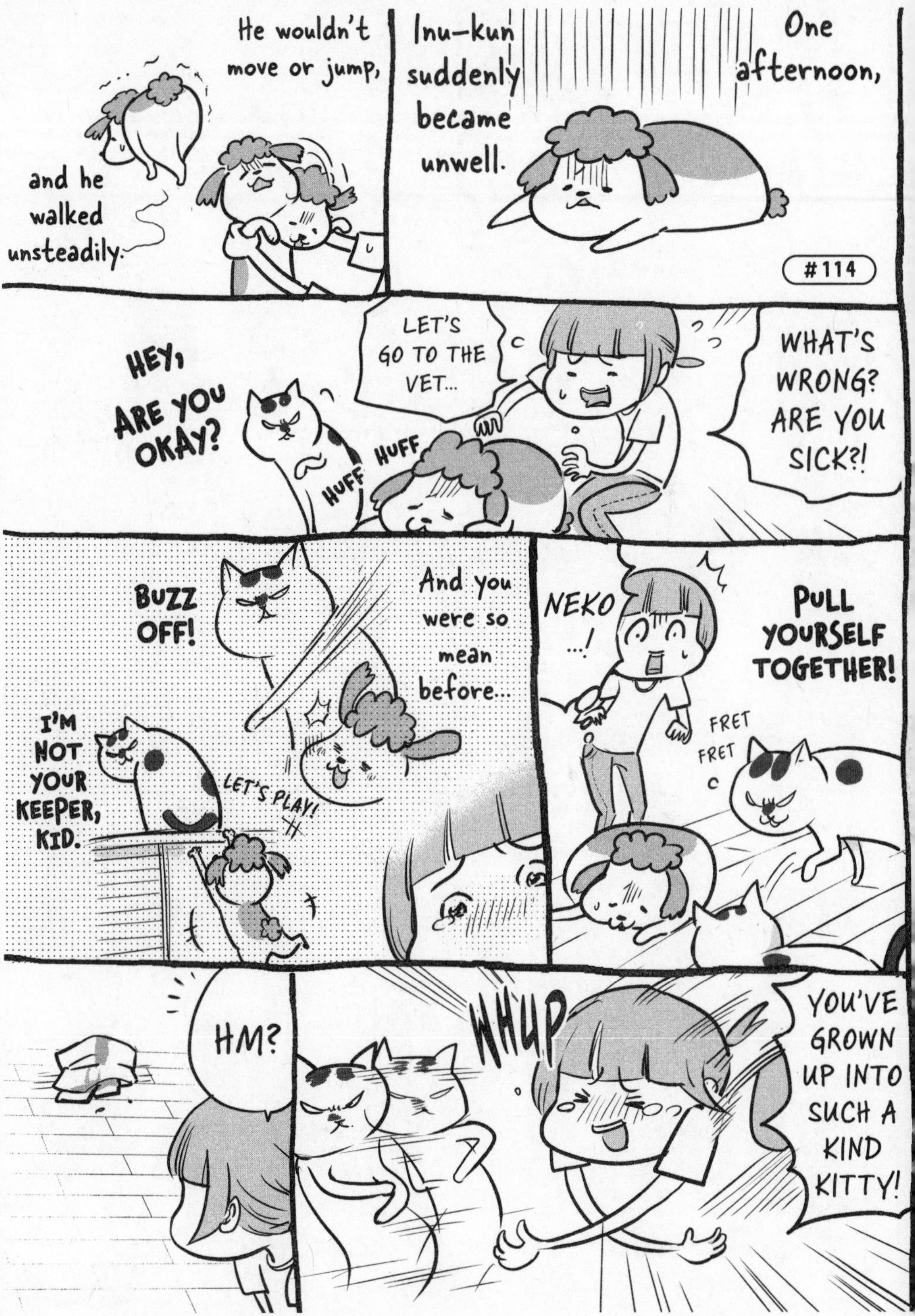
#114
One afternoon,
Inu-kun suddenly became unwell.
He wouldn't move or jump,
and he walked unsteadily.
WHAT'S WRONG? ARE YOU SICK?!
LET'S GO TO THE VET...
HUFF
HUFF
HEY, ARE YOU OKAY?
PULL YOURSELF TOGETHER!
NEKO ...!
FRET FRET
And you were so mean before...
BUZZ OFF!
LET'S PLAY!
I'M NOT YOUR KEEPER, KID.
YOU'VE GROWN UP INTO SUCH A KIND KITTY!
WHUP
HM?

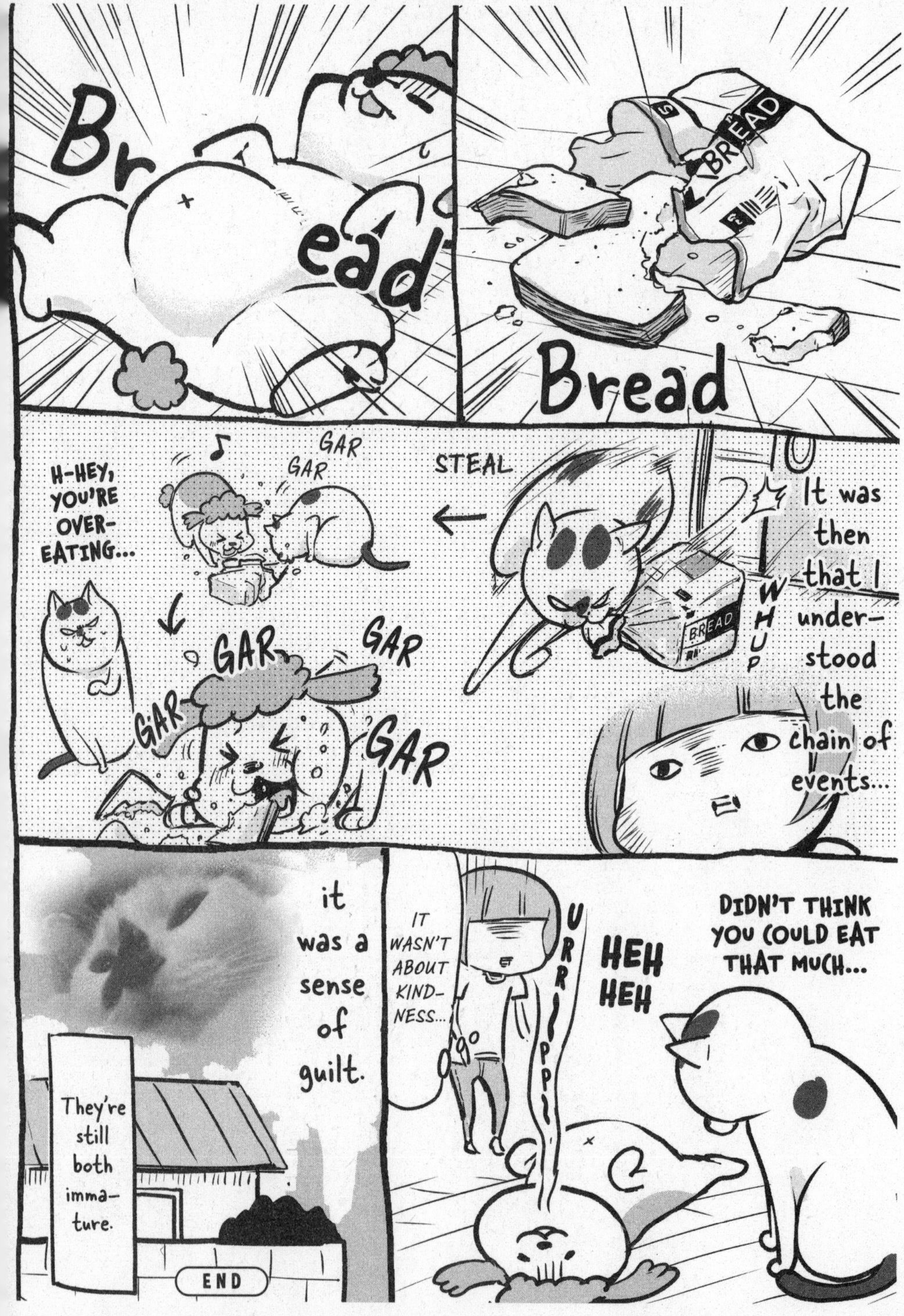
Bread
BREAD
Br ead
It was then that I under-stood the chain of events...
WHUP
BREAD
STEAL
GAR
GAR
H-HEY, YOU'RE OVER-EATING...
GAR
GAR
GAR
GAR
DIDN'T THINK YOU COULD EAT THAT MUCH...
HEH HEH
URRIPPI
IT WASN'T ABOUT KIND-NESS...
it was a sense of guilt.
They're still both imma-ture.
END

More About #114 (1)

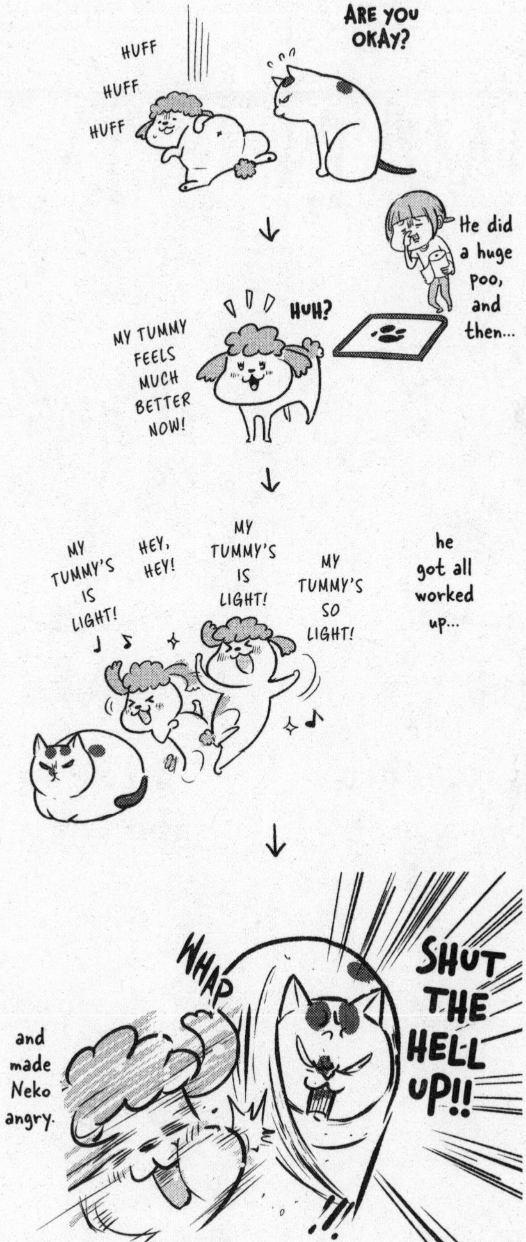
ARE YOU OKAY?
HUFF
HUFF
HUFF
He did a huge poo, and then...
HUH?
MY TUMMY FEELS MUCH BETTER NOW!
he got all worked up...
MY TUMMY'S SO LIGHT!
MY TUMMY'S IS LIGHT!
HEY, HEY!
MY TUMMY'S IS LIGHT!
SHUT THE HELL UP!!
WHAP
and made Neko angry.

WANTED

IT'S ME!

Inu

Did not steal but
ate without limit

Neko

Stole but
did not eat

Bread
5 slices

This guy's asking for a clobbering.

Newly-Drawn 4-Panel Strip

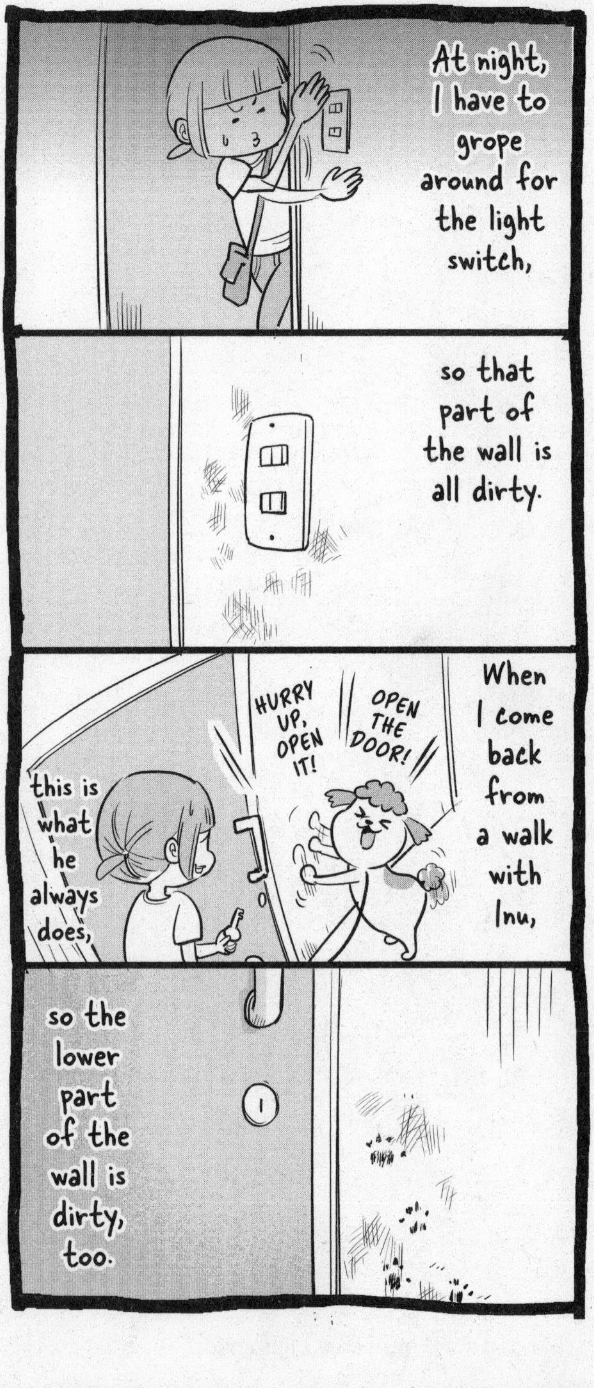
At night, I have to grope around for the light switch,
so that part of the wall is all dirty.
When I come back from a walk with Inu,
OPEN THE DOOR!
HURRY UP, OPEN IT!
this is what he always does,
so the lower part of the wall is dirty, too.

Bonus

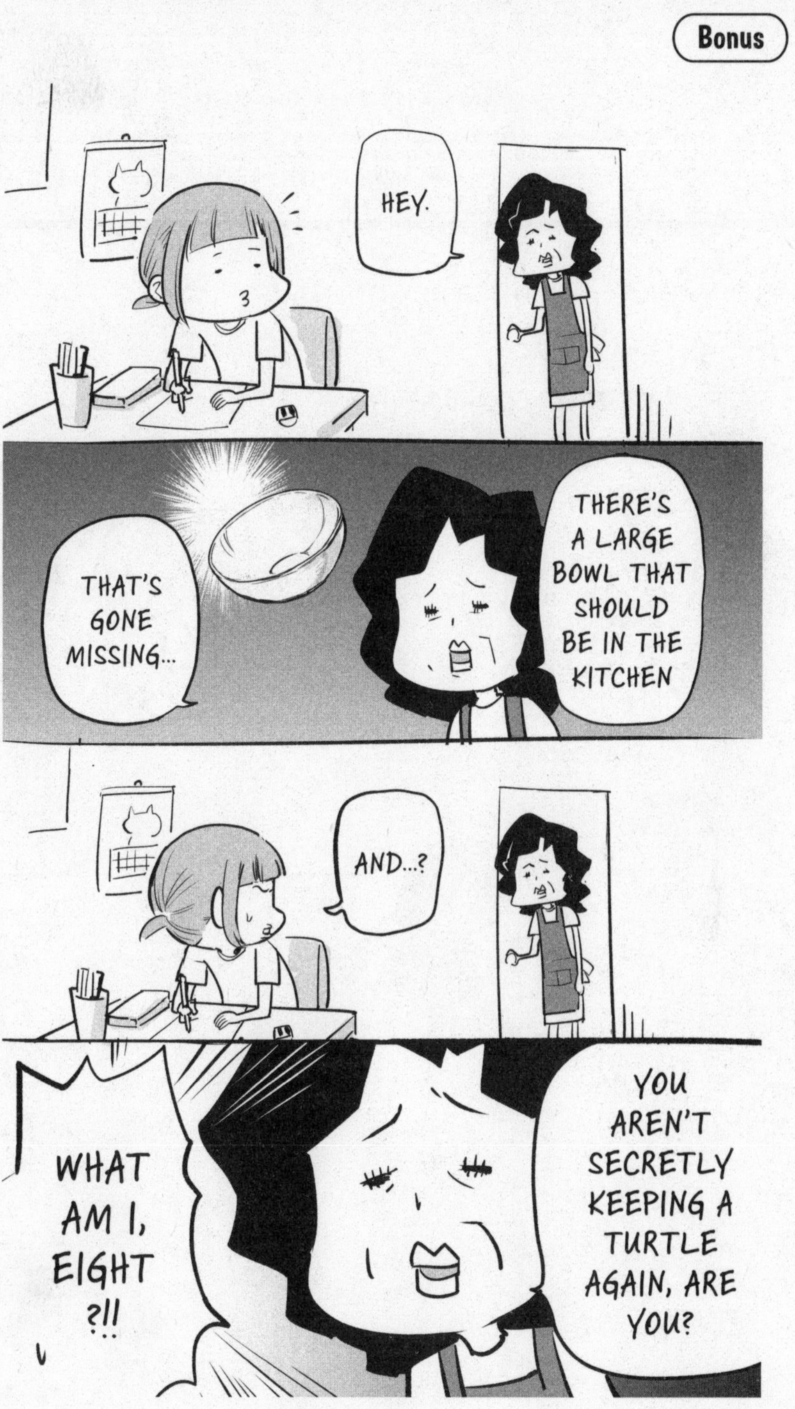
HEY.
THERE'S A LARGE BOWL THAT SHOULD BE IN THE KITCHEN
THAT'S GONE MISSING...
AND...?
YOU AREN'T SECRETLY KEEPING A TURTLE AGAIN, ARE YOU?
WHAT AM I, EIGHT ?!!

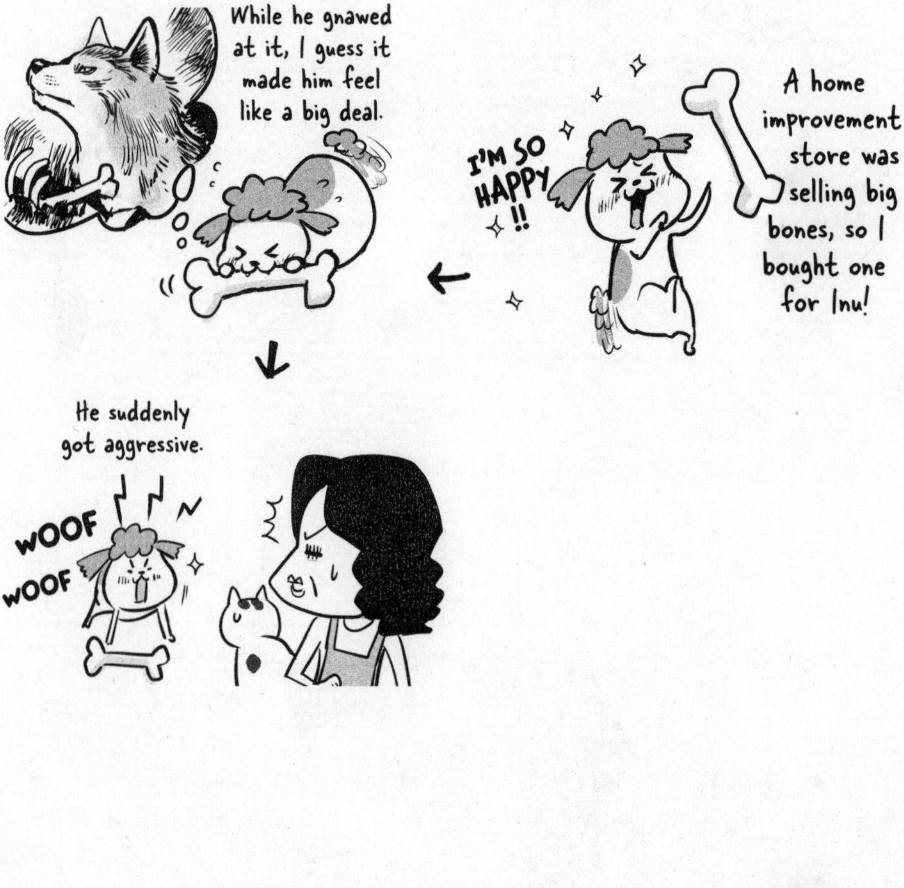
A home improvement store was selling big bones, so I bought one for Inu!
I'M SO HAPPY!!
While he gnawed at it, I guess it made him feel like a big deal.
He suddenly got aggressive.
WOOF WOOF

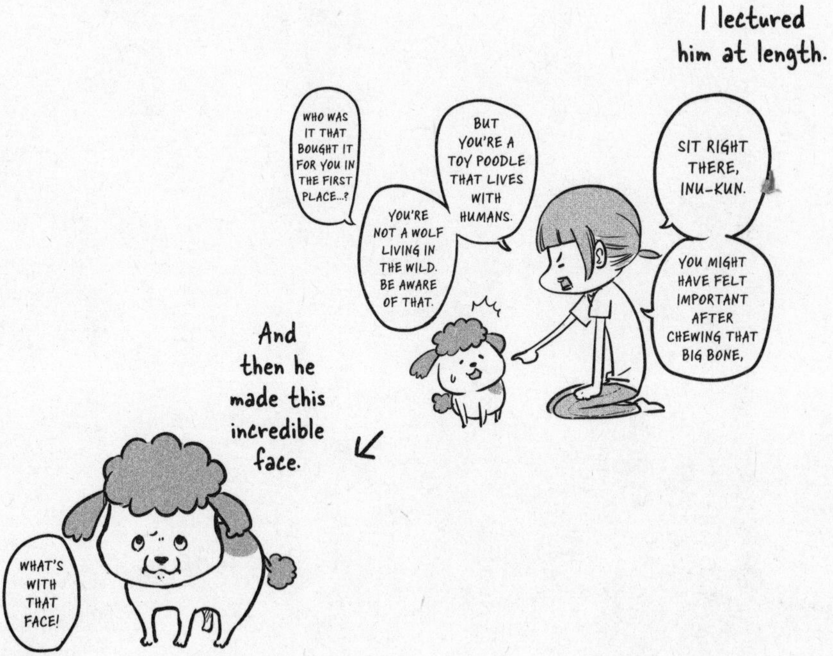
I lectured him at length.
SIT RIGHT THERE, INU-KUN.
YOU MIGHT HAVE FELT IMPORTANT AFTER CHEWING THAT BIG BONE,
BUT YOU'RE A TOY POODLE THAT LIVES WITH HUMANS.
YOU'RE NOT A WOLF LIVING IN THE WILD. BE AWARE OF THAT.
WHO WAS IT THAT BOUGHT IT FOR YOU IN THE FIRST PLACE...?
And then he made this incredible face.
WHAT'S WITH THAT FACE!

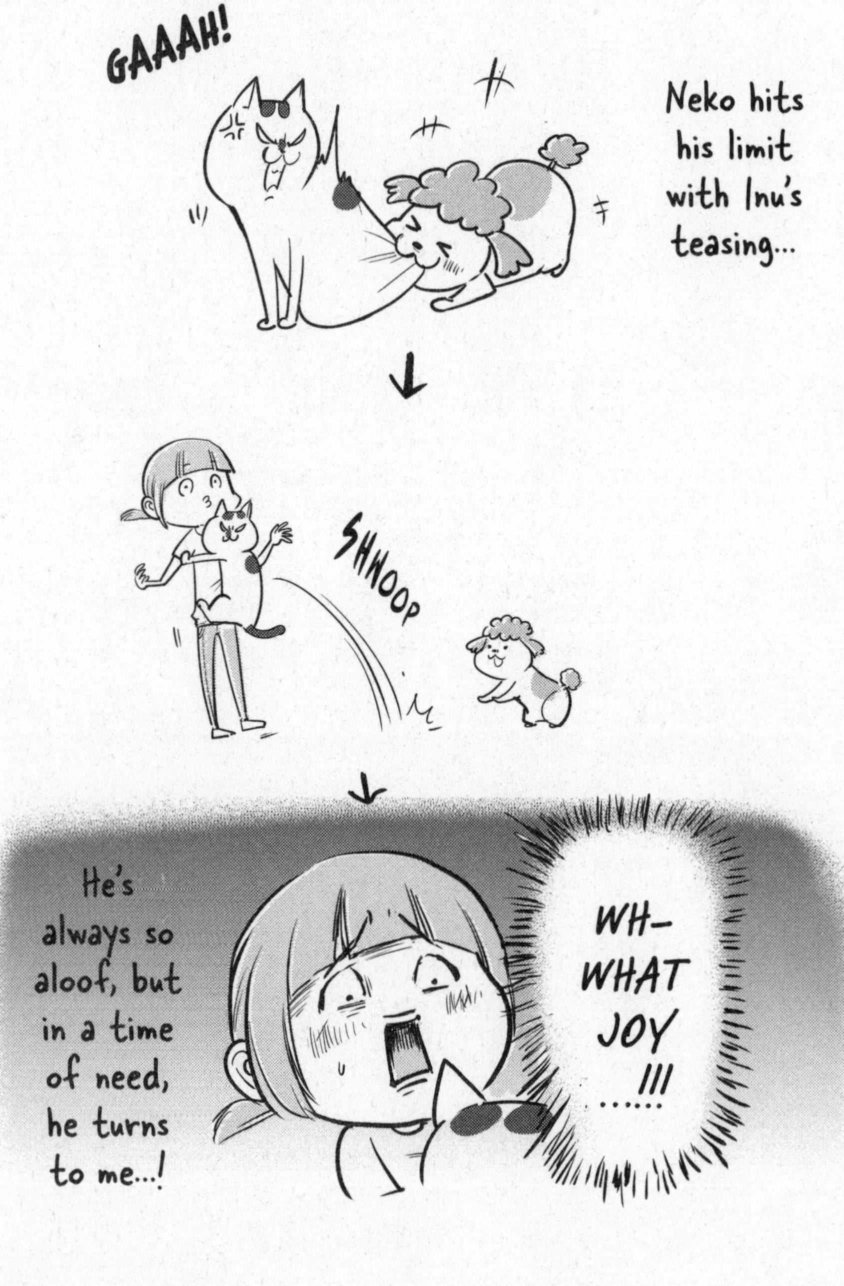
Neko hits his limit with Inu's teasing...
GAAAH!
SHWOOP
WH-WHAT JOY!!!
......
He's always so aloof, but in a time of need, he turns to me...!

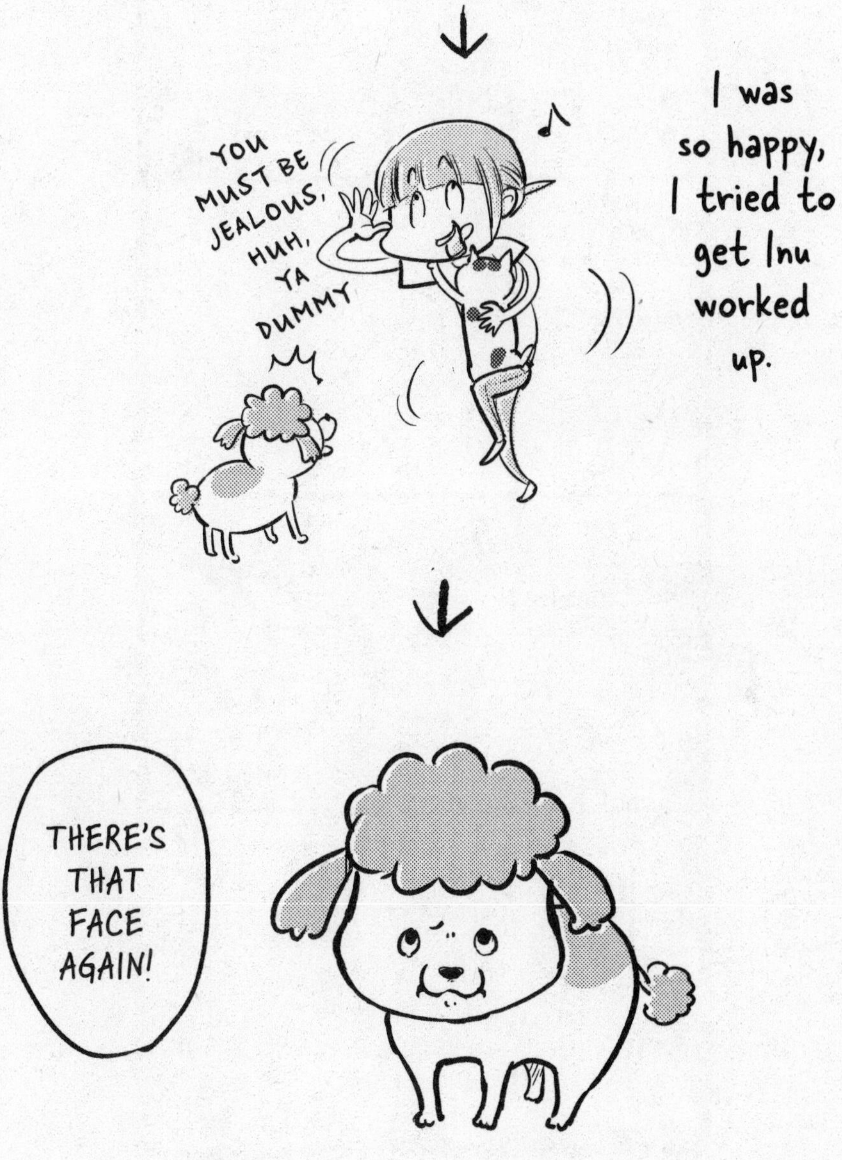
I was so happy, I tried to get Inu worked up.
YOU MUST BE JEALOUS, HUH, YA DUMMY
THERE'S THAT FACE AGAIN!

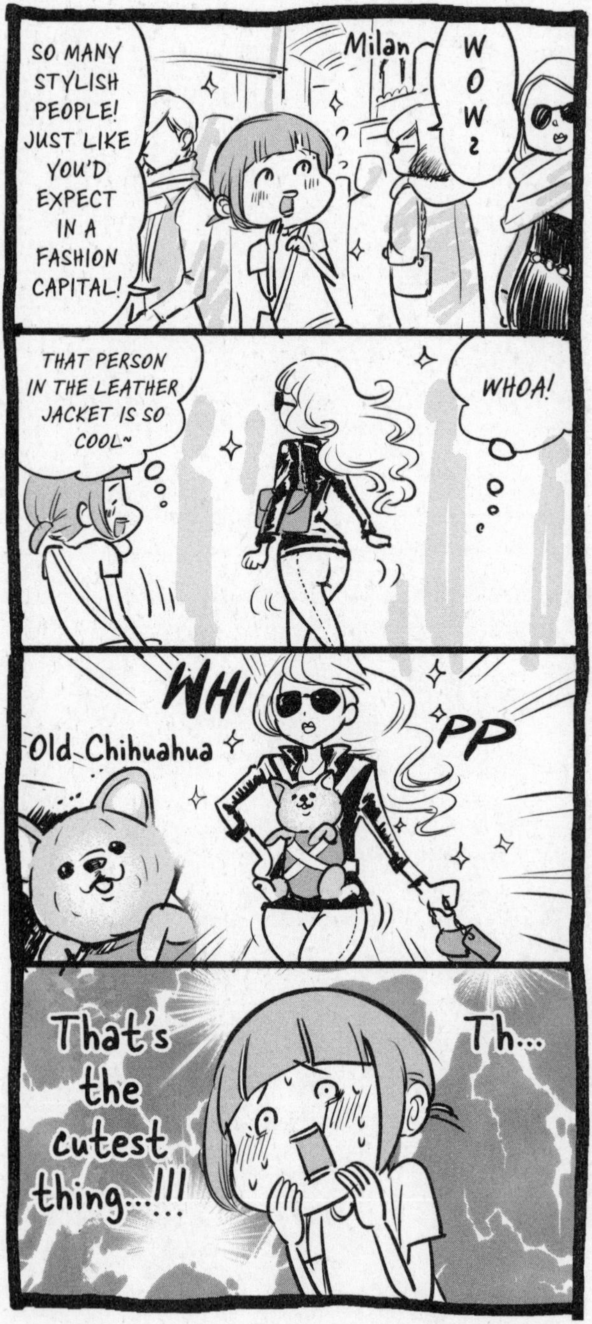
WOW?
Milan
SO MANY STYLISH PEOPLE! JUST LIKE YOU'D EXPECT IN A FASHION CAPITAL!
WHOA!
THAT PERSON IN THE LEATHER JACKET IS SO COOL~
WHI
PP
Old Chihuahua
...
Th...
That's the cutest thing...!!!

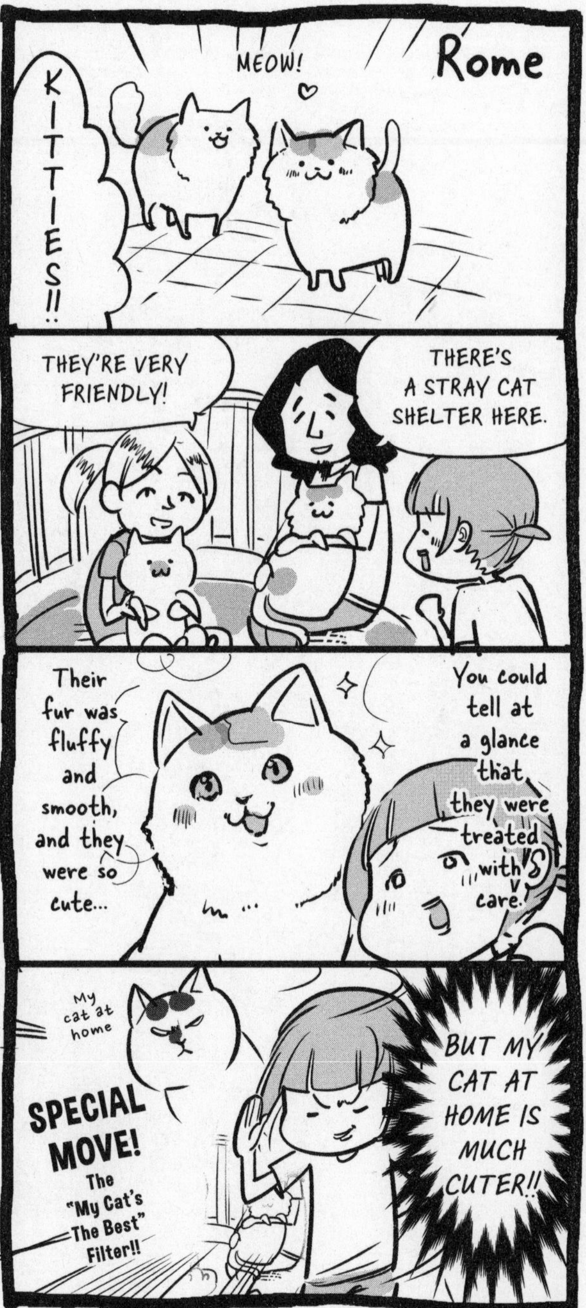
Rome
MEOW!
KITTIES!!
THERE'S A STRAY CAT SHELTER HERE.
THEY'RE VERY FRIENDLY!
You could tell at a glance that they were treated with care.
Their fur was fluffy and smooth, and they were so cute...
BUT MY CAT AT HOME IS MUCH CUTER!!
My cat at home
SPECIAL MOVE! The "My Cat's The Best" Filter!!

Walkies Style

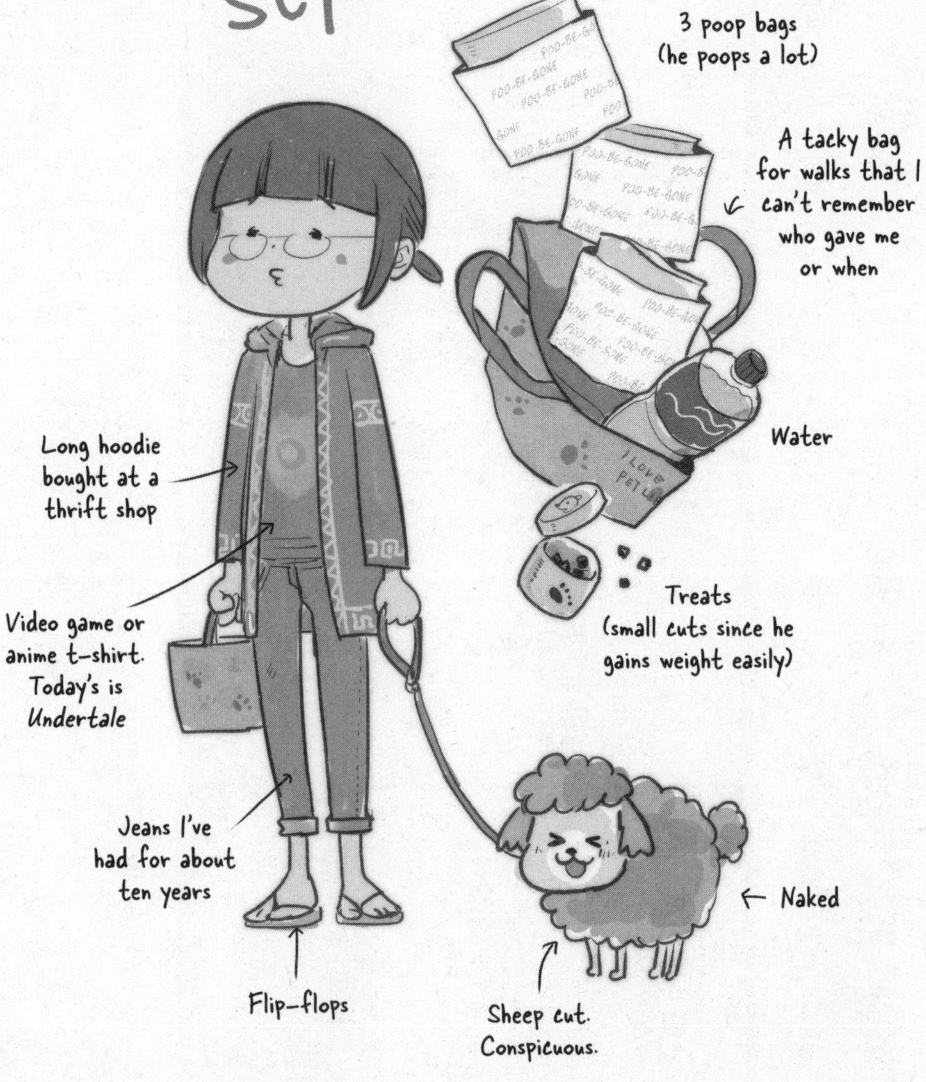

3 poop bags
(he poops a lot)
POO-BE-GONE
A tacky bag for walks that I can't remember who gave me or when
Water
Treats
(small cuts since he gains weight easily)
Long hoodie bought at a thrift shop
Video game or anime t-shirt. Today's is *Undertale*
Jeans I've had for about ten years
Flip-flops
Sheep cut. Conspicuous.
Naked

END

I'm sorry that cardboard box is so small... I *said* I was sorry...

Newly-Drawn 4-Panel Strip

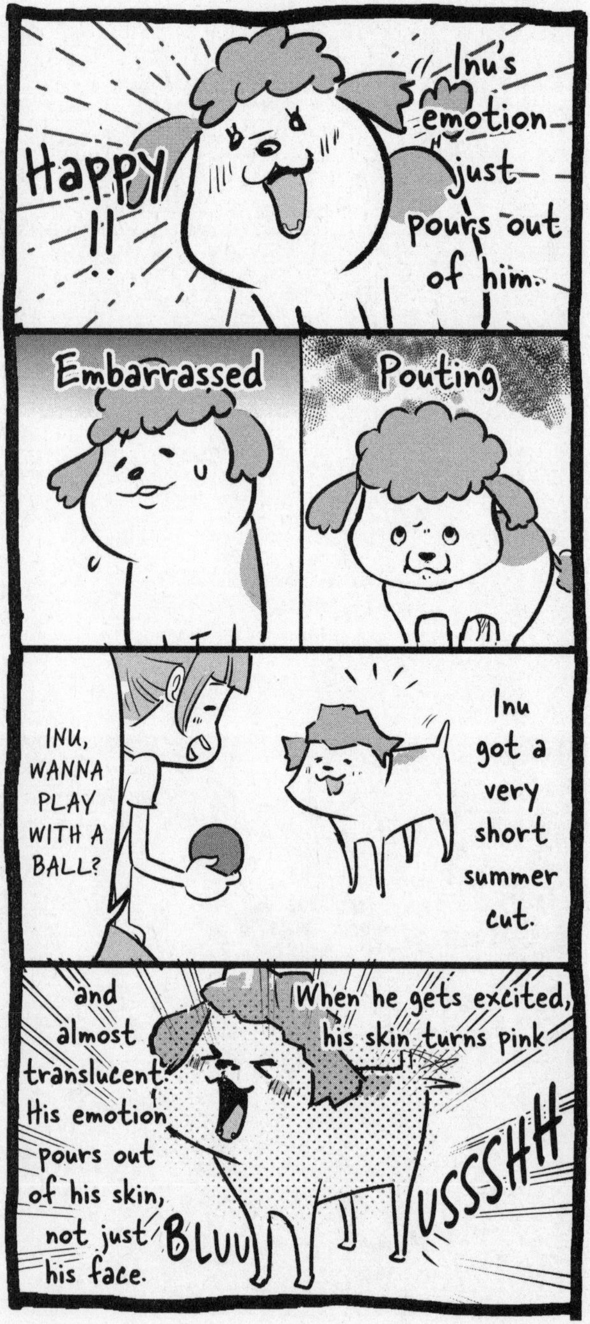
Inu's emotion just pours out of him.
Happy!!
Pouting
Embarrassed
Inu got a very short summer cut.
INU, WANNA PLAY WITH A BALL?
When he gets excited, his skin turns pink
and almost translucent. His emotion pours out of his skin, not just his face.
BLUUUSSSHH

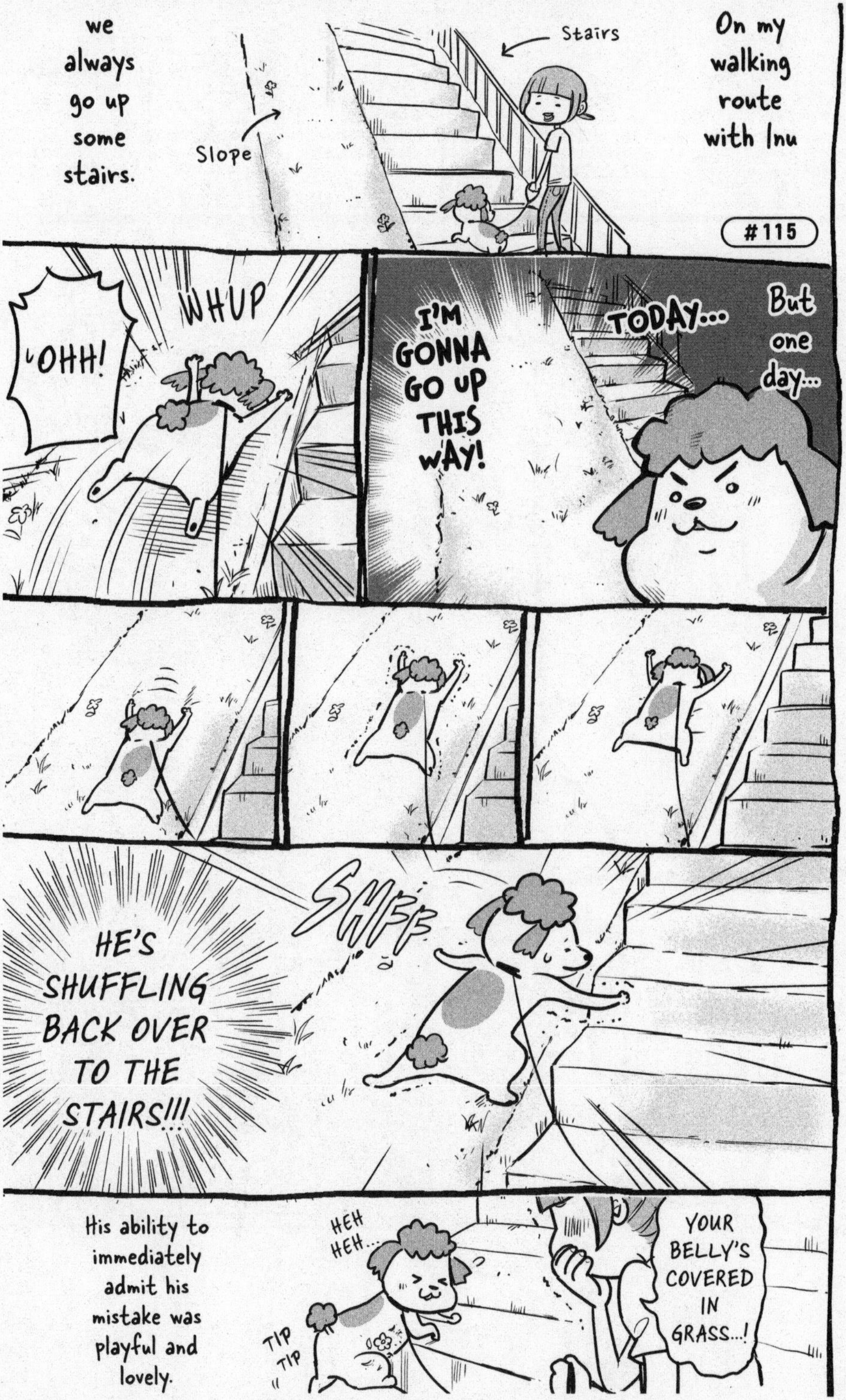
#115
On my walking route with Inu
Stairs
Slope
we always go up some stairs.
But one day...
TODAY...
I'M GONNA GO UP THIS WAY!
WHUP
OHH!
SHFF
HE'S SHUFFLING BACK OVER TO THE STAIRS!!!
YOUR BELLY'S COVERED IN GRASS...!
HEH HEH...
TIP TIP
His ability to immediately admit his mistake was playful and lovely.

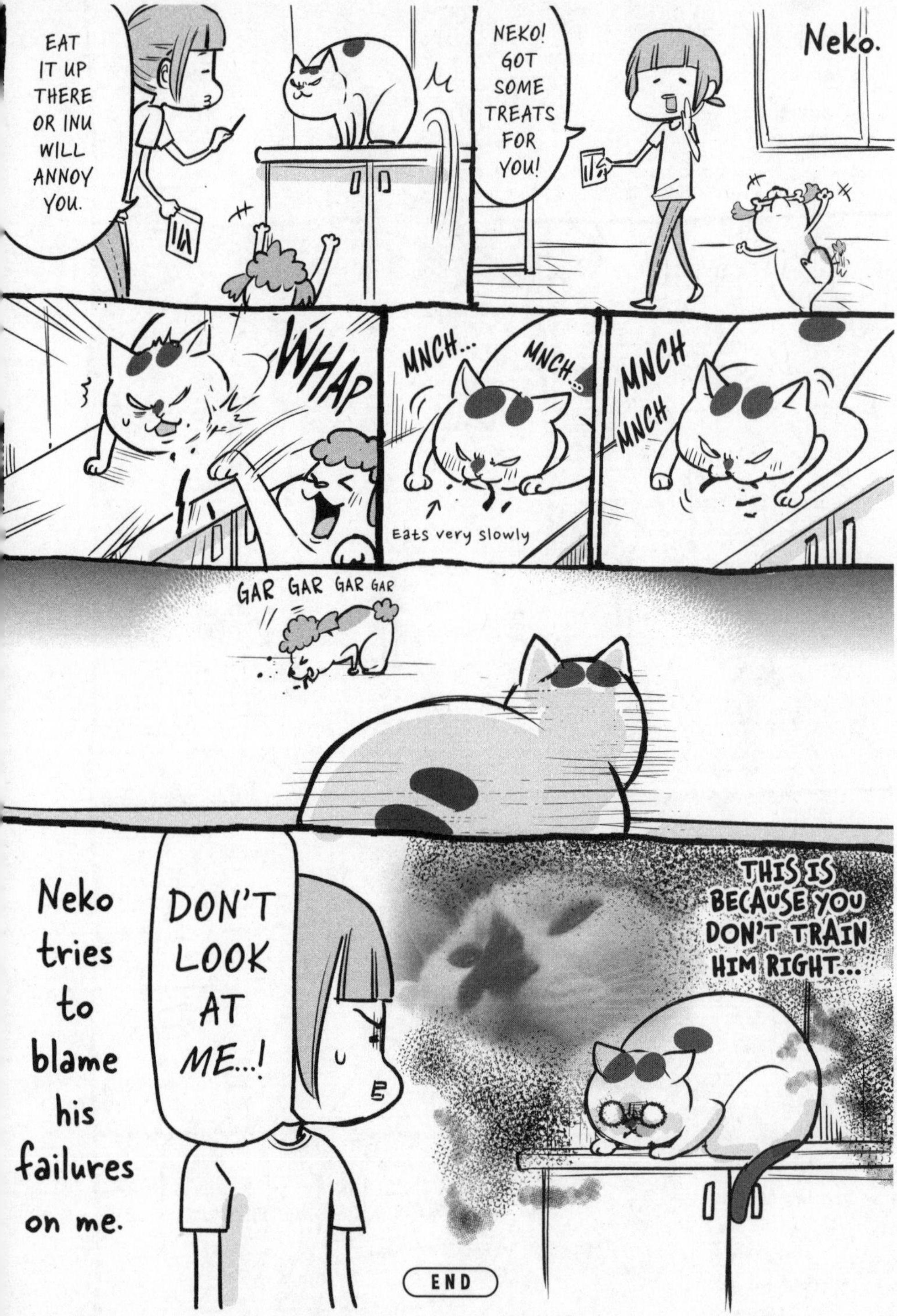
Neko.
NEKO! GOT SOME TREATS FOR YOU!
EAT IT UP THERE OR INU WILL ANNOY YOU.
MNCH MNCH
MNCH... MNCH...
Eats very slowly
WHAP
GAR GAR GAR GAR
THIS IS BECAUSE YOU DON'T TRAIN HIM RIGHT...
DON'T LOOK AT ME...!
Neko tries to blame his failures on me.

END

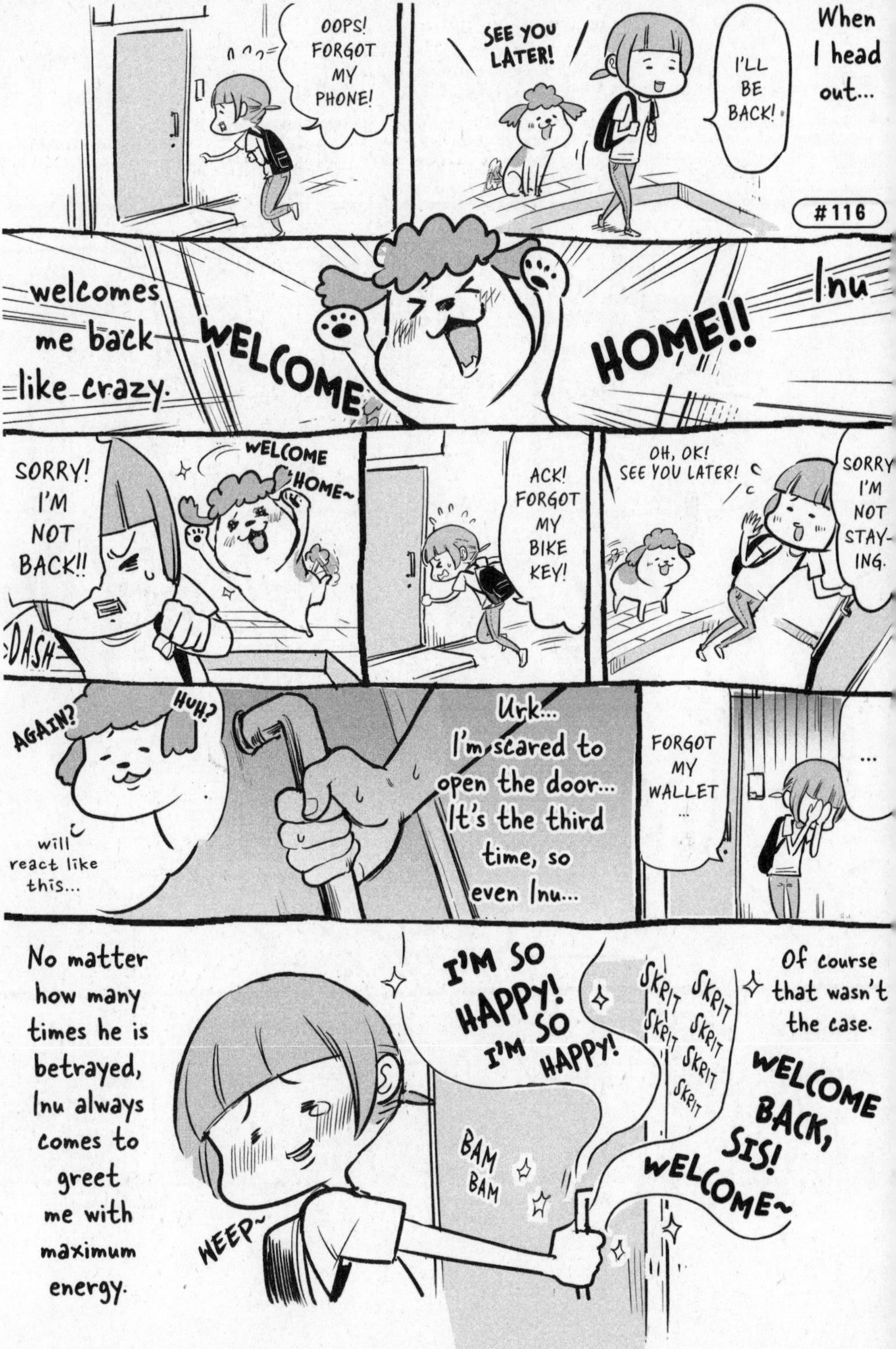
#116
When I head out...
I'LL BE BACK!
SEE YOU LATER!
OOPS! FORGOT MY PHONE!
Inu
WELCOME HOME!!
welcomes me back like crazy.
SORRY I'M NOT STAYING.
OH, OK! SEE YOU LATER!
ACK! FORGOT MY BIKE KEY!
WELCOME HOME~
SORRY! I'M NOT BACK!!
DASH
...
FORGOT MY WALLET ...
Urk... I'm scared to open the door... It's the third time, so even Inu...
HUH?
AGAIN?
will react like this...
Of course that wasn't the case.
WELCOME BACK, SIS! WELCOME~
SKRIT SKRIT SKRIT SKRIT SKRIT SKRIT SKRIT
I'M SO HAPPY! I'M SO HAPPY!
BAM BAM
WEEP~
No matter how many times he is betrayed, Inu always comes to greet me with maximum energy.

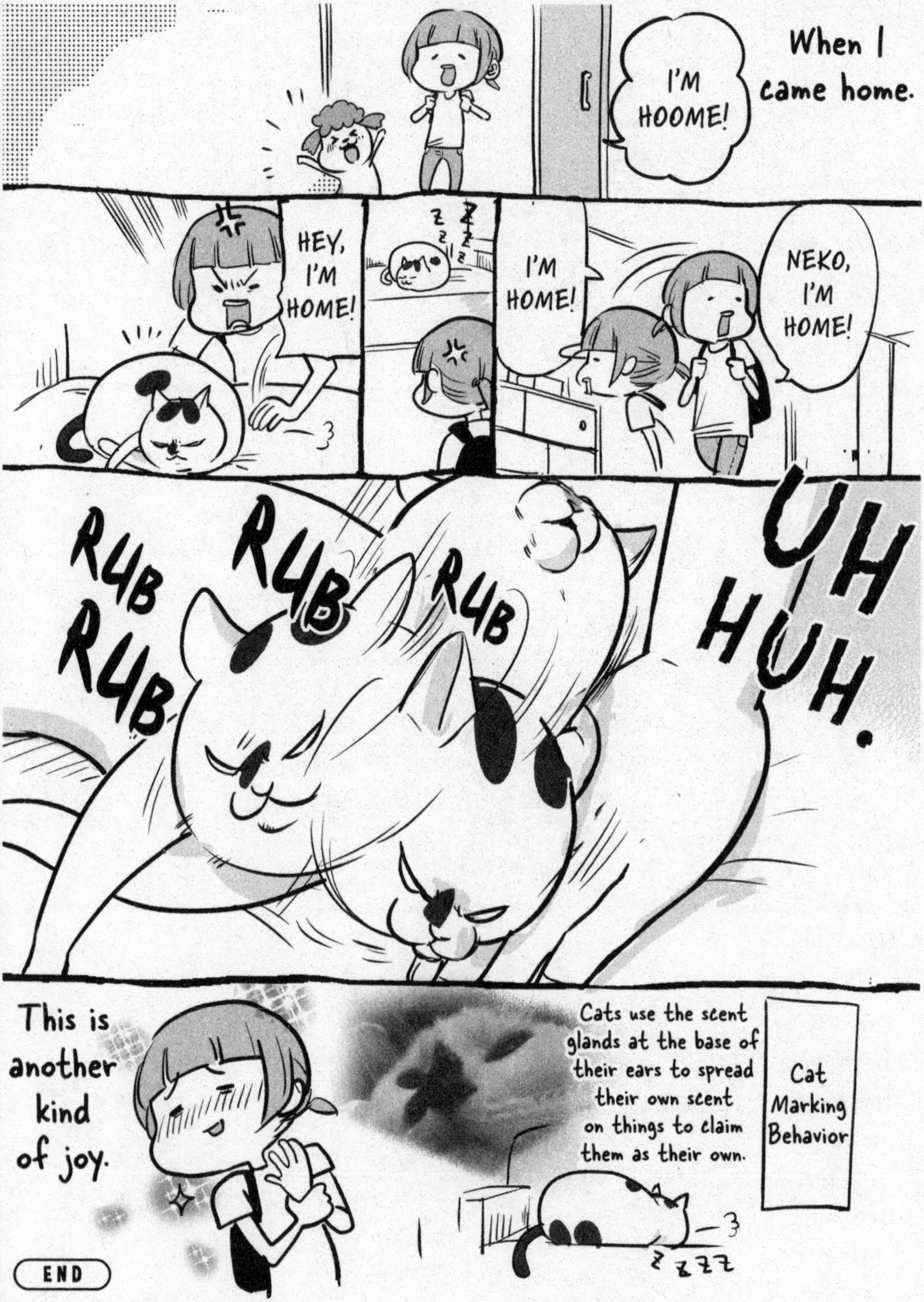
When I came home.
I'M HOOME!
NEKO, I'M HOME!
I'M HOME!
Z Z Z Z Z
HEY, I'M HOME!
UH HUH.
RUB
RUB
RUB RUB
Cat Marking Behavior
Cats use the scent glands at the base of their ears to spread their own scent on things to claim them as their own.
Z Z Z Z
This is another kind of joy.
END

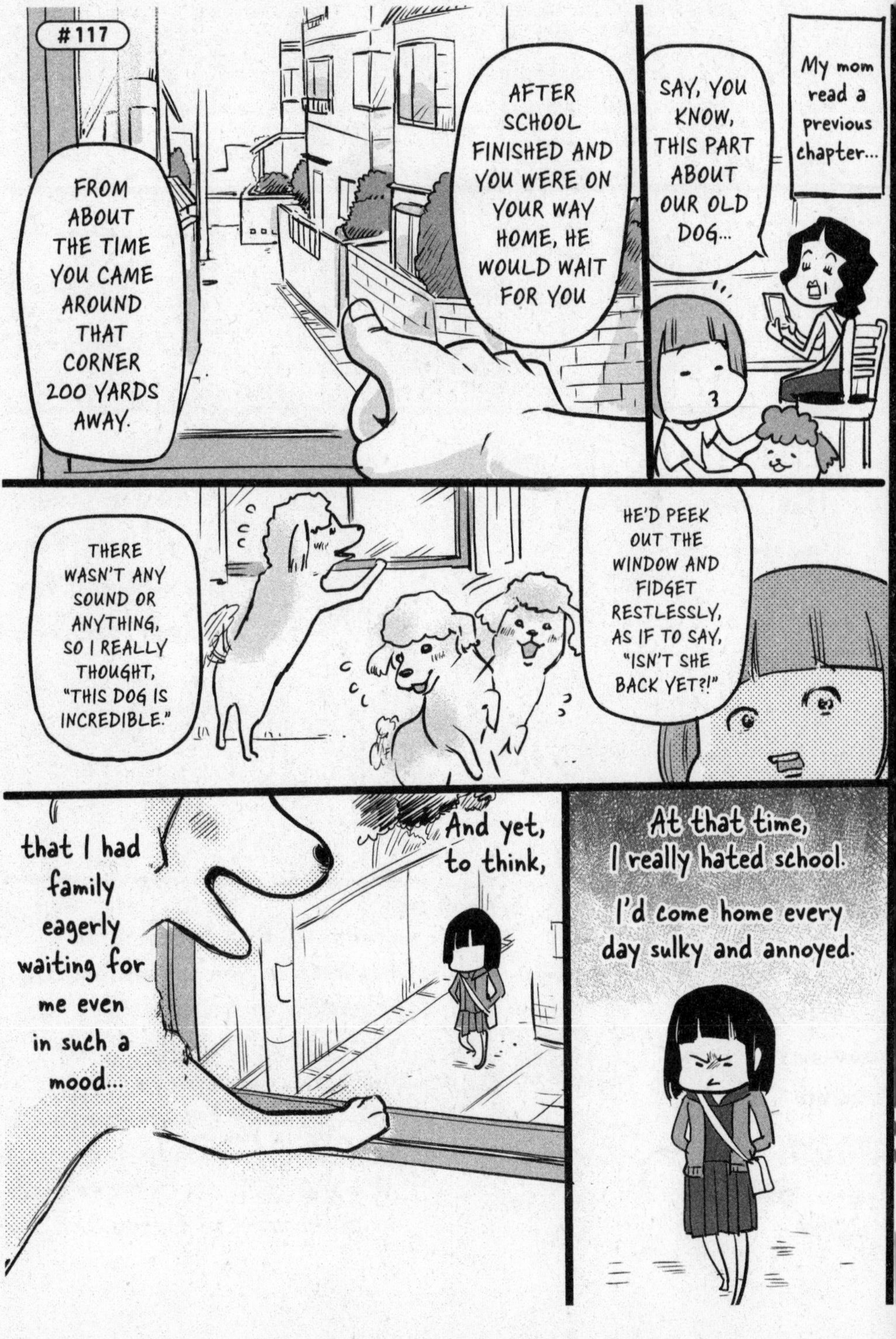
#117
My mom read a previous chapter...
SAY, YOU KNOW, THIS PART ABOUT OUR OLD DOG...
AFTER SCHOOL FINISHED AND YOU WERE ON YOUR WAY HOME, HE WOULD WAIT FOR YOU
FROM ABOUT THE TIME YOU CAME AROUND THAT CORNER 200 YARDS AWAY.
HE'D PEEK OUT THE WINDOW AND FIDGET RESTLESSLY, AS IF TO SAY, "ISN'T SHE BACK YET?!"
THERE WASN'T ANY SOUND OR ANYTHING, SO I REALLY THOUGHT, "THIS DOG IS INCREDIBLE."
At that time, I really hated school.
I'd come home every day sulky and annoyed.
And yet, to think,
that I had family eagerly waiting for me even in such a mood...

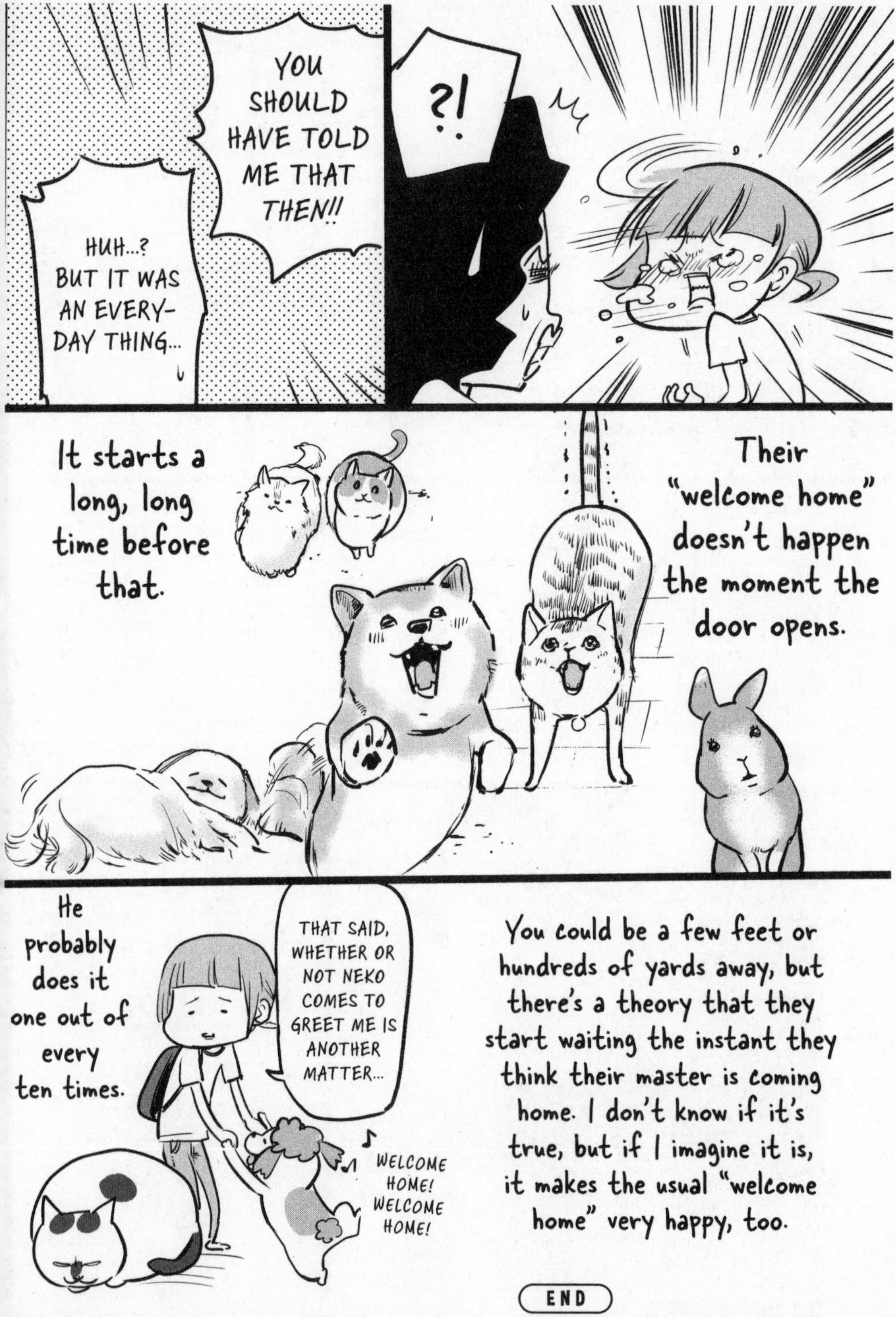
?!
YOU SHOULD HAVE TOLD ME THAT THEN!!
HUH...? BUT IT WAS AN EVERY-DAY THING...
Their "welcome home" doesn't happen the moment the door opens.
It starts a long, long time before that.
You could be a few feet or hundreds of yards away, but there's a theory that they start waiting the instant they think their master is coming home. I don't know if it's true, but if I imagine it is, it makes the usual "welcome home" very happy, too.
THAT SAID, WHETHER OR NOT NEKO COMES TO GREET ME IS ANOTHER MATTER...
He probably does it one out of every ten times.
WELCOME HOME! WELCOME HOME!
END

Inu and Neko drawn together by
the spring sunlight.

More About #116

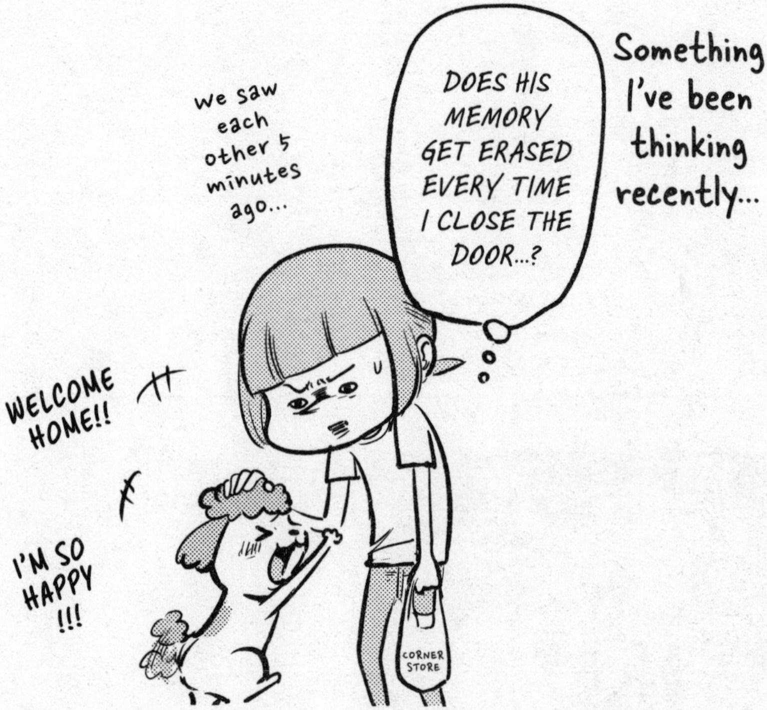

Something I've been thinking recently...
DOES HIS MEMORY GET ERASED EVERY TIME I CLOSE THE DOOR...?
we saw each other 5 minutes ago...
WELCOME HOME!!
I'M SO HAPPY!!!
CORNER STORE

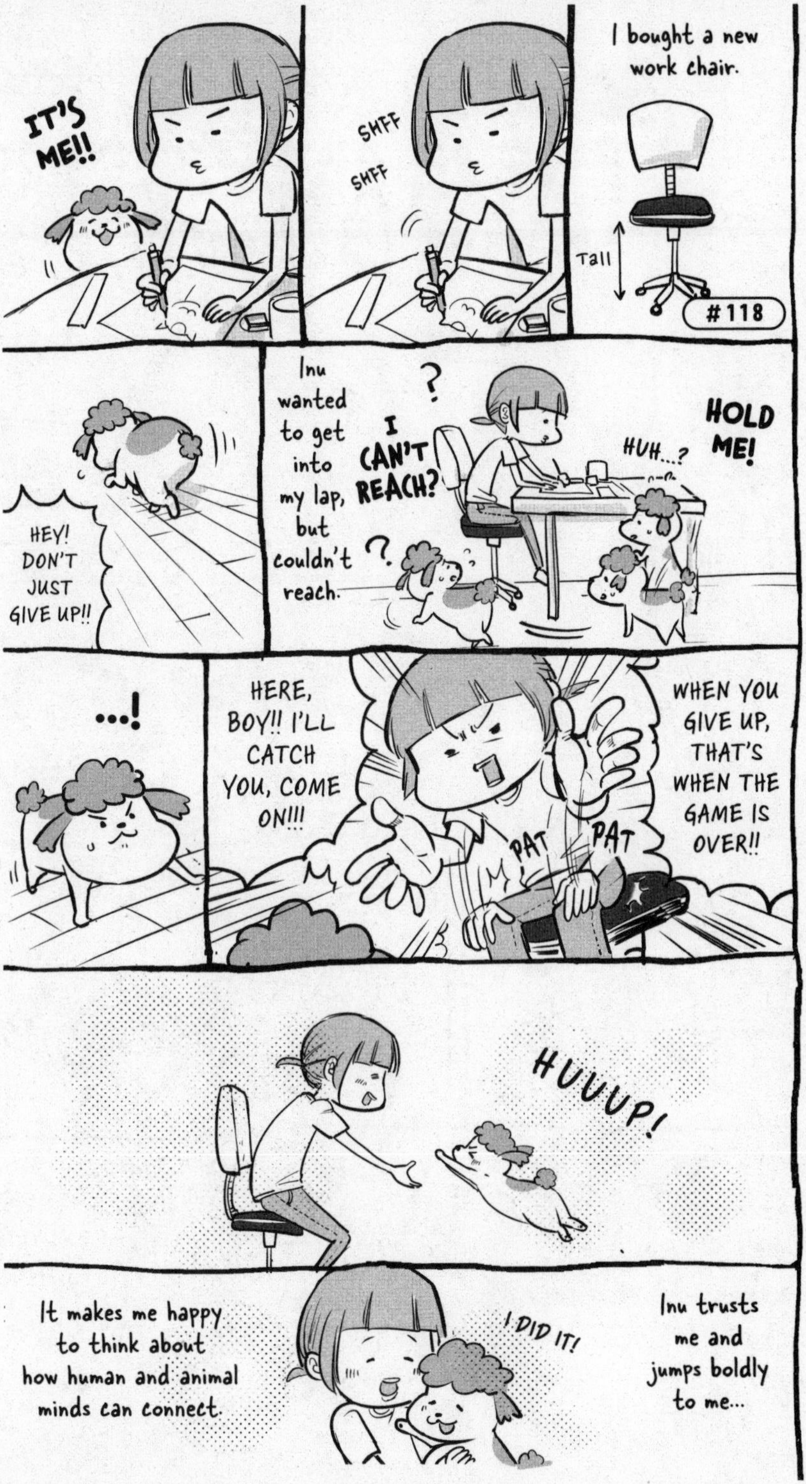
I bought a new work chair.
Tall
#118
SHFF
SHFF
IT'S ME!!
HOLD ME!
HUH...?
I CAN'T REACH?
Inu wanted to get into my lap, but couldn't reach.
HEY! DON'T JUST GIVE UP!!
WHEN YOU GIVE UP, THAT'S WHEN THE GAME IS OVER!!
HERE, BOY!! I'LL CATCH YOU, COME ON!!!
PAT PAT
...!
HUUUP!
Inu trusts me and jumps boldly to me...
I DID IT!
It makes me happy to think about how human and animal minds can connect.

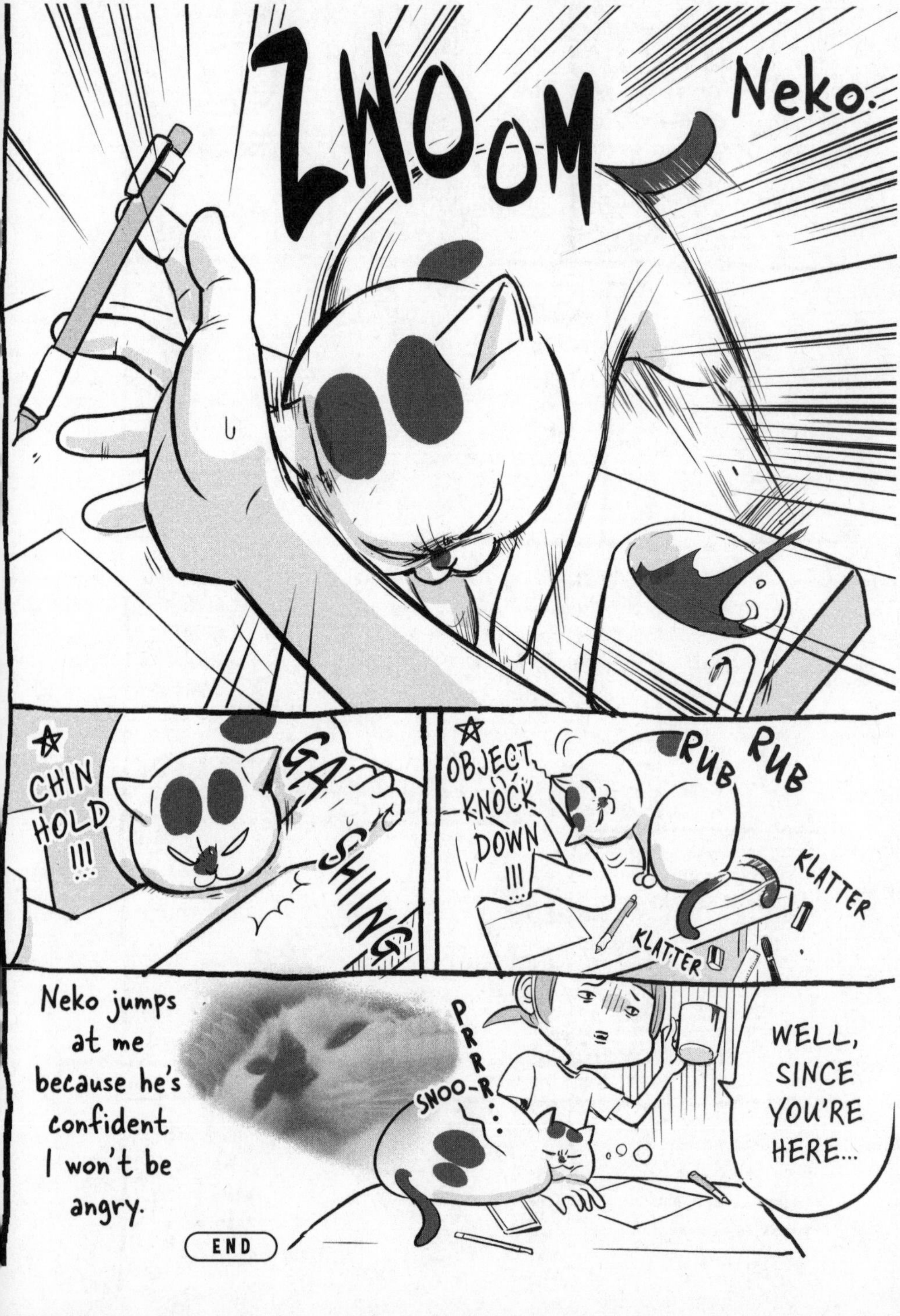
Neko.
ZWOOM
OBJECT KNOCK DOWN !!!
RUB
RUB
KLATTER
KLATTER
CHIN HOLD !!!...
GA SHING
WELL, SINCE YOU'RE HERE...
PRRRR...
SNOO-
Neko jumps at me because he's confident I won't be angry.
END

#119

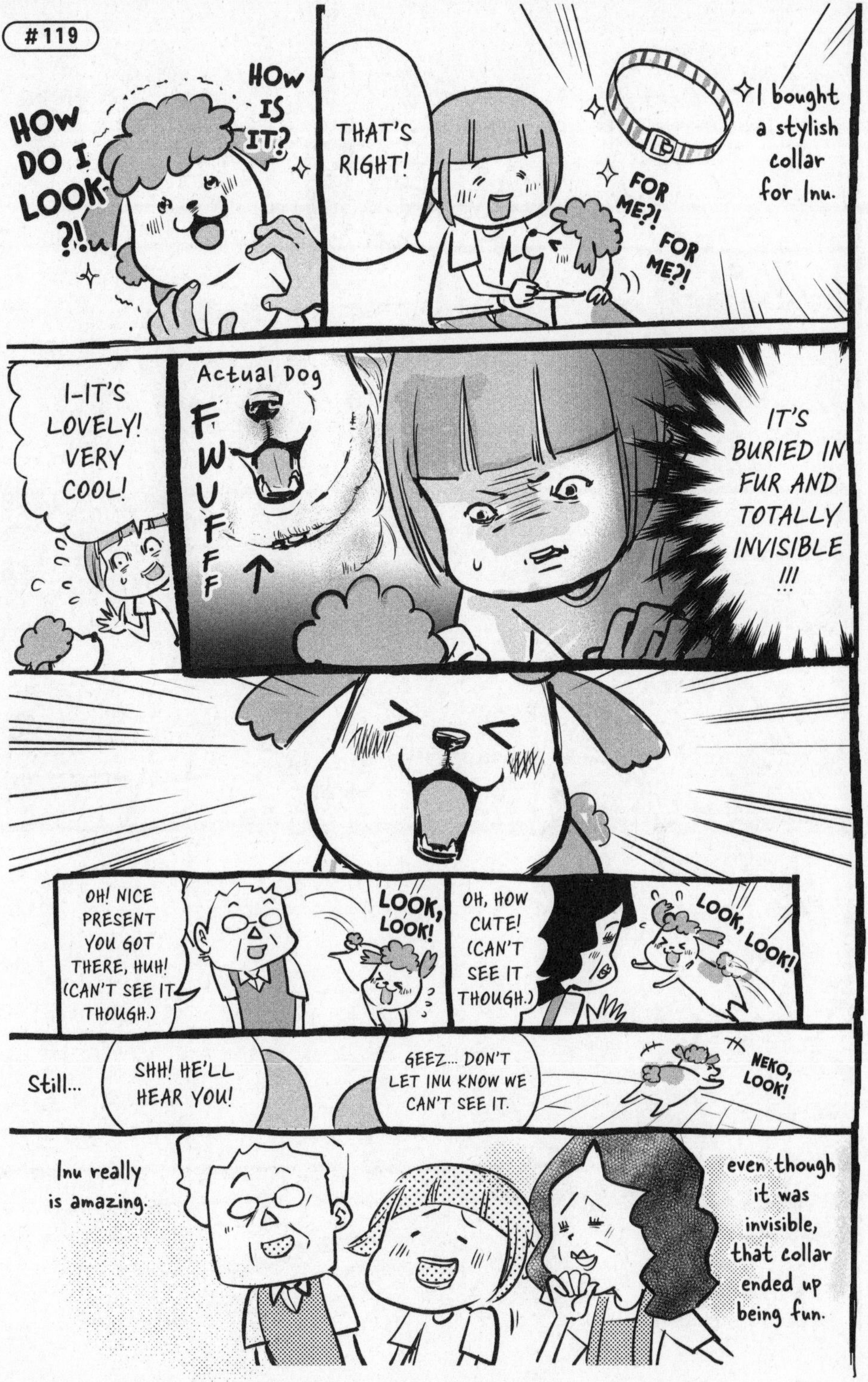
I bought a stylish collar for Inu.
FOR ME?!
FOR ME?!
THAT'S RIGHT!
HOW IS IT?
HOW DO I LOOK?!
IT'S BURIED IN FUR AND TOTALLY INVISIBLE!!!
Actual Dog
FWUFFF
I-IT'S LOVELY! VERY COOL!
LOOK, LOOK!
OH, HOW CUTE! (CAN'T SEE IT THOUGH.)
LOOK, LOOK!
OH! NICE PRESENT YOU GOT THERE, HUH! (CAN'T SEE IT THOUGH.)
NEKO, LOOK!
GEEZ... DON'T LET INU KNOW WE CAN'T SEE IT.
SHH! HE'LL HEAR YOU!
Still...
even though it was invisible, that collar ended up being fun.
Inu really is amazing.

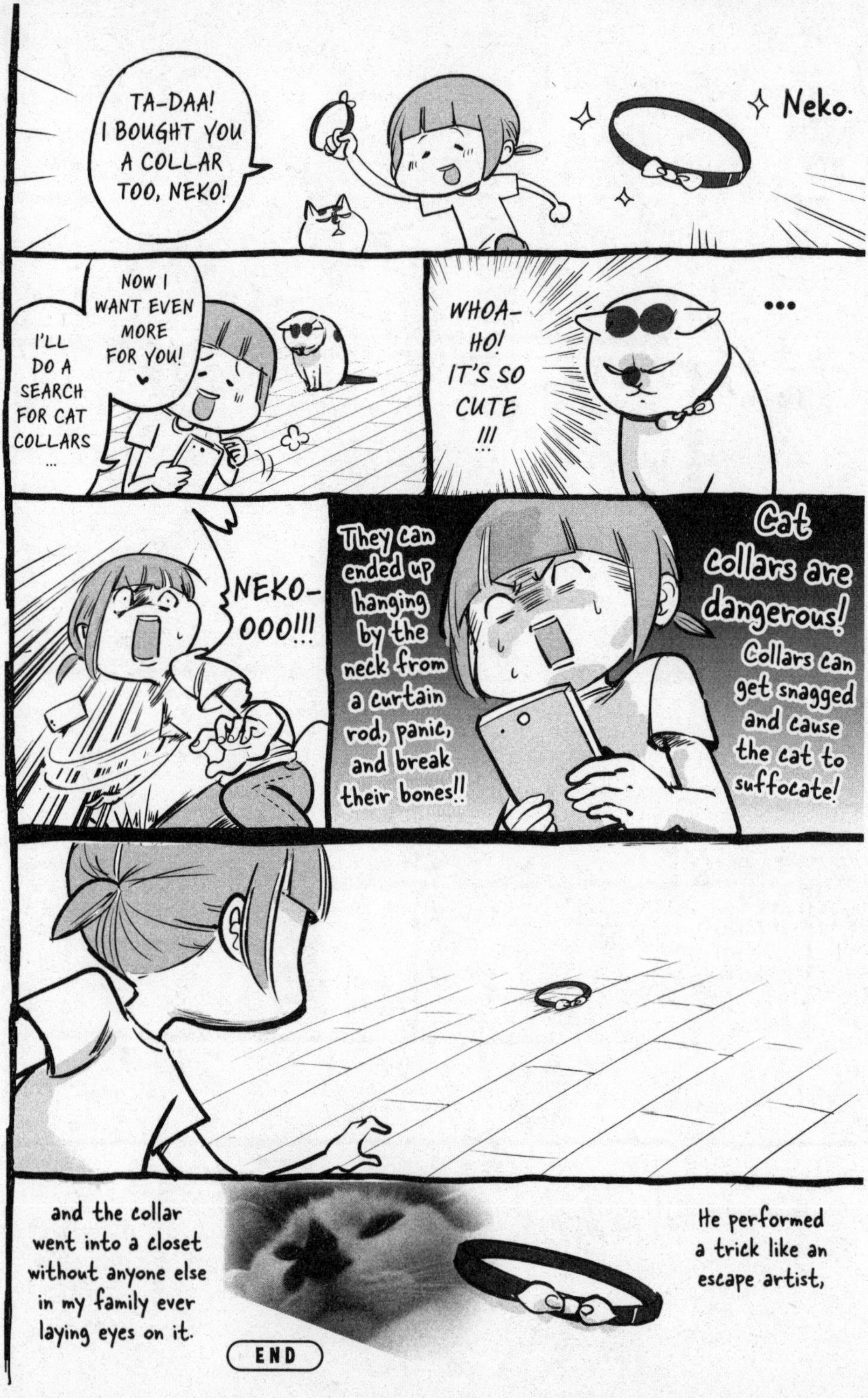
Neko.
TA-DAA! I BOUGHT YOU A COLLAR TOO, NEKO!
...
WHOA-HO! IT'S SO CUTE!!!
NOW I WANT EVEN MORE FOR YOU!
I'LL DO A SEARCH FOR CAT COLLARS...
Cat collars are dangerous!
Collars can get snagged and cause the cat to suffocate!
They can ended up hanging by the neck from a curtain rod, panic, and break their bones!!
NEKO-OOO!!!
He performed a trick like an escape artist,
and the collar went into a closet without anyone else in my family ever laying eyes on it.
END

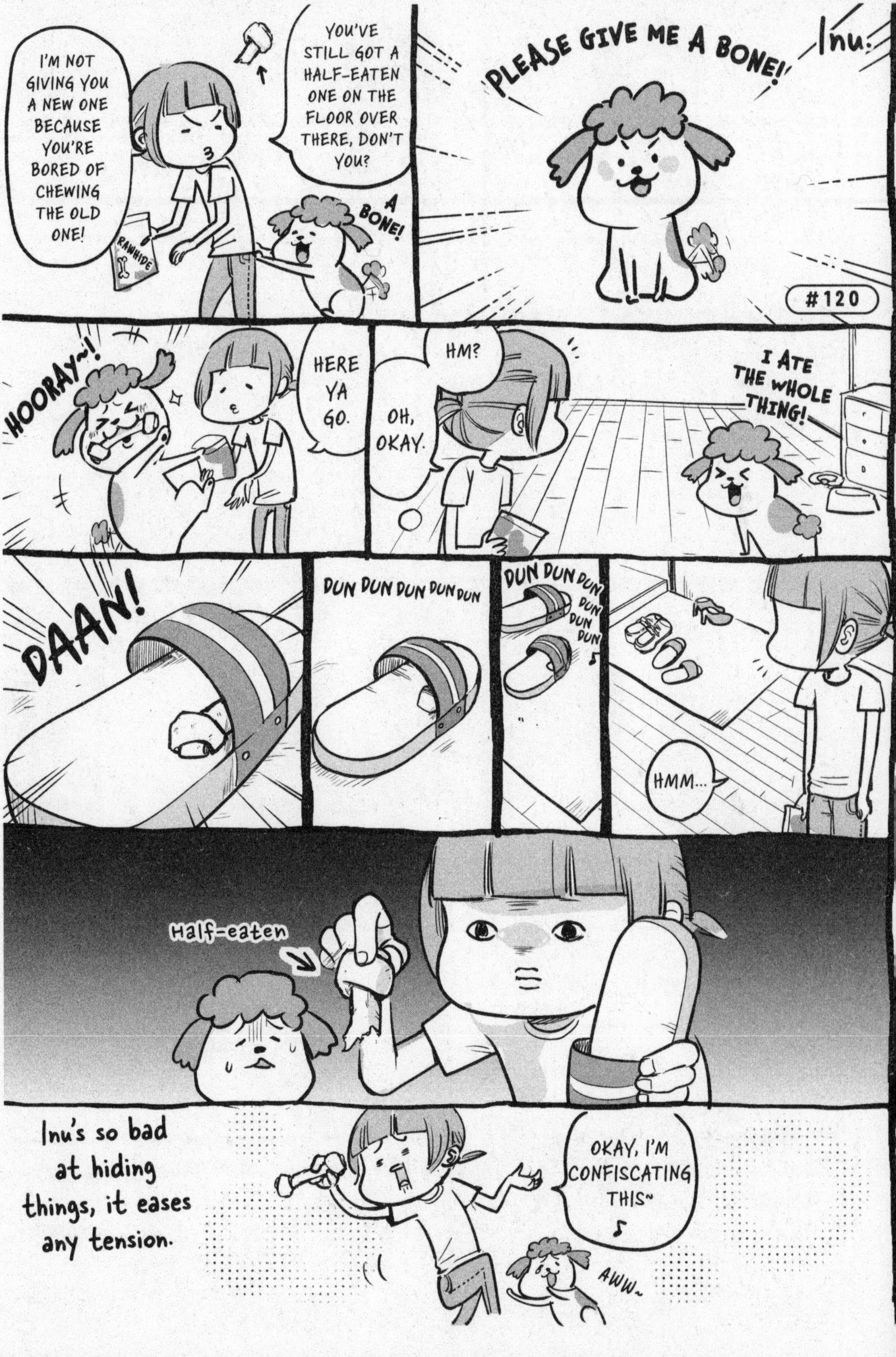
Inu.
PLEASE GIVE ME A BONE!
#120
YOU'VE STILL GOT A HALF-EATEN ONE ON THE FLOOR OVER THERE, DON'T YOU?
A BONE!
I'M NOT GIVING YOU A NEW ONE BECAUSE YOU'RE BORED OF CHEWING THE OLD ONE!
RAWHIDE
I ATE THE WHOLE THING!
HM?
OH, OKAY.
HERE YA GO.
HOORAY~!
HMM...
DUN DUN DUN DUN DUN DUN
DUN DUN DUN DUN DUN
DAAN!
Half-eaten
OKAY, I'M CONFISCATING THIS~
AWW~
Inu's so bad at hiding things, it eases any tension.

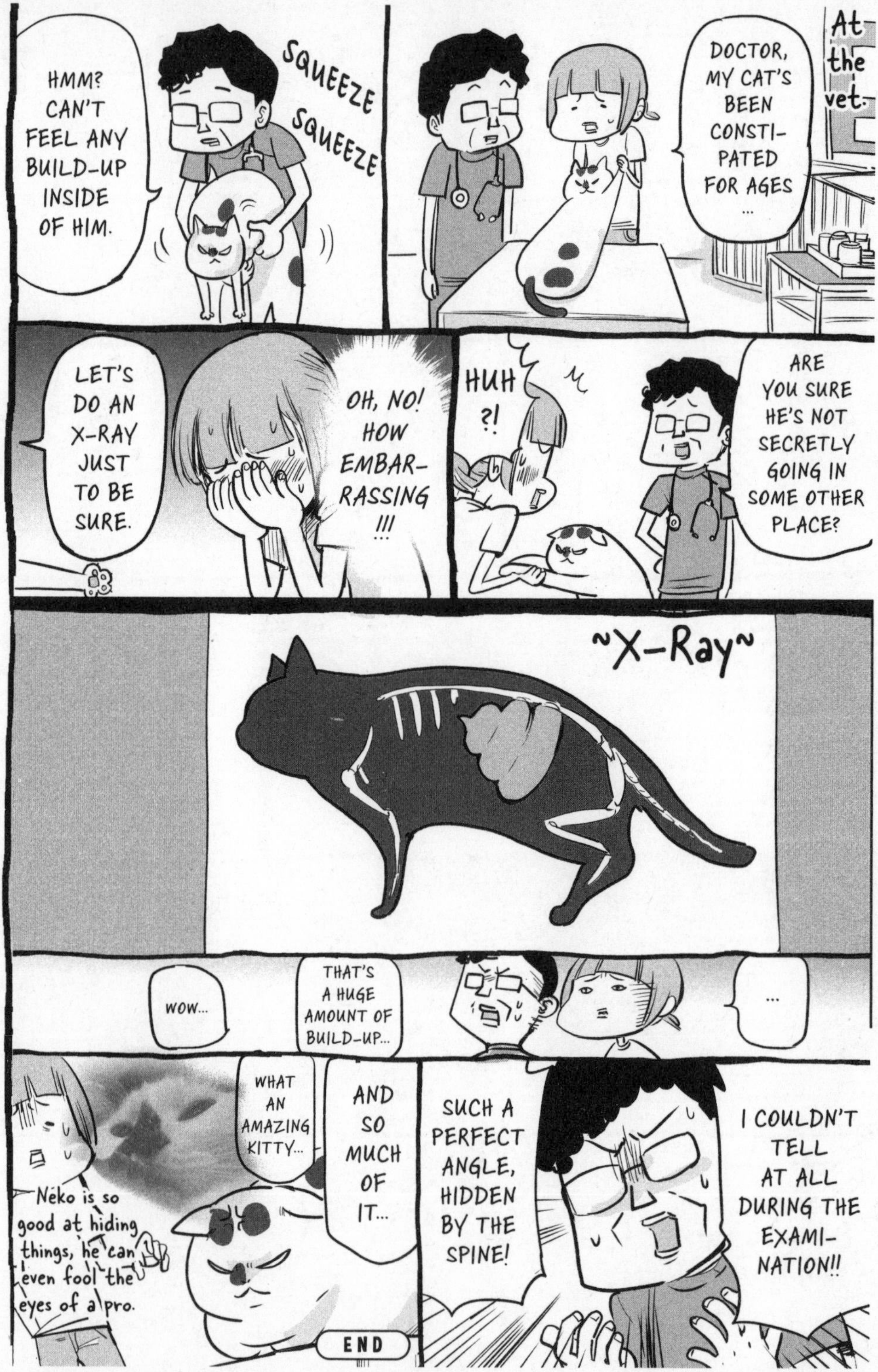
At the vet.
DOCTOR, MY CAT'S BEEN CONSTI-PATED FOR AGES ...
SQUEEZE SQUEEZE
HMM? CAN'T FEEL ANY BUILD-UP INSIDE OF HIM.
ARE YOU SURE HE'S NOT SECRETLY GOING IN SOME OTHER PLACE?
HUH ?!
OH, NO! HOW EMBAR-RASSING !!!
LET'S DO AN X-RAY JUST TO BE SURE.
~X-Ray~
...
THAT'S A HUGE AMOUNT OF BUILD-UP...
WOW...
I COULDN'T TELL AT ALL DURING THE EXAMI-NATION!!
SUCH A PERFECT ANGLE, HIDDEN BY THE SPINE!
AND SO MUCH OF IT...
WHAT AN AMAZING KITTY...
Neko is so good at hiding things, he can even fool the eyes of a pro.
END

More About #120

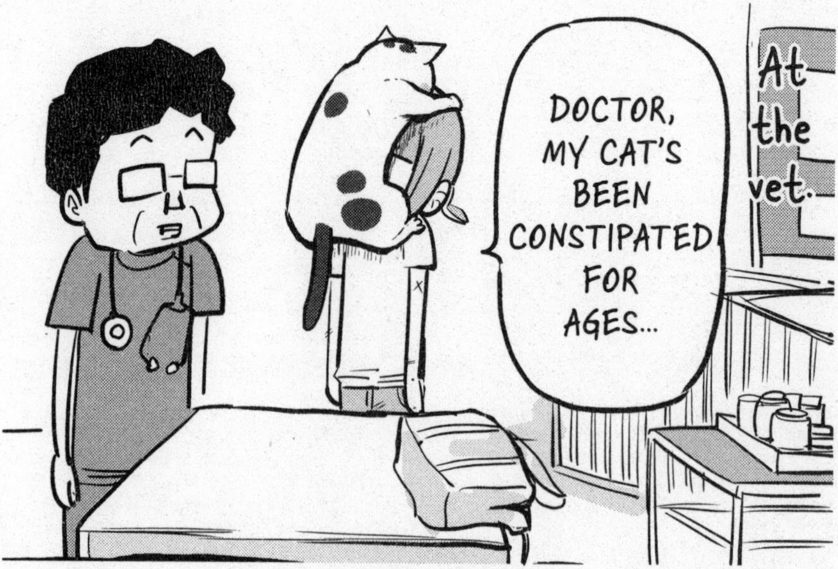
At the vet.
DOCTOR, MY CAT'S BEEN CONSTIPATED FOR AGES...

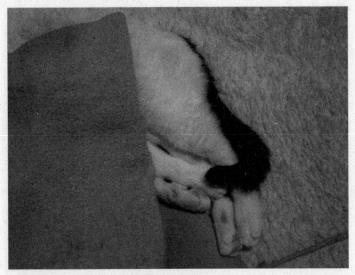

I can see you. I can totally see you.

Newly-Drawn 4-Panel Strip

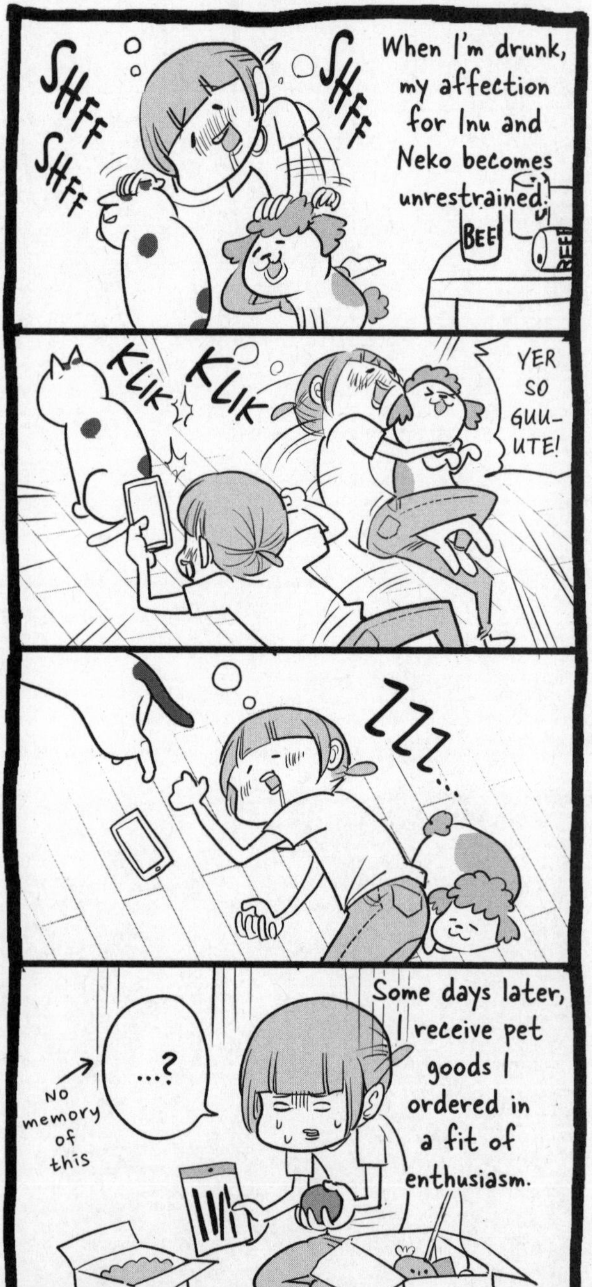
When I'm drunk, my affection for Inu and Neko becomes unrestrained.
SHFF
SHFF SHFF
YER SO GUU-UTE!
KLIK
KLIK
ZZZ...
Some days later, I receive pet goods I ordered in a fit of enthusiasm.
...?
NO memory of this

Booze is truly scary.

#121

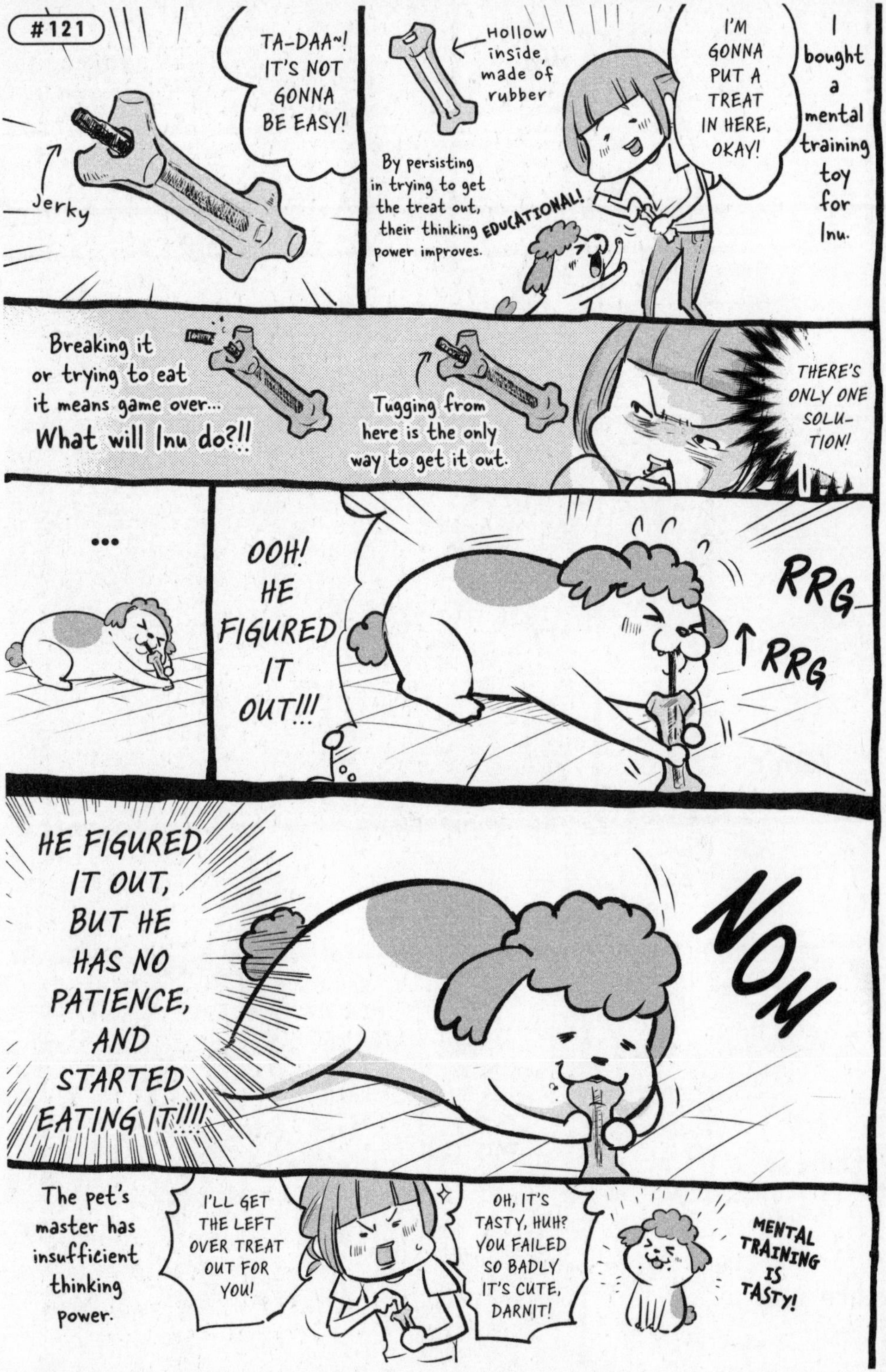
I bought a mental training toy for Inu.
I'M GONNA PUT A TREAT IN HERE, OKAY!
Hollow inside, made of rubber
By persisting in trying to get the treat out, their thinking power improves.
EDUCATIONAL!
TA-DAA~! IT'S NOT GONNA BE EASY!
Jerky
THERE'S ONLY ONE SOLU-TION!
Tugging from here is the only way to get it out.
Breaking it or trying to eat it means game over...
What will Inu do?!!
RRG
RRG
OOH! HE FIGURED IT OUT!!!
...
NOM
HE FIGURED IT OUT, BUT HE HAS NO PATIENCE, AND STARTED EATING IT!!!!!
MENTAL TRAINING IS TASTY!
OH, IT'S TASTY, HUH? YOU FAILED SO BADLY IT'S CUTE, DARNIT!
I'LL GET THE LEFT OVER TREAT OUT FOR YOU!
The pet's master has insufficient thinking power.

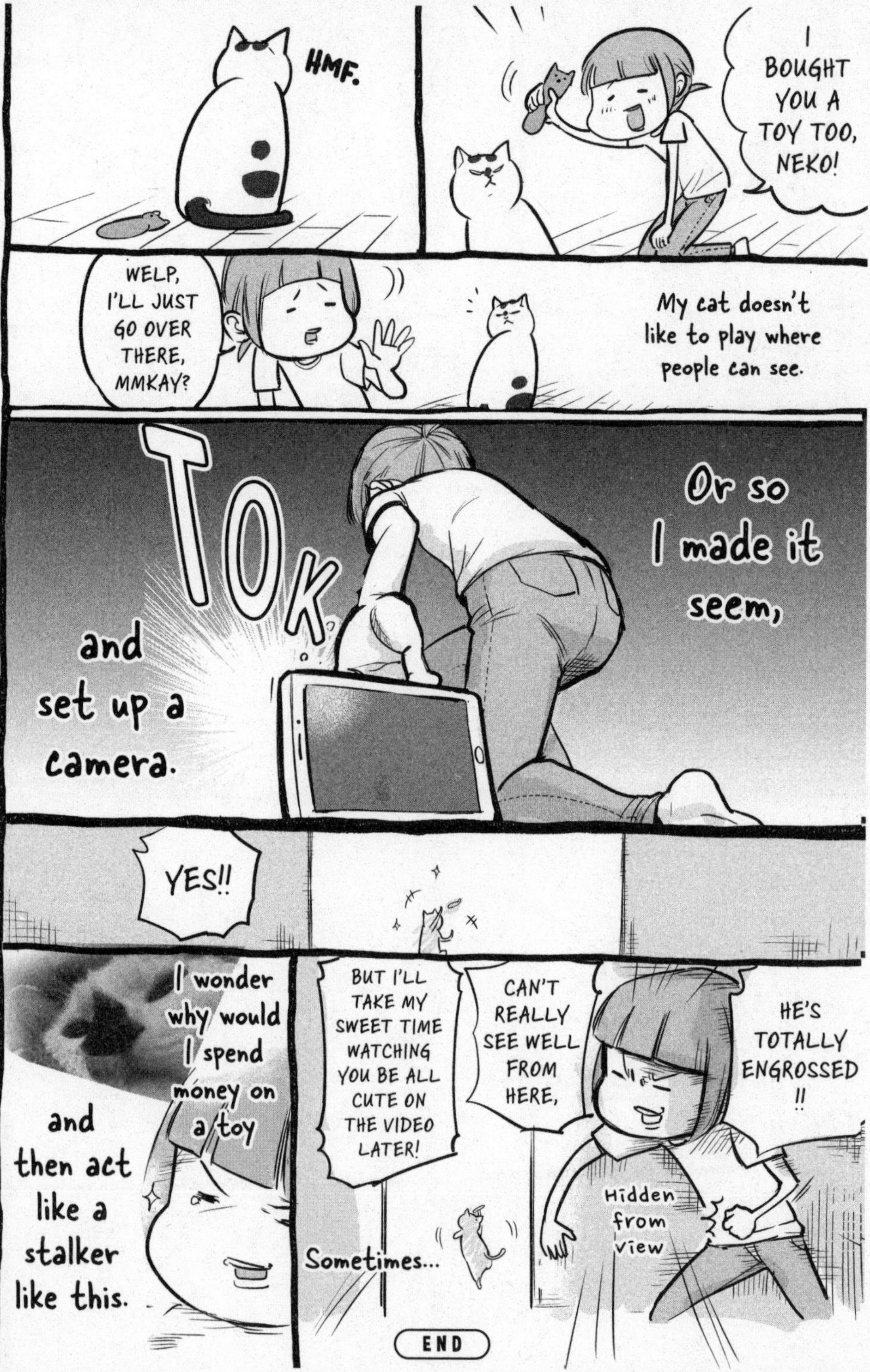
I BOUGHT YOU A TOY TOO, NEKO!
HMF.
My cat doesn't like to play where people can see.
WELP, I'LL JUST GO OVER THERE, MMKAY?
Or so I made it seem,
TOK
and set up a camera.
YES!!
HE'S TOTALLY ENGROSSED !!
CAN'T REALLY SEE WELL FROM HERE,
Hidden from view
BUT I'LL TAKE MY SWEET TIME WATCHING YOU BE ALL CUTE ON THE VIDEO LATER!
Sometimes...
I wonder why would I spend money on a toy
and then act like a stalker like this.
END

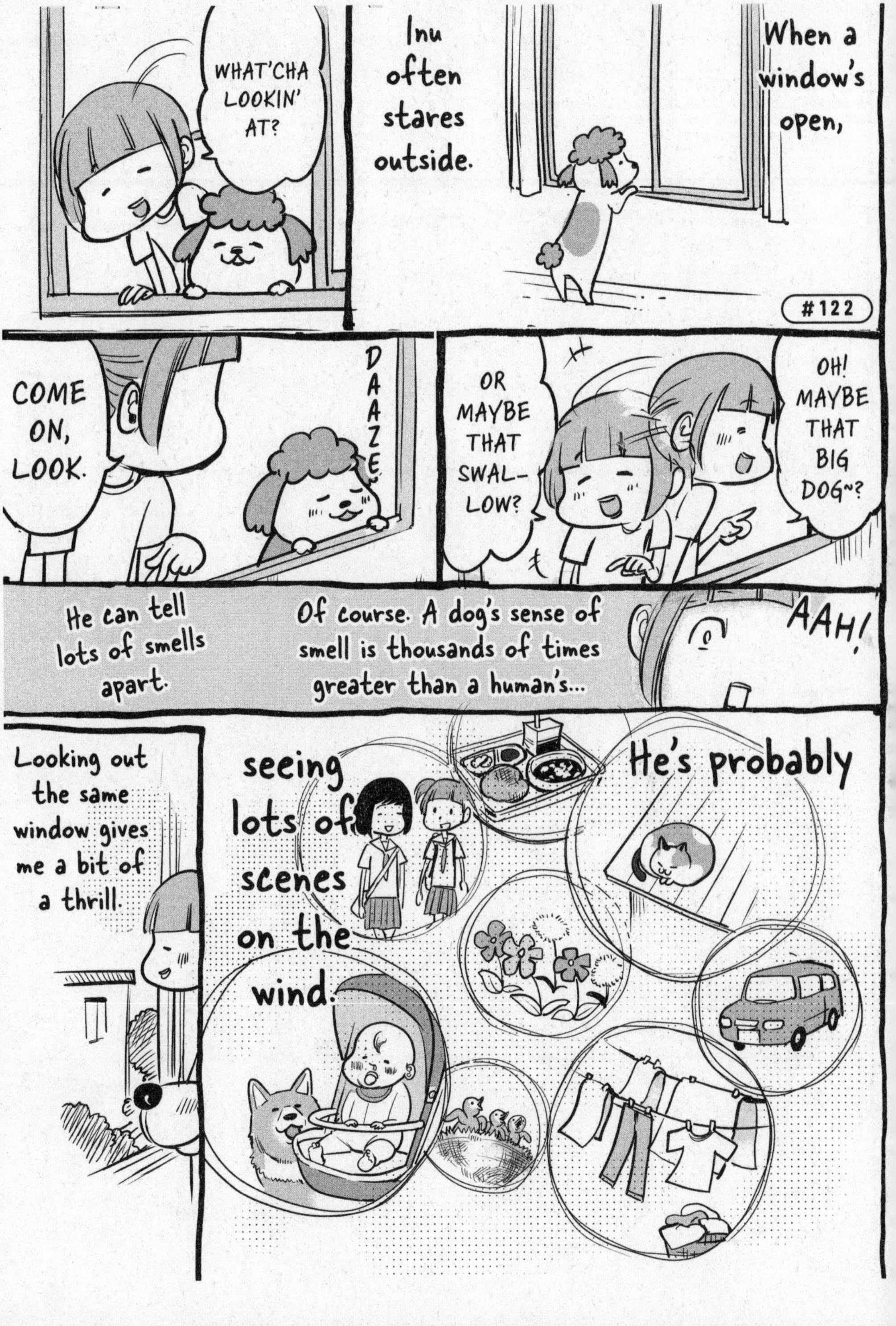
When a window's open,
#122
Inu often stares outside.
WHAT'CHA LOOKIN' AT?
OH! MAYBE THAT BIG DOG~?
OR MAYBE THAT SWAL-LOW?
DAAAZE
COME ON, LOOK.
AAH!
Of course. A dog's sense of smell is thousands of times greater than a human's...
He can tell lots of smells apart.
He's probably seeing lots of scenes on the wind.
Looking out the same window gives me a bit of a thrill.

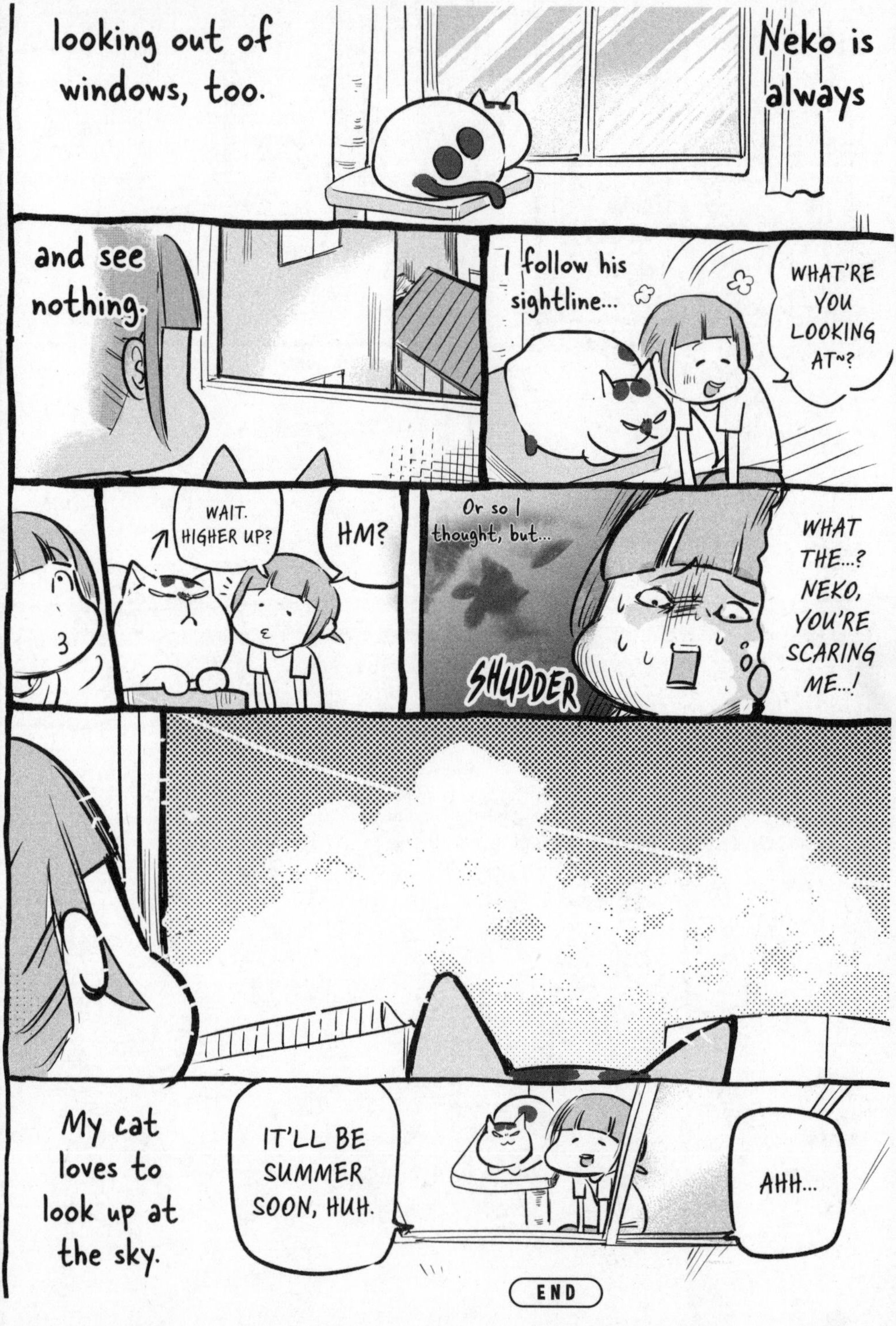

Neko is always
looking out of windows, too.
I follow his sightline...
WHAT'RE YOU LOOKING AT~?
and see nothing.
Or so I thought, but...
SHUDDER
WHAT THE...? NEKO, YOU'RE SCARING ME...!
HM?
WAIT. HIGHER UP?
AHH...
IT'LL BE SUMMER SOON, HUH.
My cat loves to look up at the sky.
END

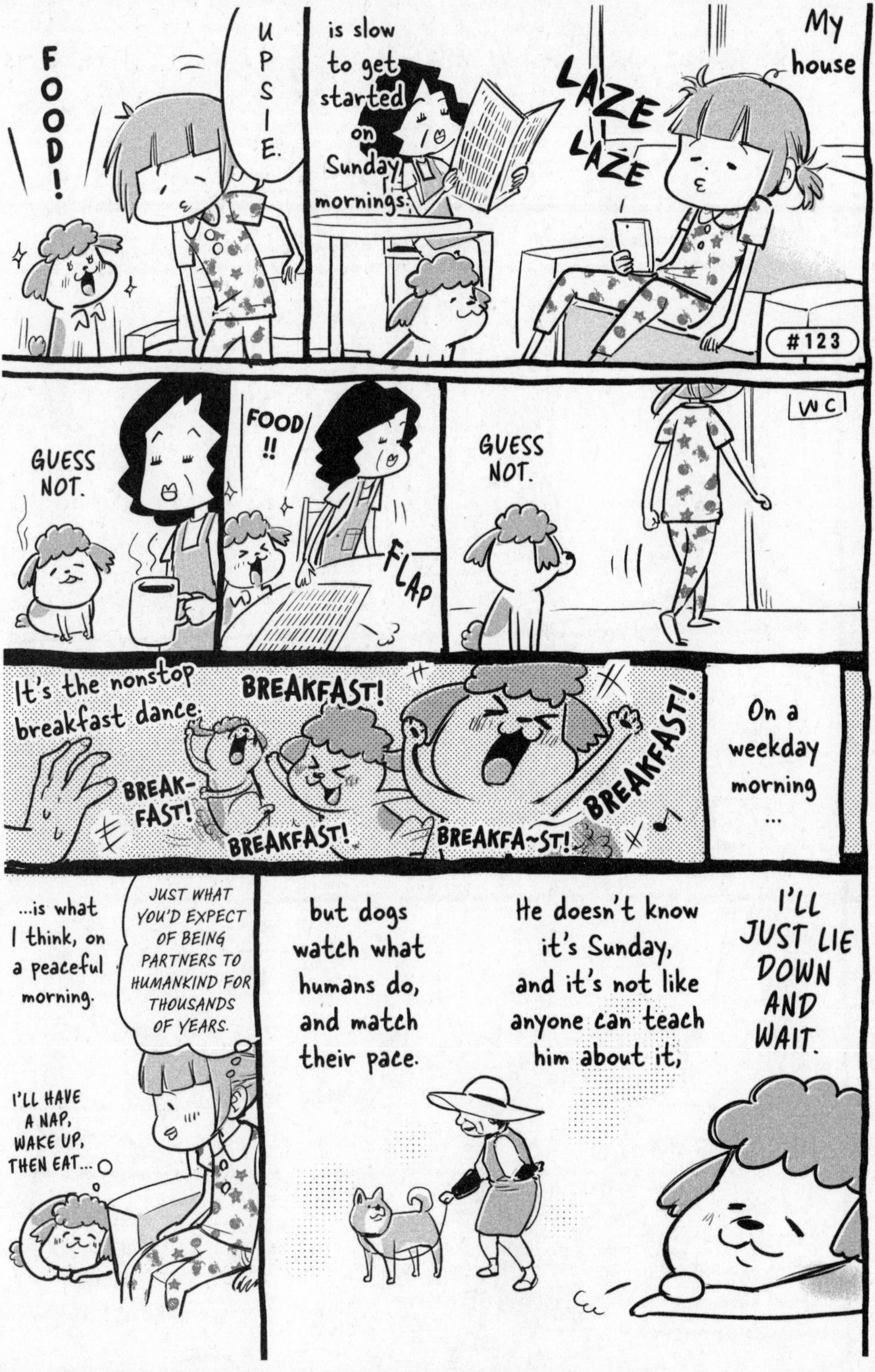
My house
LAZE LAZE
#123
is slow to get started on Sunday mornings.
UPSIE.
FOOD!
WC
GUESS NOT.
FOOD!!
FLAP
GUESS NOT.
On a weekday morning ...
BREAKFAST!
BREAKFA~ST!
BREAKFAST!
BREAKFAST!
It's the nonstop breakfast dance.
BREAK-FAST!
I'LL JUST LIE DOWN AND WAIT.
He doesn't know it's Sunday, and it's not like anyone can teach him about it,
but dogs watch what humans do, and match their pace.
JUST WHAT YOU'D EXPECT OF BEING PARTNERS TO HUMANKIND FOR THOUSANDS OF YEARS.
...is what I think, on a peaceful morning.
I'LL HAVE A NAP, WAKE UP, THEN EAT...

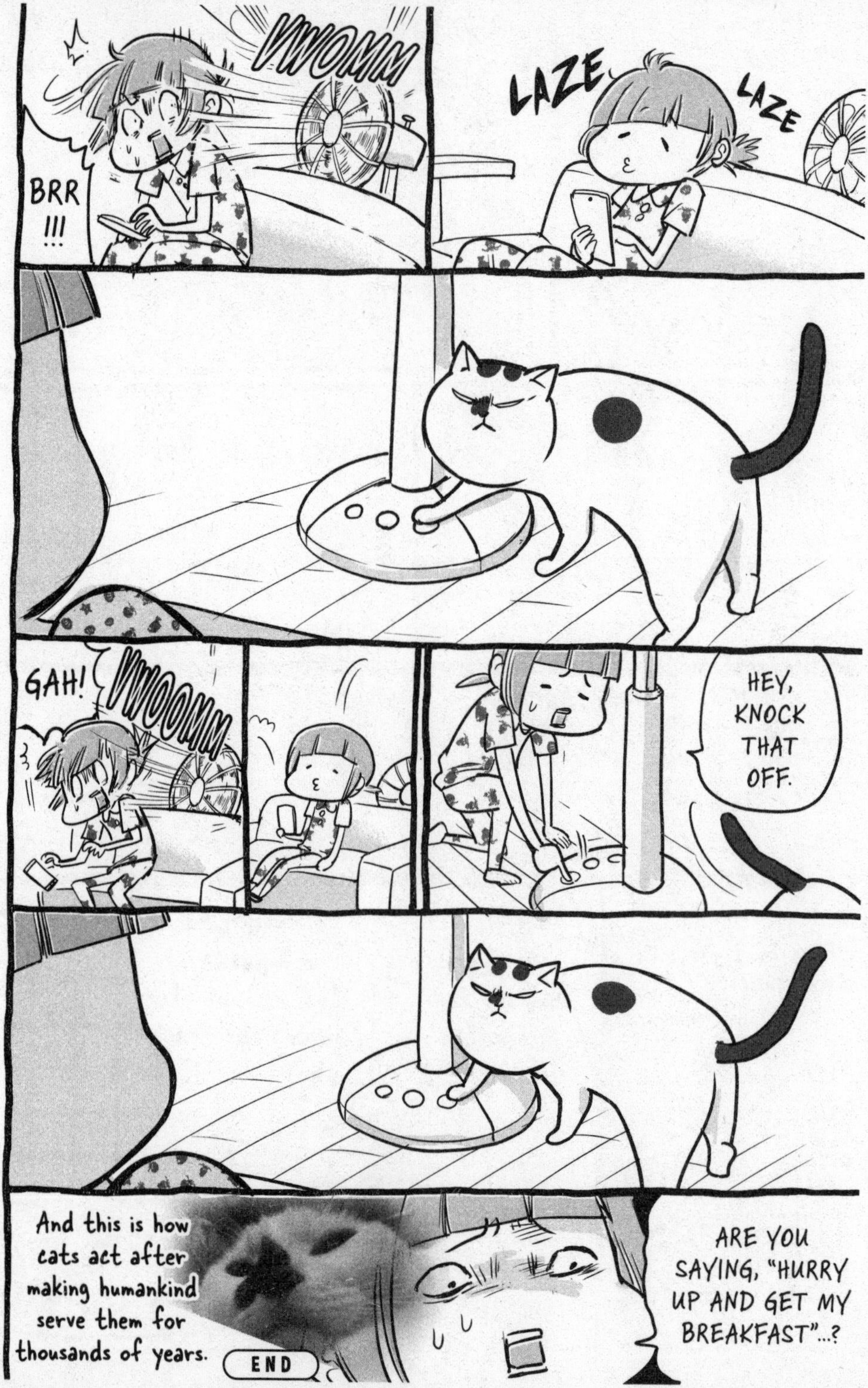
LAZE
LAZE
VWOMM
BRR!!!
HEY, KNOCK THAT OFF.
GAH!
VWOOMM
ARE YOU SAYING, "HURRY UP AND GET MY BREAKFAST"...?
And this is how cats act after making humankind serve them for thousands of years.
END

At the back, on the right... do you see him?

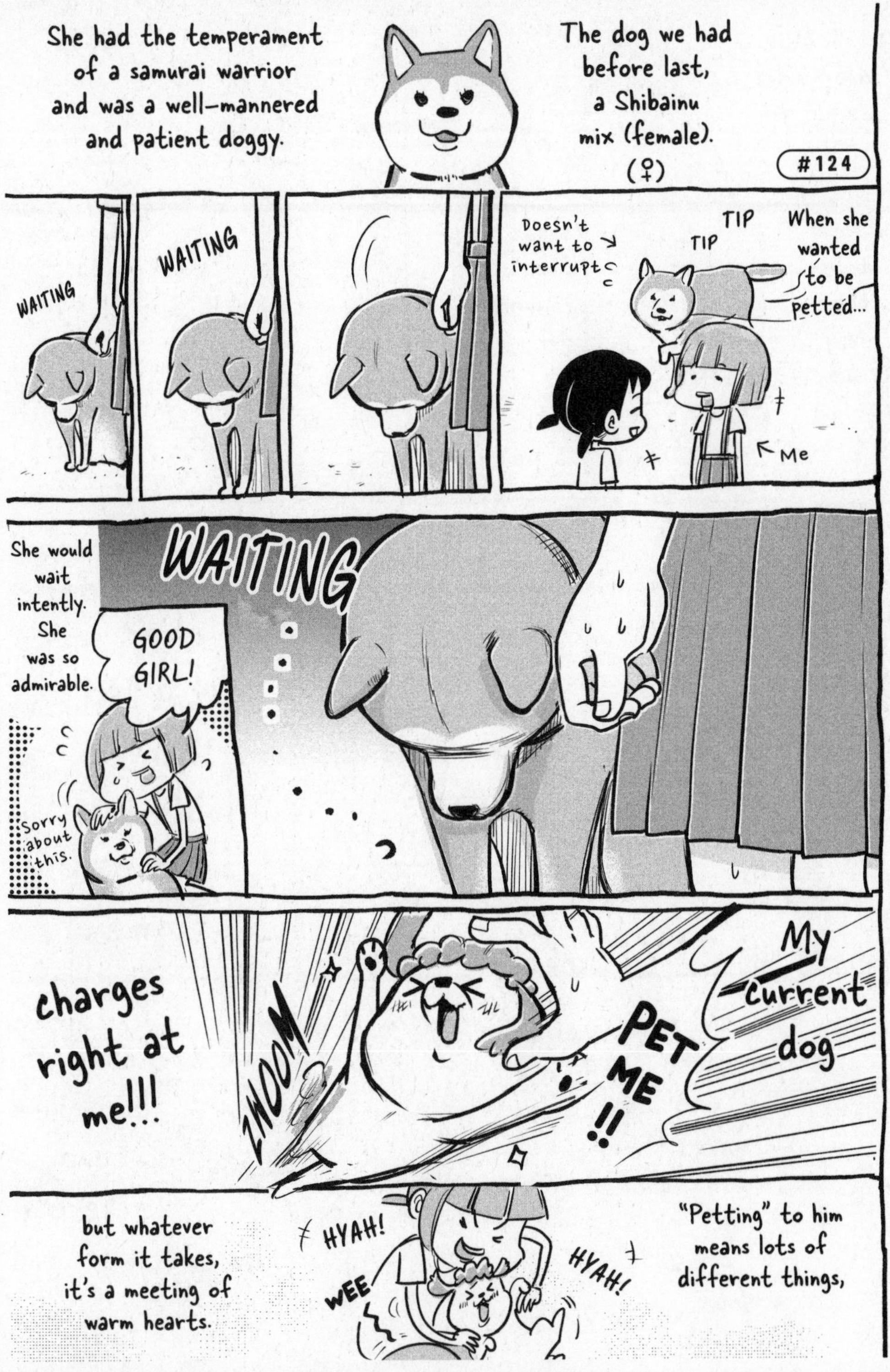

The dog we had before last, a Shibainu mix (female). (♀)
#124
She had the temperament of a samurai warrior and was a well-mannered and patient doggy.
When she wanted to be petted...
TIP
TIP
Doesn't want to interrupt
Me
WAITING
WAITING
WAITING
She would wait intently. She was so admirable.
GOOD GIRL!
Sorry about this.
My current dog
PET ME!!
ZWOOM
charges right at me!!!
"Petting" to him means lots of different things,
HYAH!
HYAH!
WEE
but whatever form it takes, it's a meeting of warm hearts.

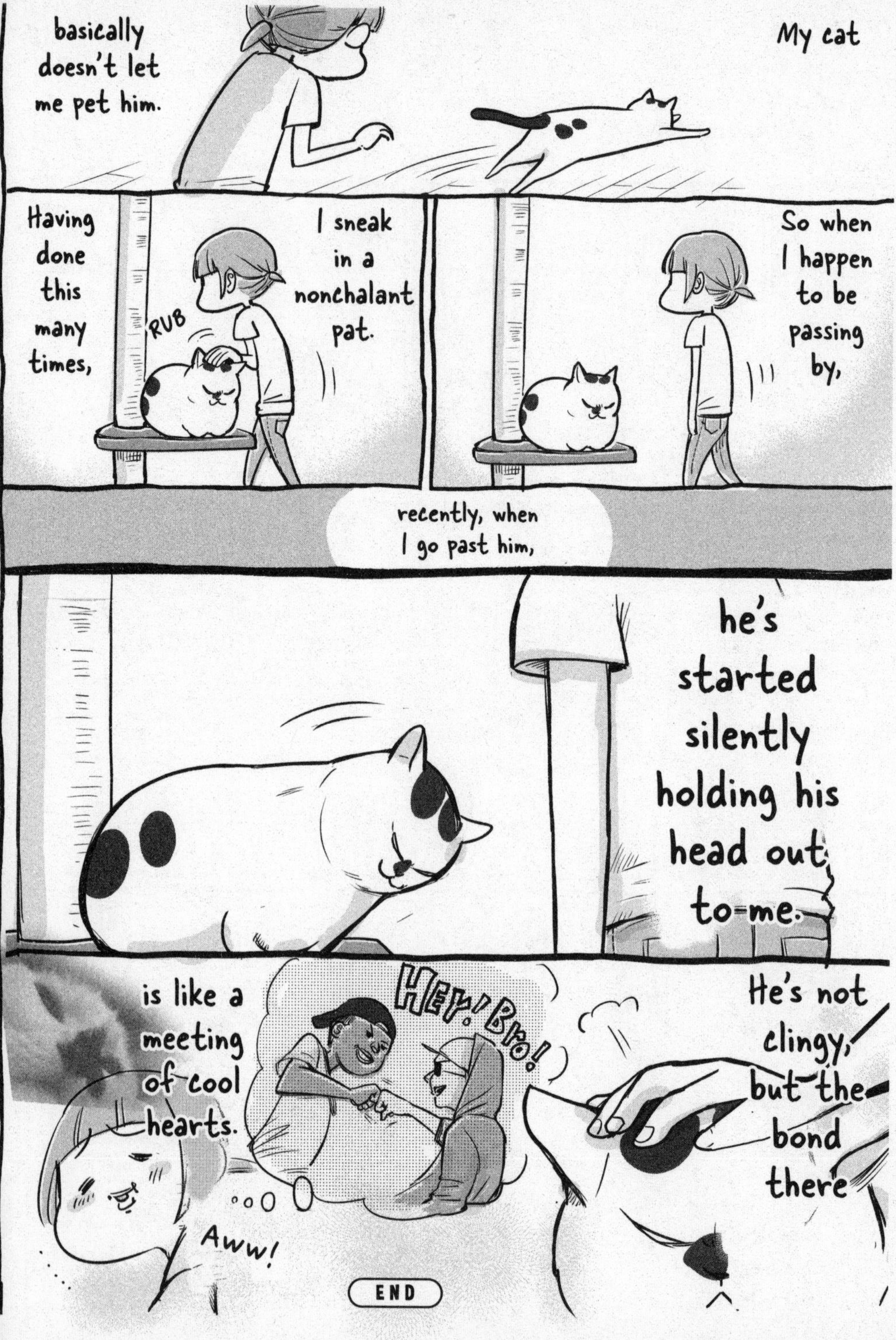
My cat
basically doesn't let me pet him.
So when I happen to be passing by,
I sneak in a nonchalant pat.
RUB
Having done this many times,
recently, when I go past him,
he's started silently holding his head out to me.
He's not clingy, but the bond there
HEY! BRO!
is like a meeting of cool hearts.
Aww!
END

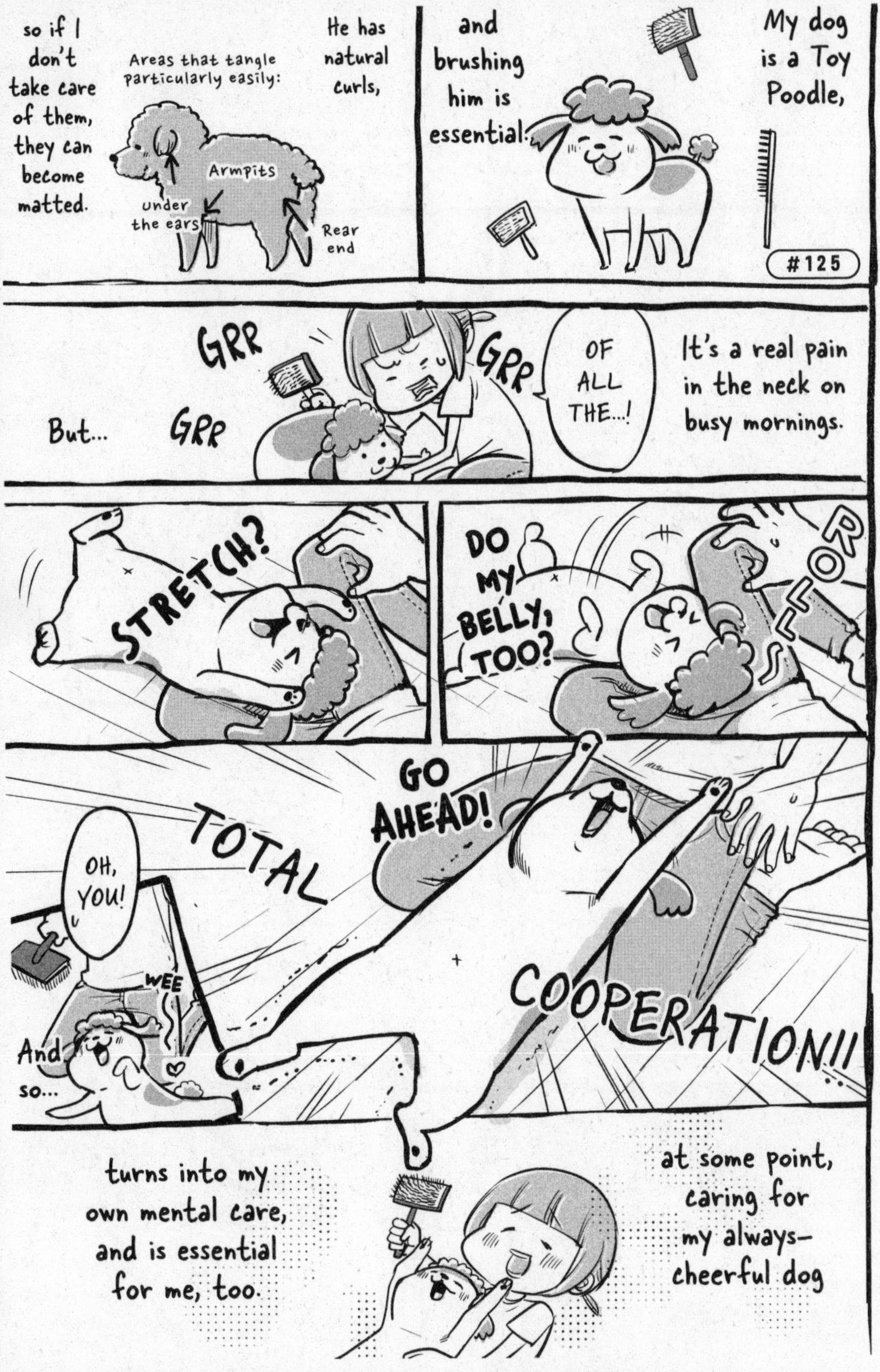

#125
My dog is a Toy Poodle,
and brushing him is essential.
He has natural curls,
Areas that tangle particularly easily:
Armpits
under the ears
Rear end
so if I don't take care of them, they can become matted.
It's a real pain in the neck on busy mornings.
OF ALL THE...!
GRR
GRR
GRR
But...
ROLLS
DO MY BELLY, TOO?
STRETCH?
GO AHEAD!
TOTAL COOPERATION!!
OH, YOU!
WEE
And so...
at some point, caring for my always-cheerful dog
turns into my own mental care, and is essential for me, too.

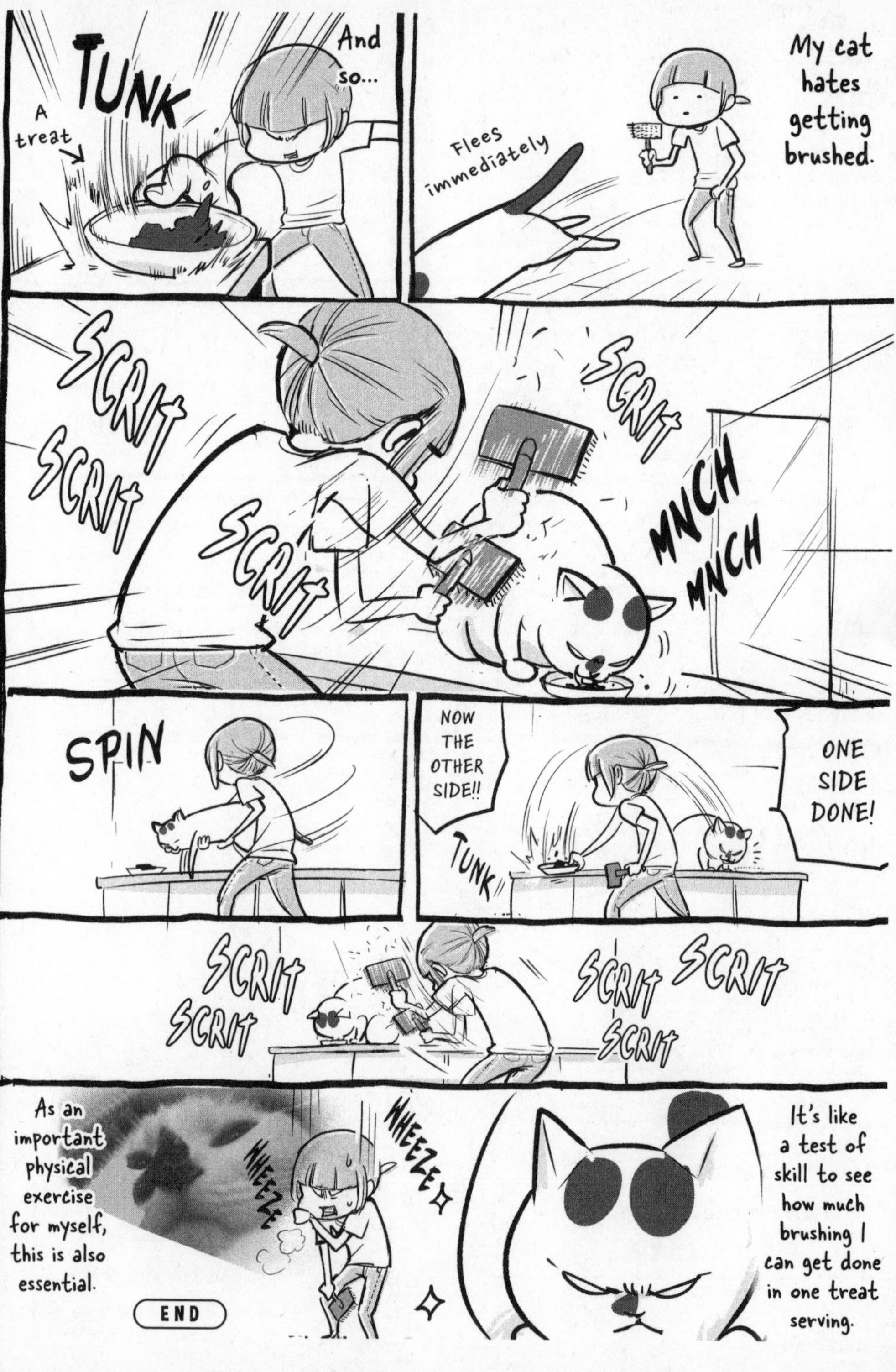
My cat hates getting brushed.
Flees immediately
And so...
TUNK
A treat
SCRIT
MNCH MNCH
SCRIT
SCRIT
SCRIT
ONE SIDE DONE!
NOW THE OTHER SIDE!!
TUNK
SPIN
SCRIT
SCRIT
SCRIT
SCRIT
SCRIT
SCRIT
It's like a test of skill to see how much brushing I can get done in one treat serving.
WHEEZE
WHEEZE
As an important physical exercise for myself, this is also essential.
END

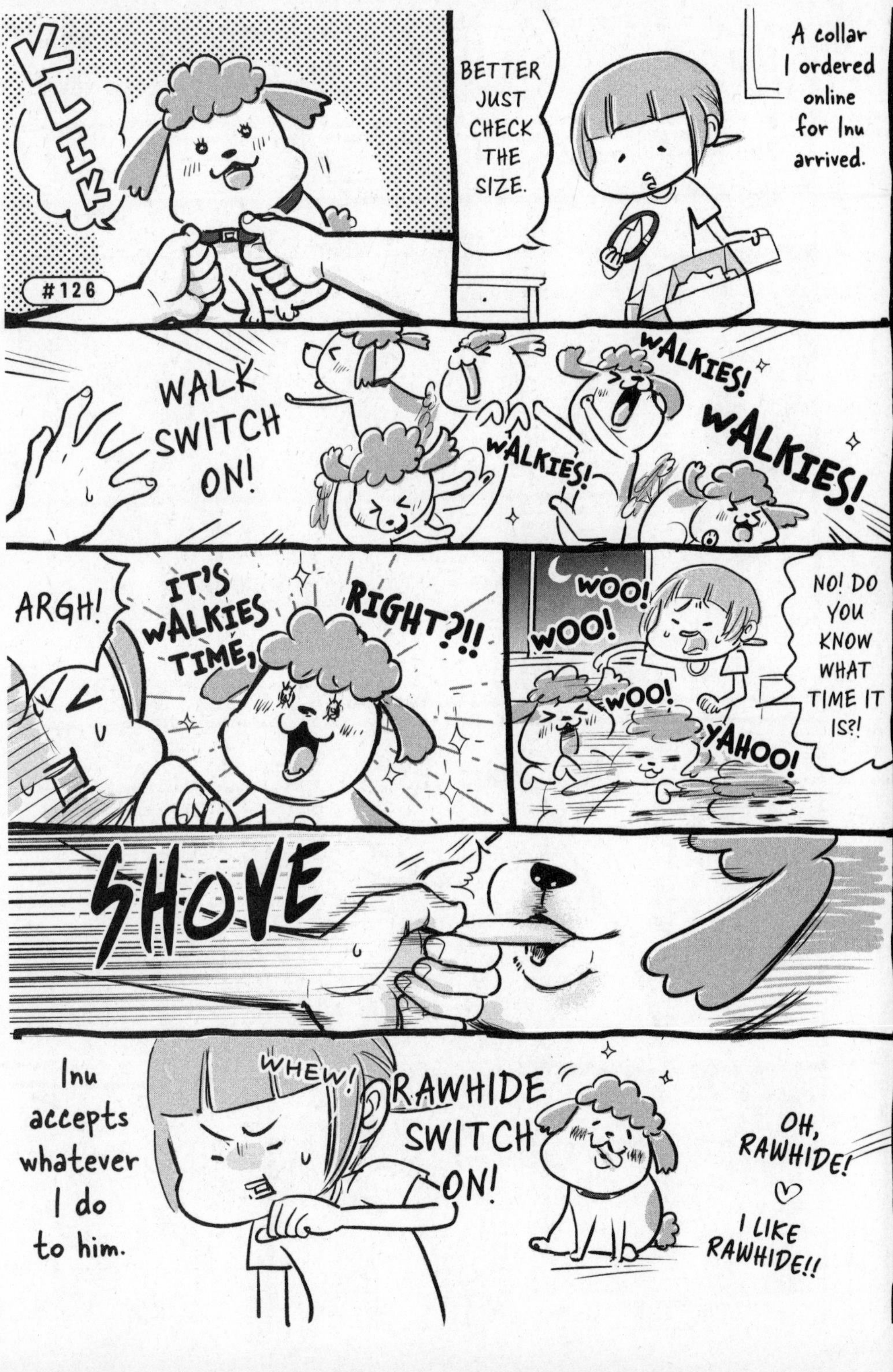
A collar I ordered online for Inu arrived.
BETTER JUST CHECK THE SIZE.
KLIK
#126
wALKIES!
wALKIES!
wALKIES!
WALK SWITCH ON!
NO! DO YOU KNOW WHAT TIME IT IS?!
WOO!
WOO!
WOO!
YAHOO!
IT'S wALKIES TIME, RIGHT?!!
ARGH!
SHOVE
OH, RAWHIDE! ♡
I LIKE RAWHIDE!!
RAWHIDE SWITCH ON!
WHEW!
Inu accepts whatever I do to him.

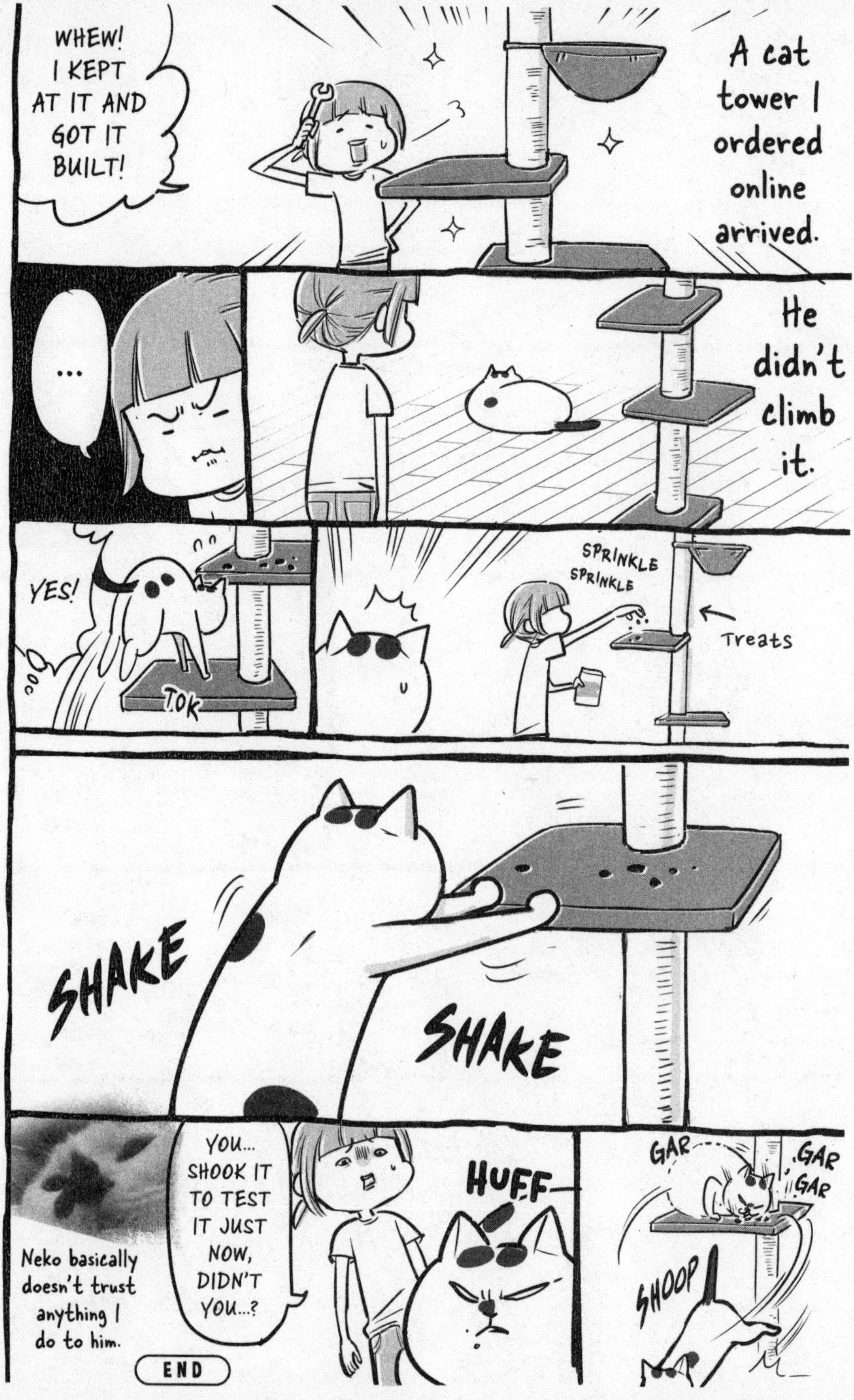
A cat tower I ordered online arrived.
WHEW! I KEPT AT IT AND GOT IT BUILT!
He didn't climb it.
...
SPRINKLE SPRINKLE
Treats
YES!
TOK
SHAKE
SHAKE
GAR
GAR
GAR
SHOOP
HUFF
YOU... SHOOK IT TO TEST IT JUST NOW, DIDN'T YOU...?
Neko basically doesn't trust anything I do to him.
END

More About #125

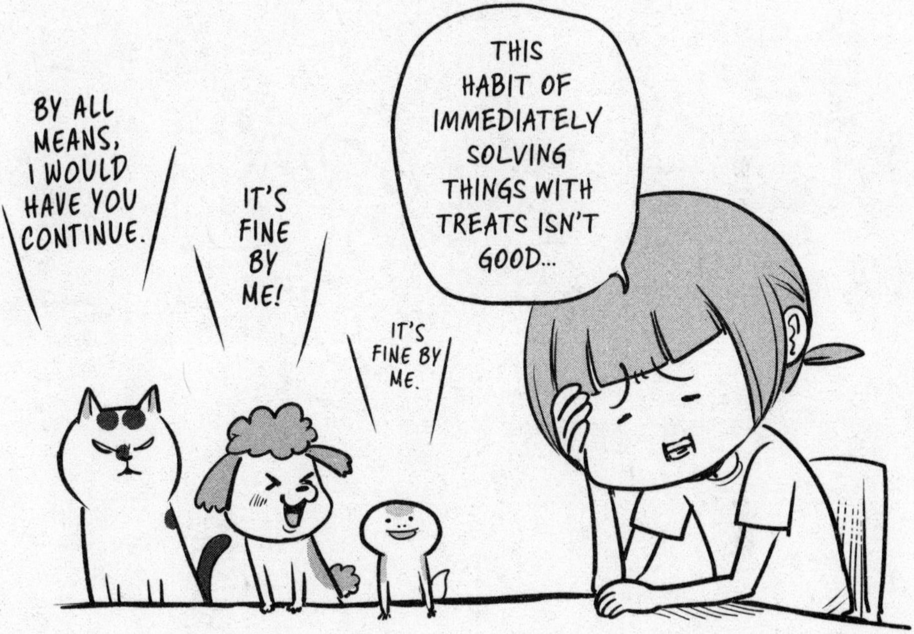
THIS HABIT OF IMMEDIATELY SOLVING THINGS WITH TREATS ISN'T GOOD...
IT'S FINE BY ME.
IT'S FINE BY ME!
BY ALL MEANS, I WOULD HAVE YOU CONTINUE.

More About #126

There is also the

Nonstop Walkies Dance.

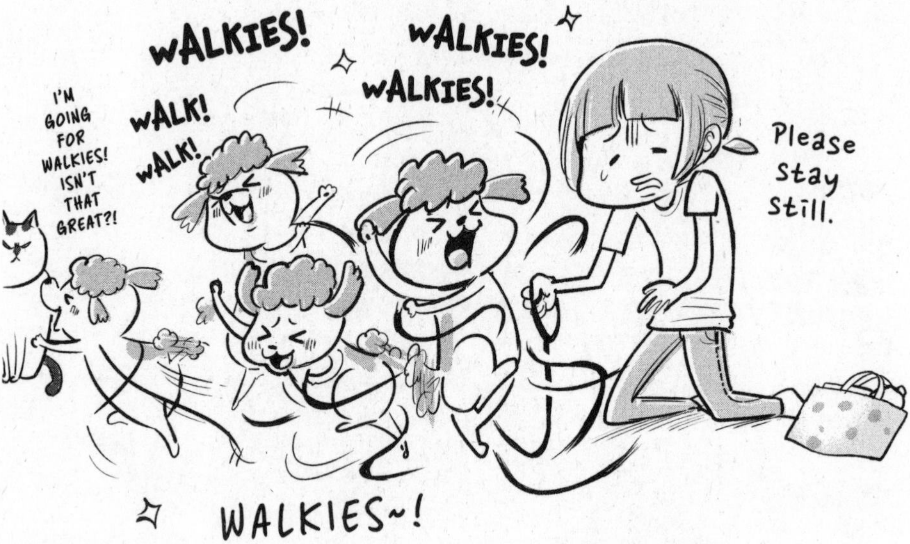
Please stay still.
wALKIES!
wALKIES!
wALKIES!
wALK!
wALK!
I'M GOING FOR WALKIES! ISN'T THAT GREAT?!
WALKIES~!

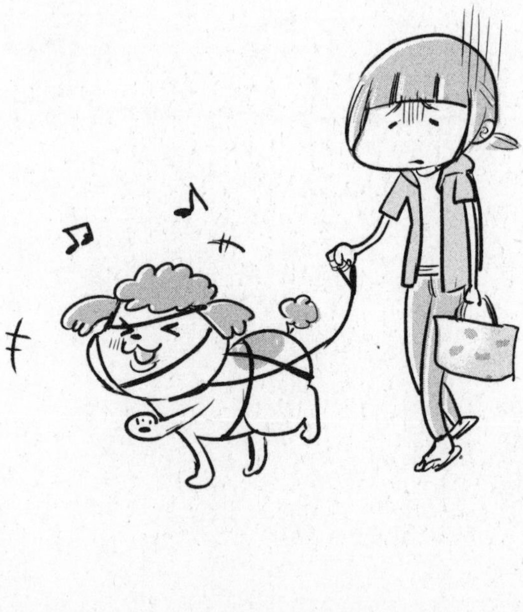

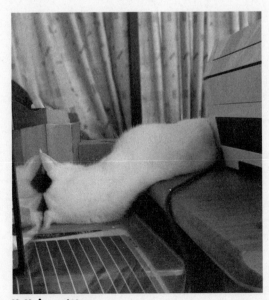

H-He's melting.

Newly-Drawn 4-Panel Strip

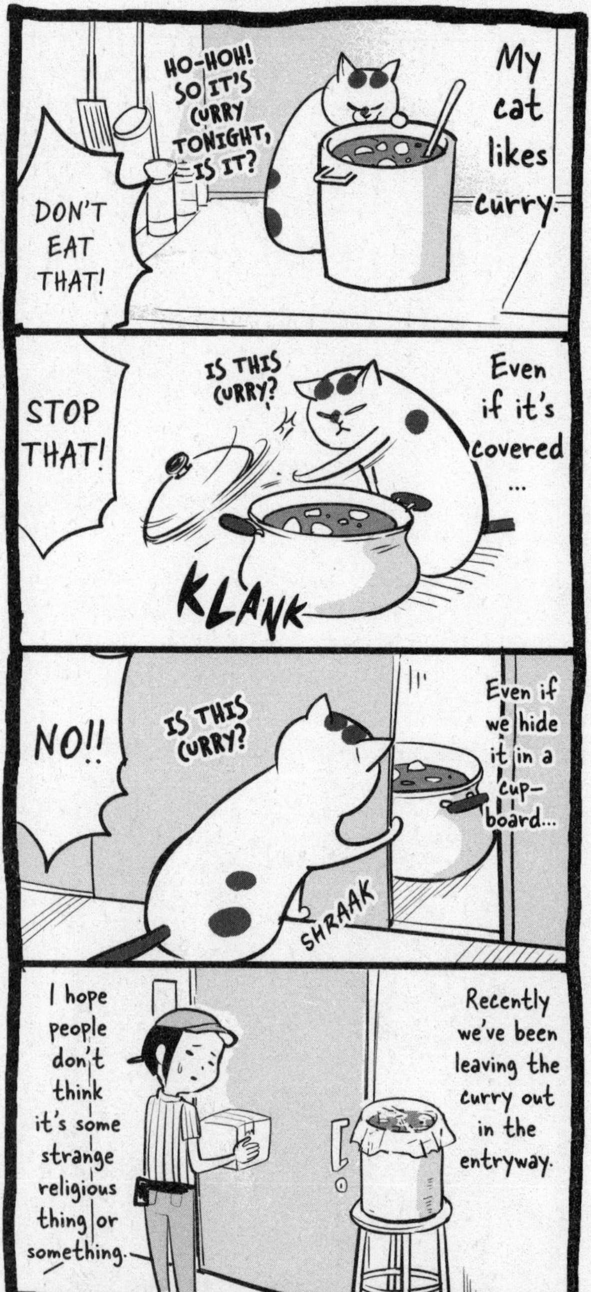
My cat likes curry.
HO-HOH! SO IT'S CURRY TONIGHT, IS IT?
DON'T EAT THAT!
Even if it's covered...
IS THIS CURRY?
STOP THAT!
KLANK
Even if we hide it in a cup-board...
IS THIS CURRY?
NO!!
SHRAAK
Recently we've been leaving the curry out in the entryway.
I hope people don't think it's some strange religious thing or something.

Bonus

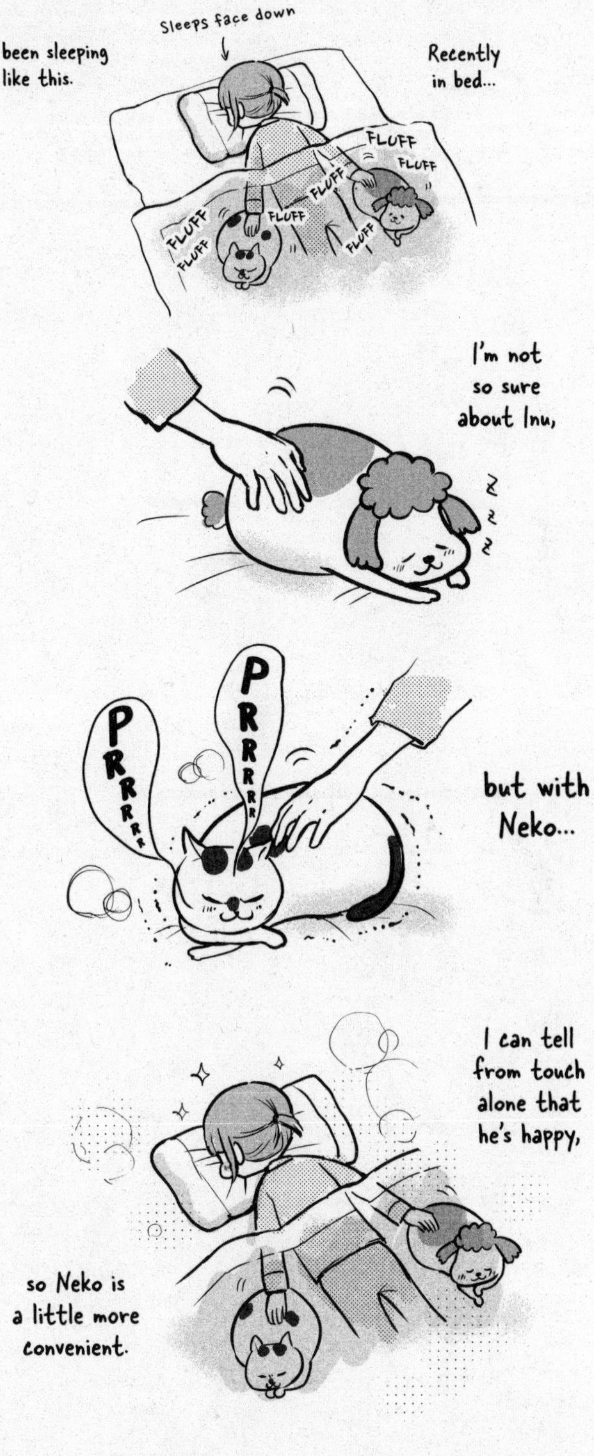
Recently in bed...
Sleeps face down
I've been sleeping like this.
FLUFF
FLUFF
FLUFF
FLUFF
FLUFF
FLUFF
FLUFF
I'm not so sure about Inu,
Z Z Z
but with Neko...
PRRRRR
PRRRRR
I can tell from touch alone that he's happy,
so Neko is a little more convenient.

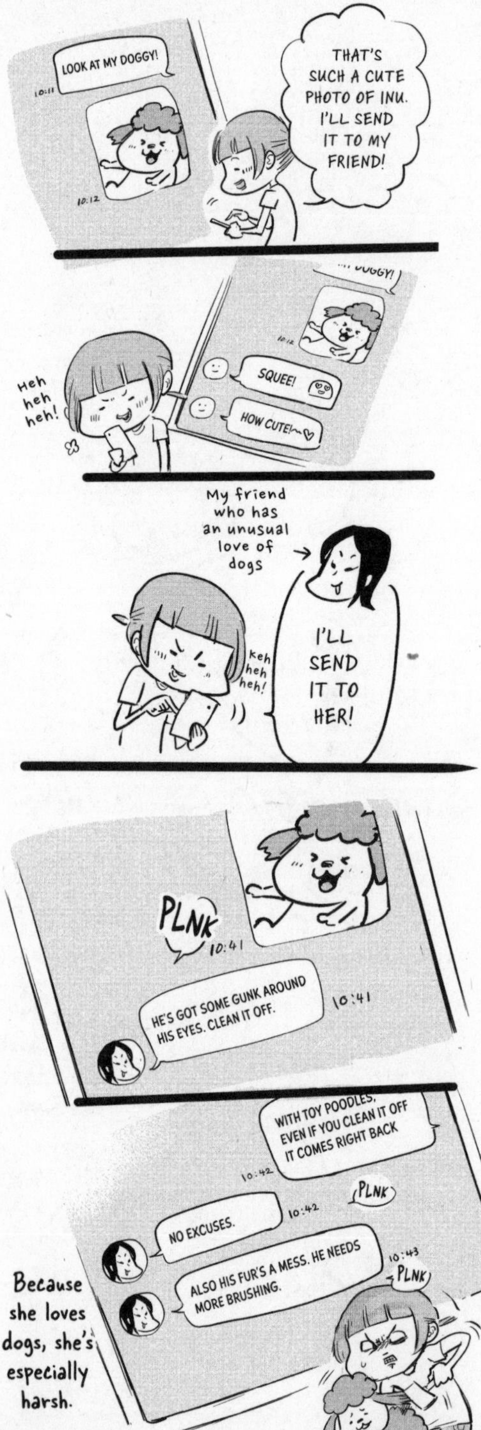
THAT'S SUCH A CUTE PHOTO OF INU. I'LL SEND IT TO MY FRIEND!
LOOK AT MY DOGGY!
SQUEE!
HOW CUTE!~♡
Heh heh heh!
My friend who has an unusual love of dogs
I'LL SEND IT TO HER!
keh heh heh!
PLNK
10:41
10:41
HE'S GOT SOME GUNK AROUND HIS EYES. CLEAN IT OFF.
WITH TOY POODLES, EVEN IF YOU CLEAN IT OFF IT COMES RIGHT BACK
10:42
PLNK
10:42
NO EXCUSES.
10:43
PLNK
ALSO HIS FUR'S A MESS. HE NEEDS MORE BRUSHING.
Because she loves dogs, she's especially harsh.

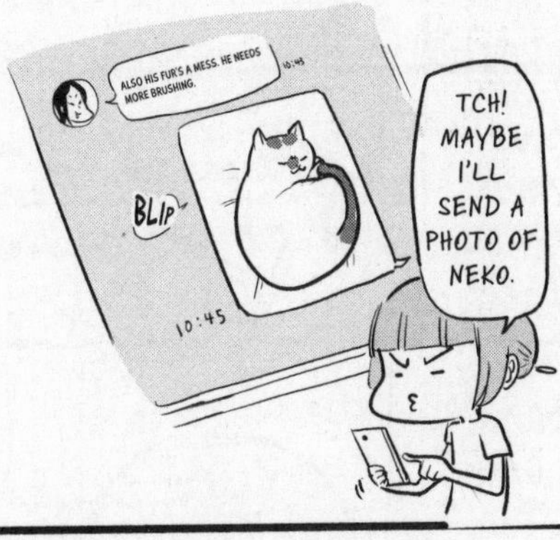
TCH! MAYBE I'LL SEND A PHOTO OF NEKO.
ALSO HIS FUR'S A MESS. HE NEEDS MORE BRUSHING.
BLIP
10:45

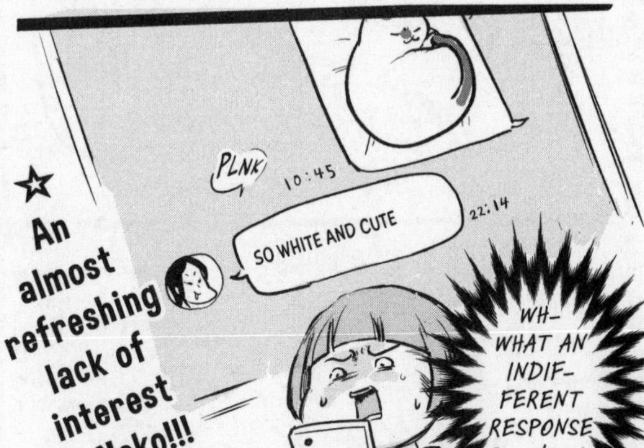
PLNK
10:45
22:14
SO WHITE AND CUTE
WH- WHAT AN INDIF-FERENT RESPONSE!
☆ An almost refreshing lack of interest in Neko!!!

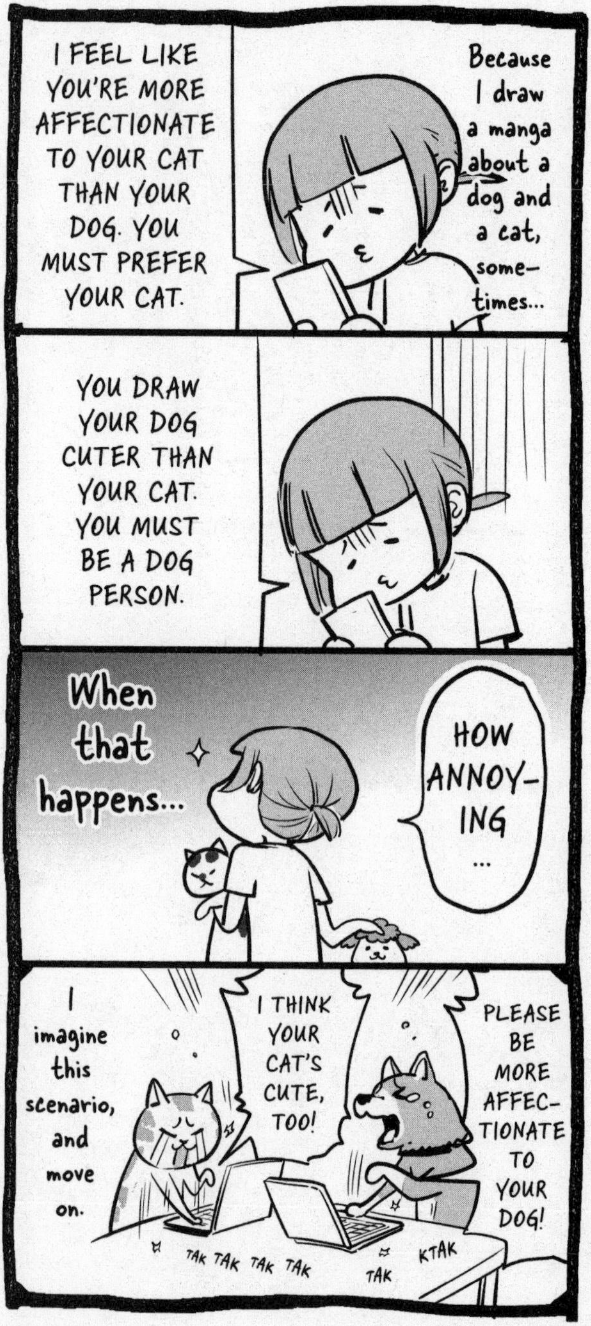
Because I draw a manga about a dog and a cat, some-times...
I FEEL LIKE YOU'RE MORE AFFECTIONATE TO YOUR CAT THAN YOUR DOG. YOU MUST PREFER YOUR CAT.
YOU DRAW YOUR DOG CUTER THAN YOUR CAT. YOU MUST BE A DOG PERSON.
HOW ANNOY-ING...
When that happens...
PLEASE BE MORE AFFEC-TIONATE TO YOUR DOG!
I THINK YOUR CAT'S CUTE, TOO!
I imagine this scenario, and move on.
KTAK
TAK
TAK TAK TAK TAK

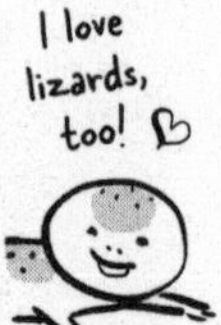
I love lizards, too!

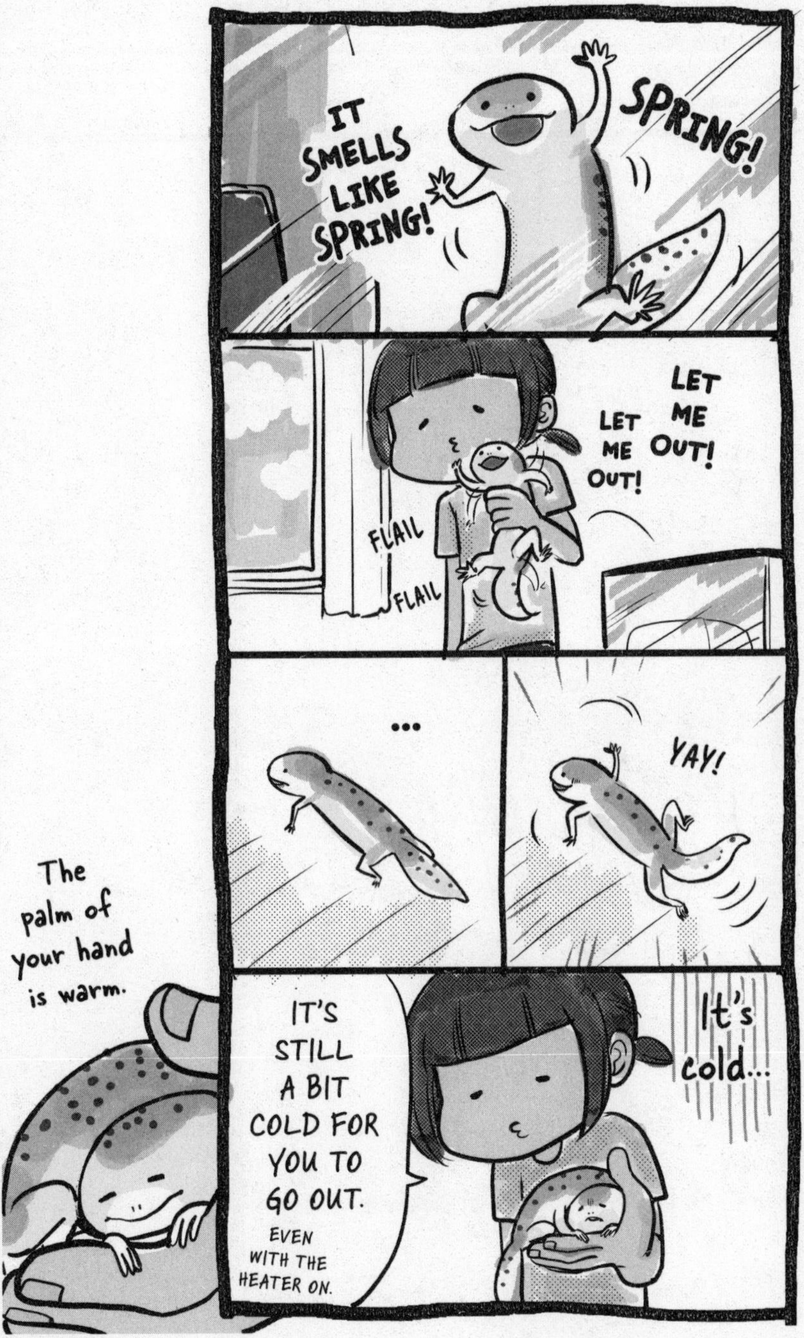
SPRING!
IT SMELLS LIKE SPRING!
LET ME OUT!
LET ME OUT!
FLAIL
FLAIL
YAY!
...
It's cold...
IT'S STILL A BIT COLD FOR YOU TO GO OUT.
EVEN WITH THE HEATER ON.
The palm of your hand is warm.

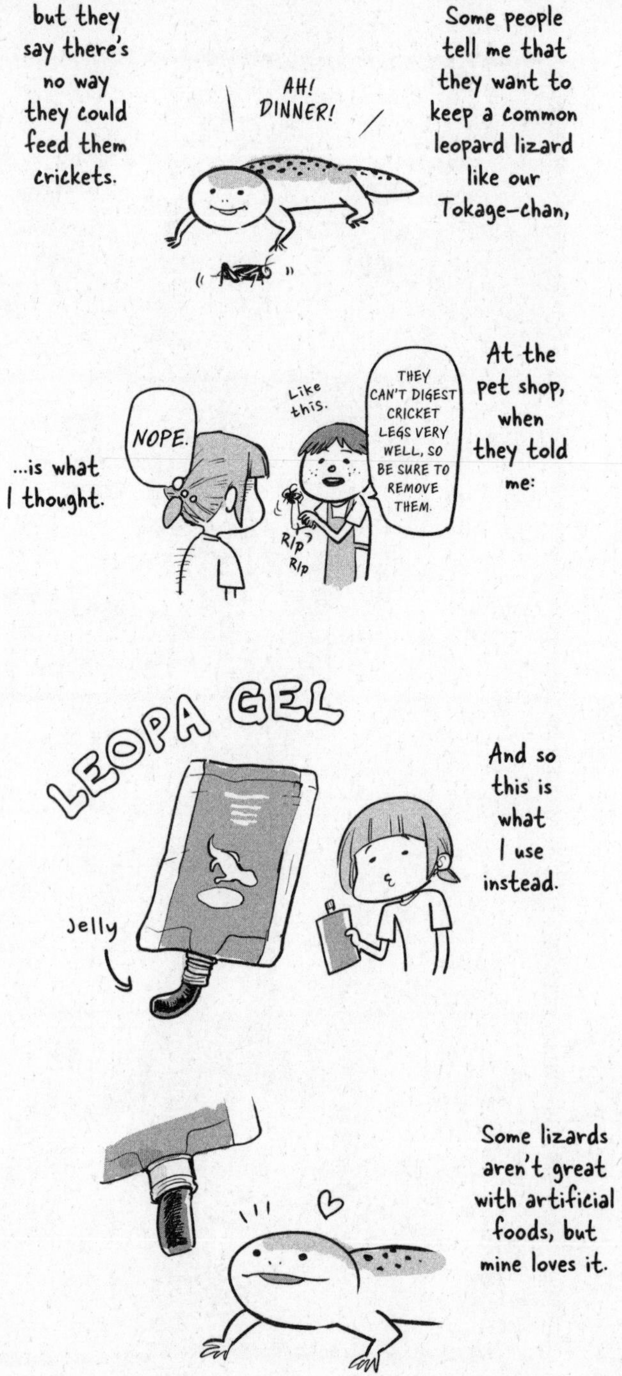
Some people tell me that they want to keep a common leopard lizard like our Tokage-chan,
AH! DINNER!
but they say there's no way they could feed them crickets.
At the pet shop, when they told me:
THEY CAN'T DIGEST CRICKET LEGS VERY WELL, SO BE SURE TO REMOVE THEM.
Like this.
RIP RIP
NOPE.
...is what I thought.
And so this is what I use instead.
LEOPA GEL
Jelly
Some lizards aren't great with artificial foods, but mine loves it.

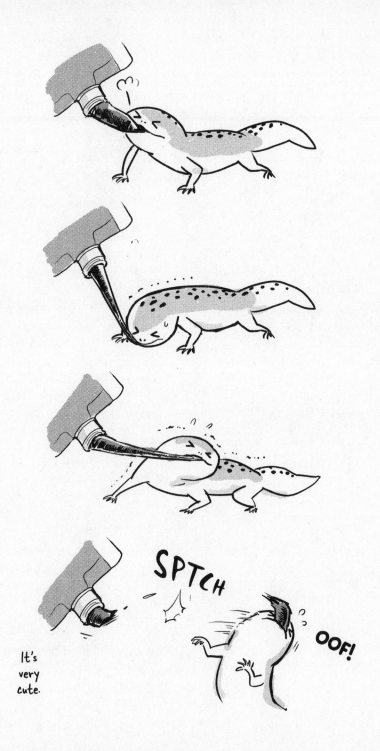

SPTCH

OOF!

It's
very
cute.

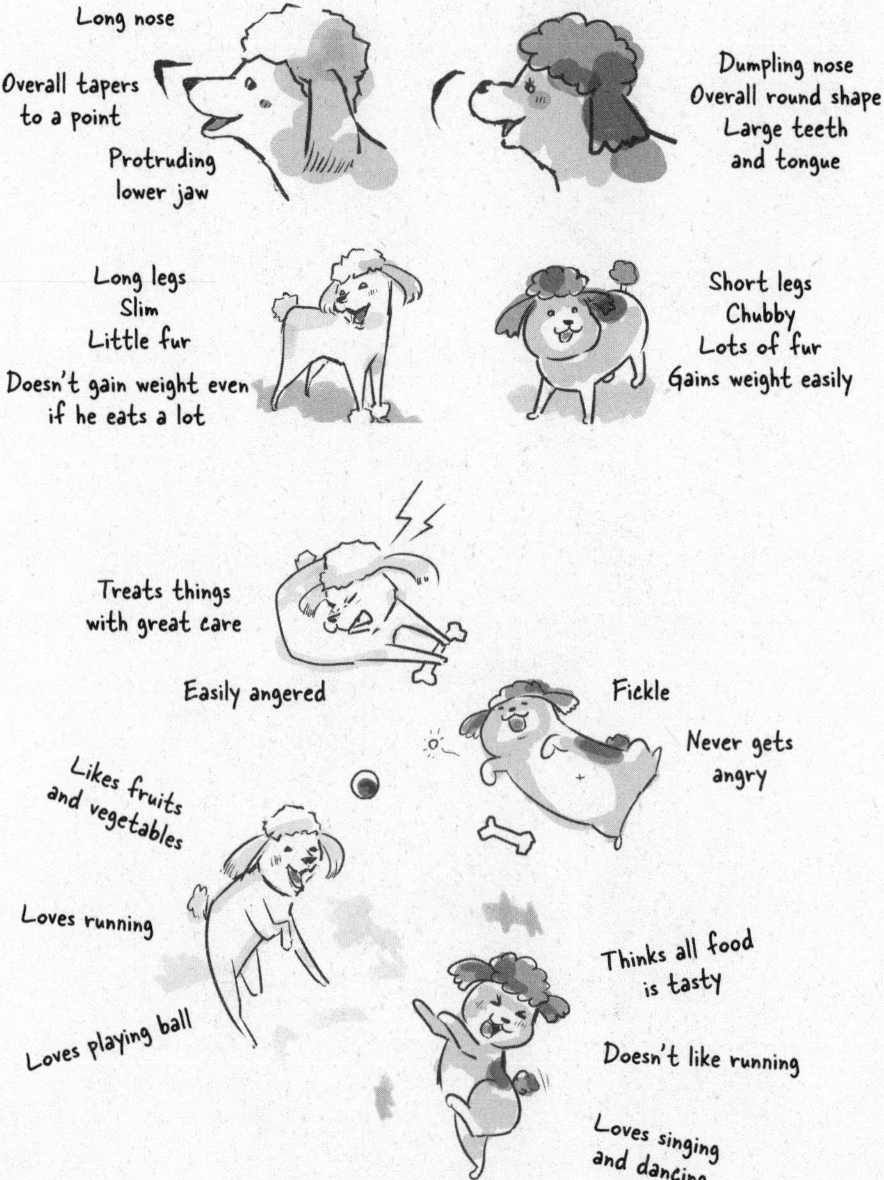

Long nose
Overall tapers to a point
Protruding lower jaw
Dumpling nose
Overall round shape
Large teeth and tongue
Long legs
Slim
Little fur
Doesn't gain weight even if he eats a lot
Short legs
Chubby
Lots of fur
Gains weight easily
Treats things with great care
Easily angered
Fickle
Never gets angry
Likes fruits and vegetables
Loves running
Loves playing ball
Thinks all food is tasty
Doesn't like running
Loves singing and dancing

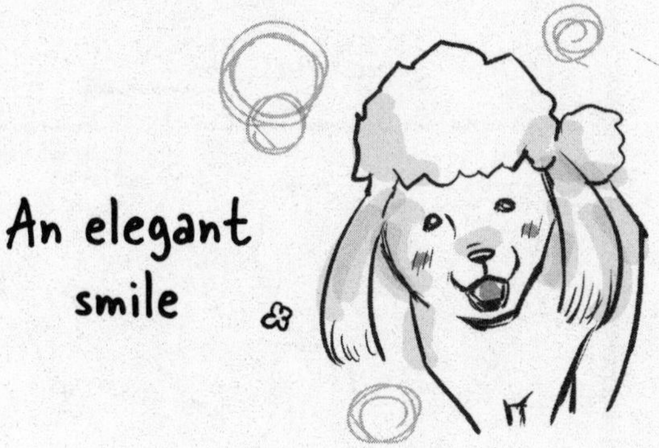
An elegant smile

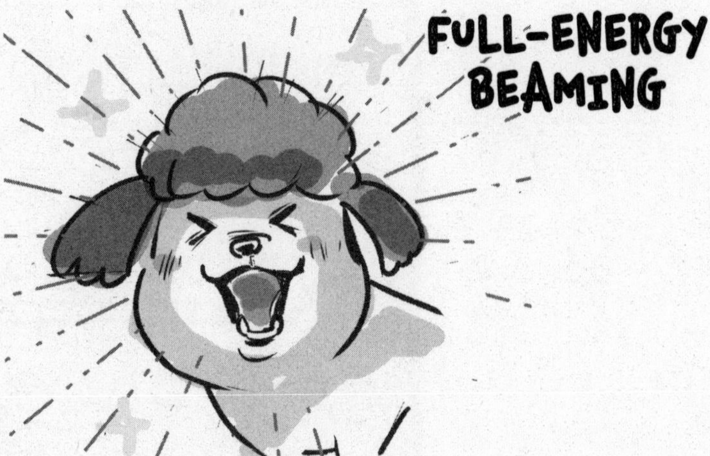
FULL-ENERGY BEAMING

END

Newly-Drawn 4-Panel Strip

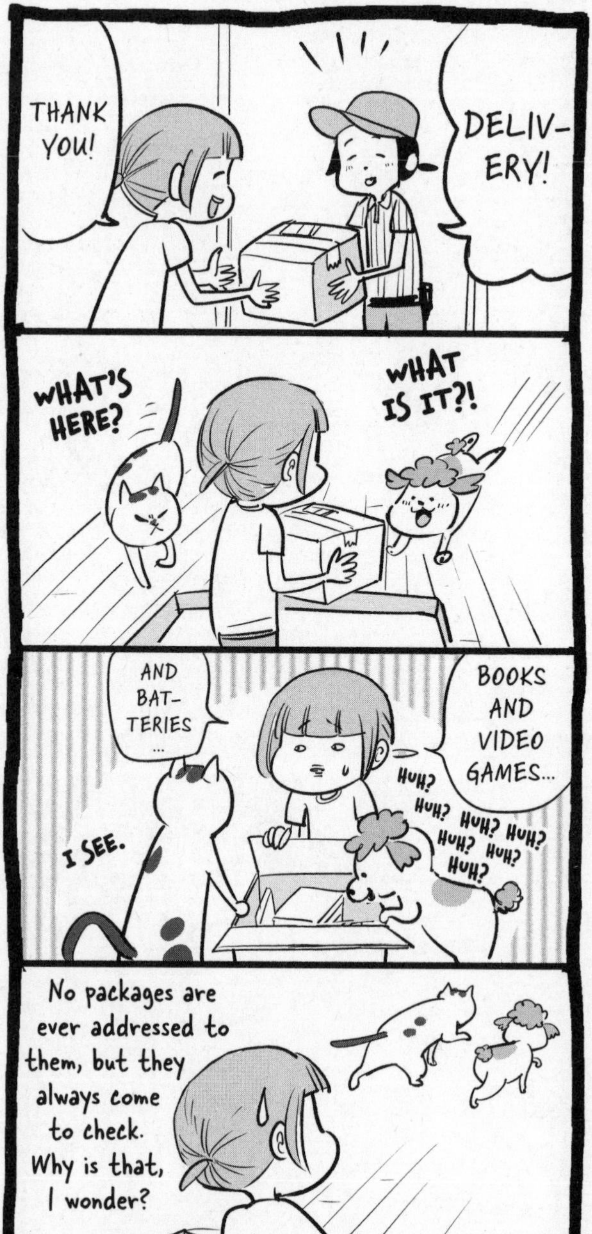
DELIV-ERY!
THANK YOU!
WHAT IS IT?!
WHAT'S HERE?
BOOKS AND VIDEO GAMES...
AND BAT-TERIES ...
HUH? HUH? HUH? HUH? HUH? HUH? HUH?
I SEE.
No packages are ever addressed to them, but they always come to check. Why is that, I wonder?

Newly-Drawn Comic: Grooming

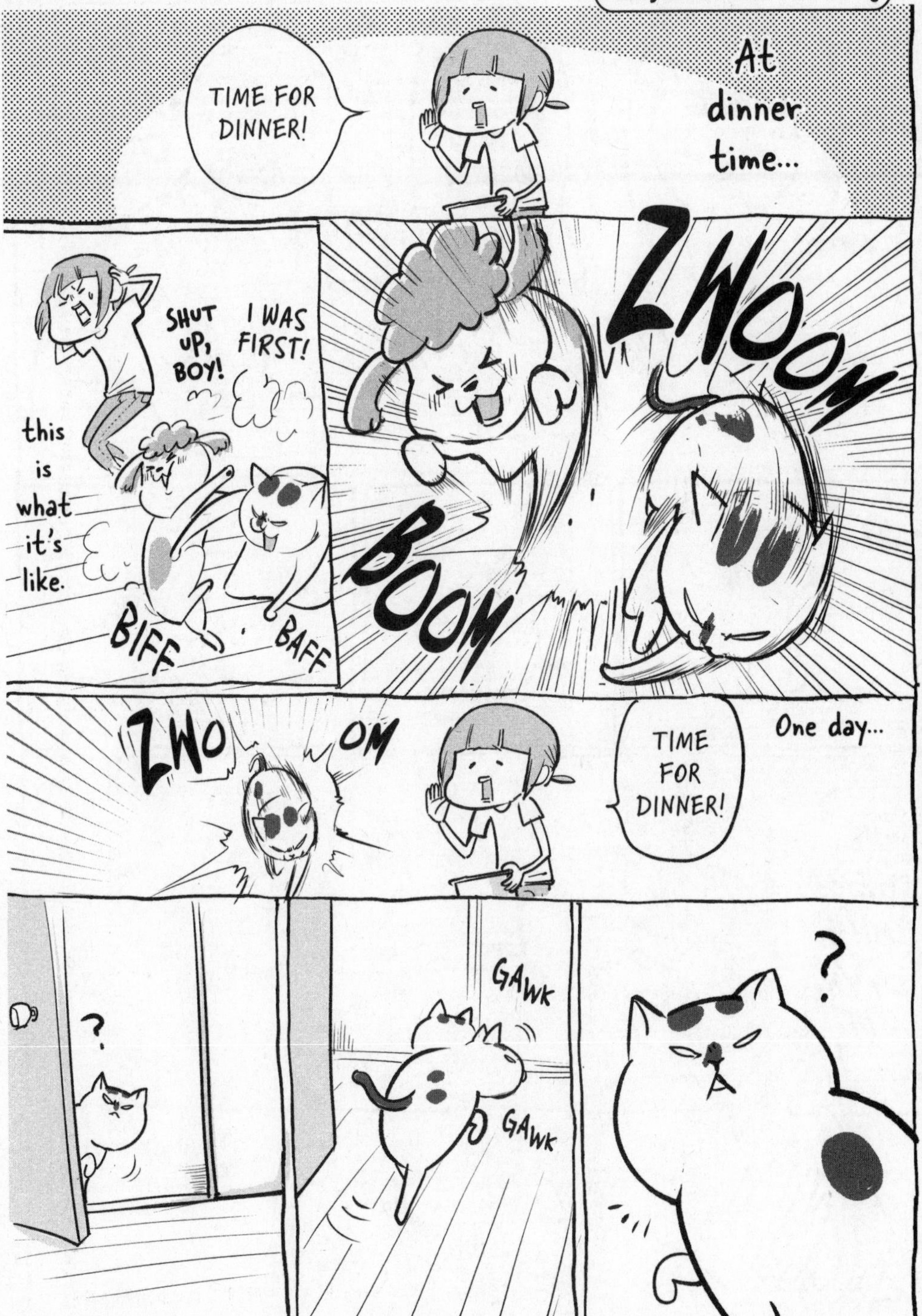
At dinner time...
TIME FOR DINNER!
ZWOOM
BOOM
I WAS FIRST!
SHUT UP, BOY!
this is what it's like.
BAFF
BIFF
One day...
TIME FOR DINNER!
ZWO OM
?
GAWK
GAWK
?

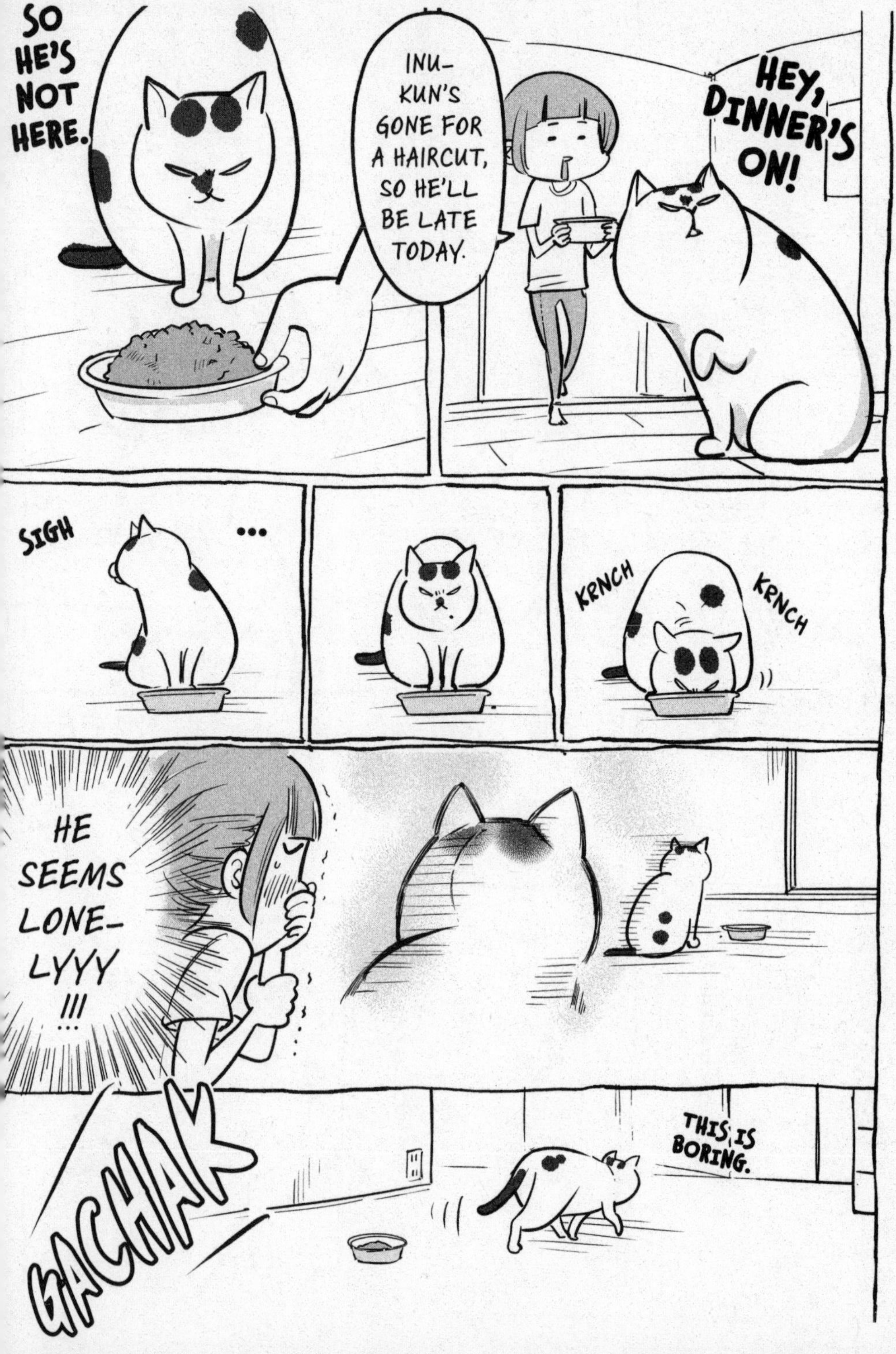
HEY, DINNER'S ON!
INU-KUN'S GONE FOR A HAIRCUT, SO HE'LL BE LATE TODAY.
SO HE'S NOT HERE.
KRNCH
KRNCH
...
SIGH
HE SEEMS LONE-LYYY !!! ...
THIS IS BORING.
GACHAK

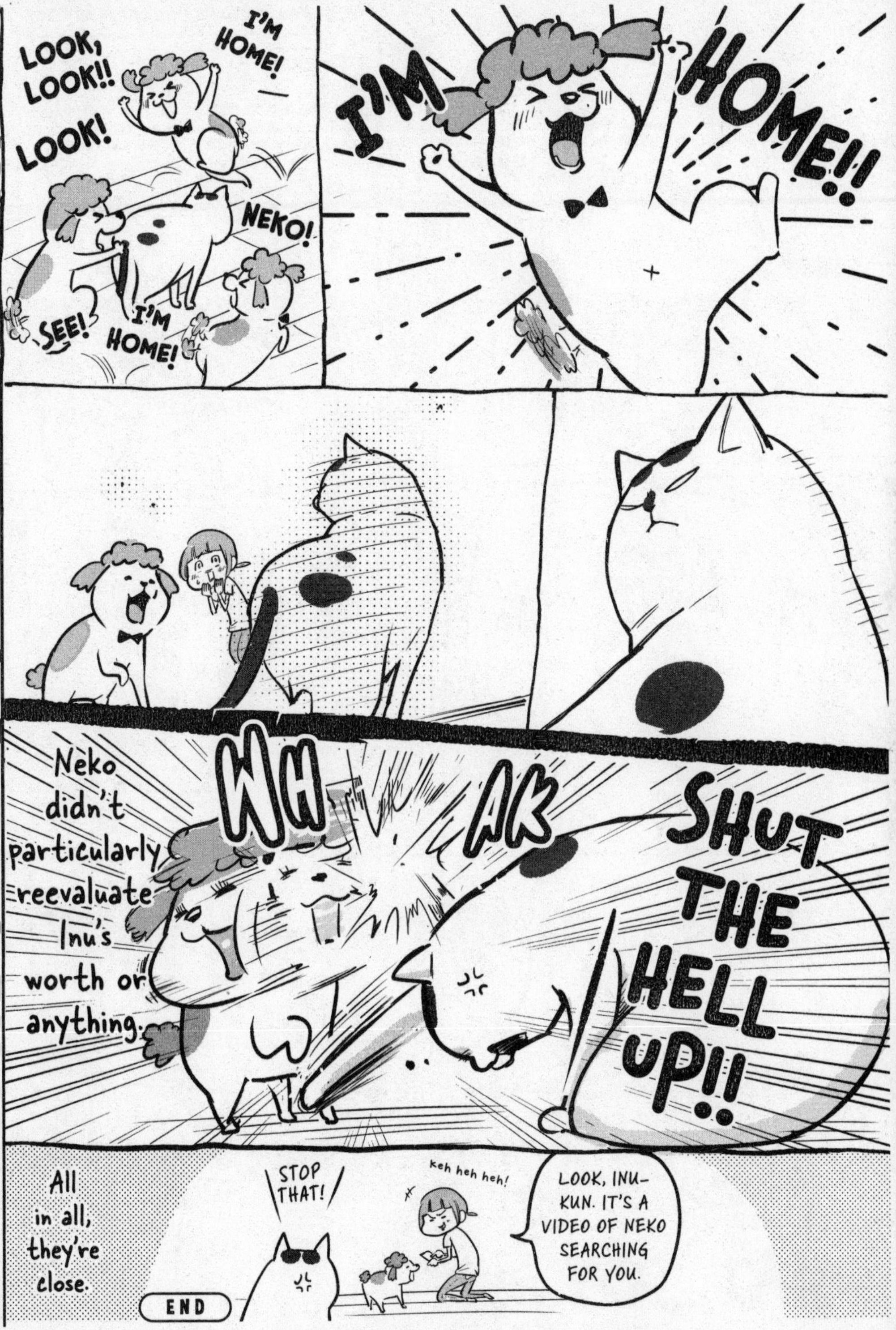
I'M HOME!!
I'M HOME!
LOOK, LOOK!!
LOOK!
NEKO!
I'M HOME!
SEE!
SHUT THE HELL UP!!
WHAK
Neko didn't particularly reevaluate Inu's worth or anything.
LOOK, INU-KUN. IT'S A VIDEO OF NEKO SEARCHING FOR YOU.
keh heh heh!
STOP THAT!
All in all, they're close.
END

Newly-Drawn Comic: Kukur Tihar

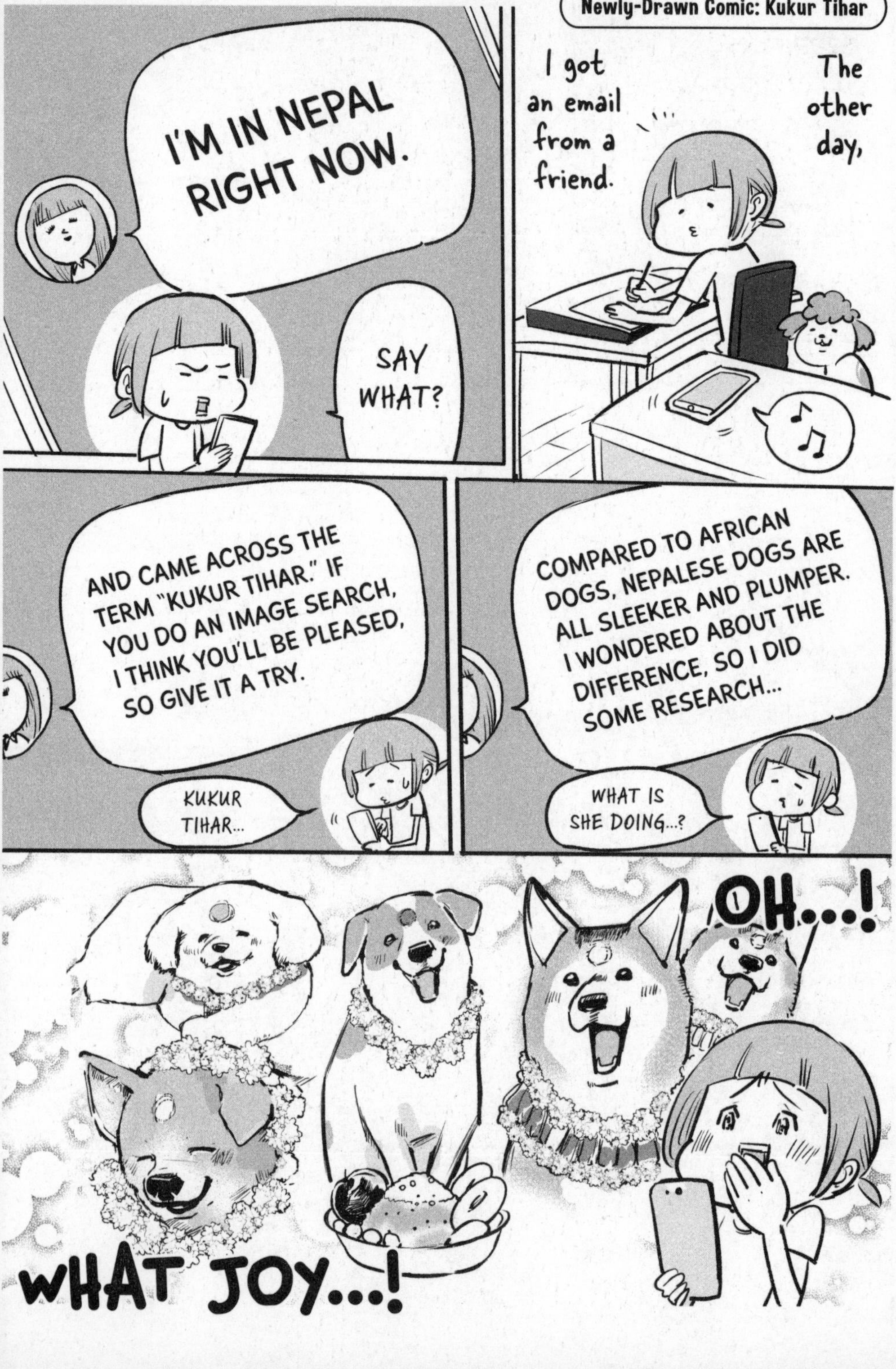
The other day,
I got an email from a friend.
I'M IN NEPAL RIGHT NOW.
SAY WHAT?
COMPARED TO AFRICAN DOGS, NEPALESE DOGS ARE ALL SLEEKER AND PLUMPER. I WONDERED ABOUT THE DIFFERENCE, SO I DID SOME RESEARCH...
WHAT IS SHE DOING...?
AND CAME ACROSS THE TERM "KUKUR TIHAR." IF YOU DO AN IMAGE SEARCH, I THINK YOU'LL BE PLEASED, SO GIVE IT A TRY.
KUKUR TIHAR...
OH...!
WHAT JOY...!

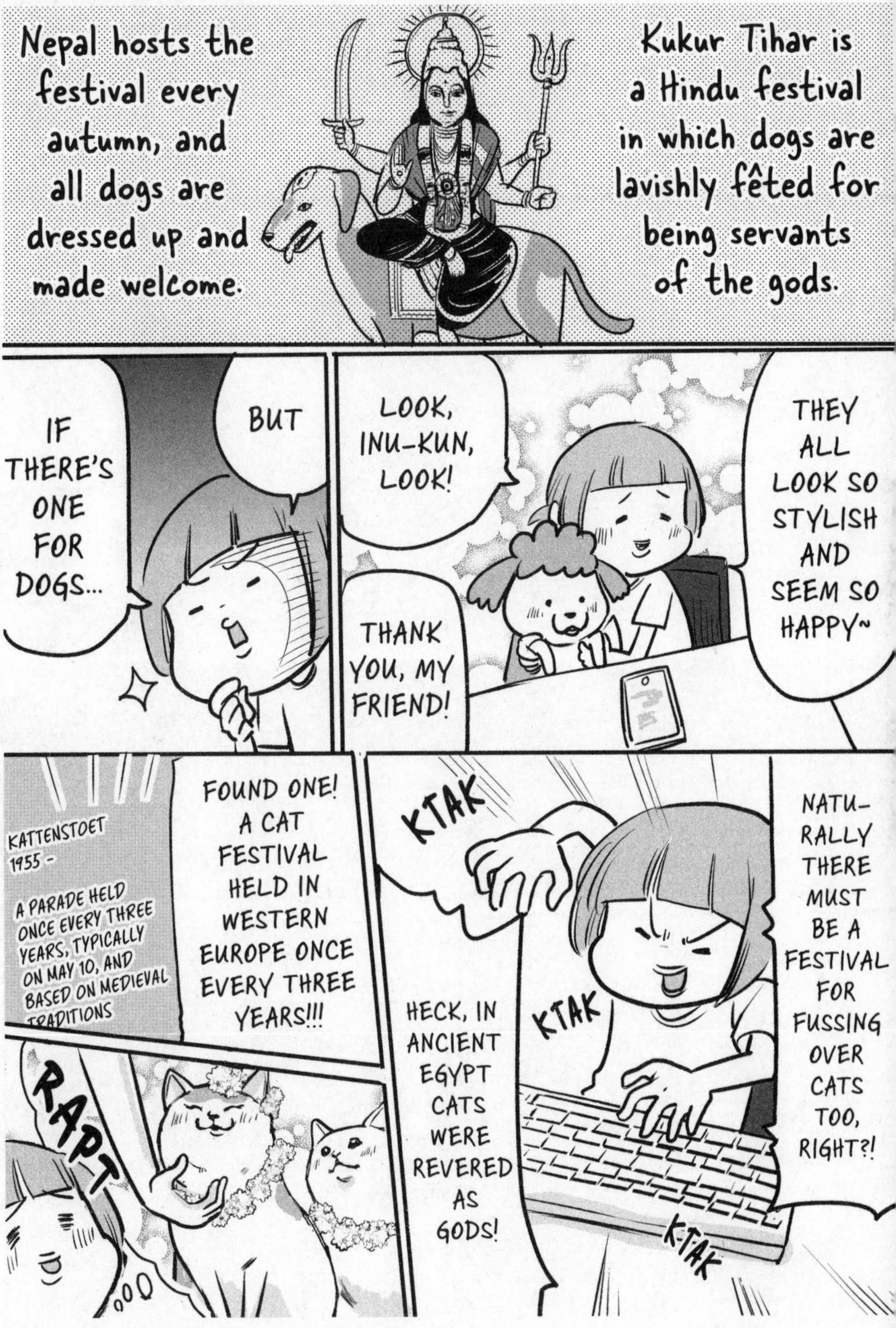
Kukur Tihar is a Hindu festival in which dogs are lavishly fêted for being servants of the gods.
Nepal hosts the festival every autumn, and all dogs are dressed up and made welcome.
THEY ALL LOOK SO STYLISH AND SEEM SO HAPPY~
LOOK, INU-KUN, LOOK!
THANK YOU, MY FRIEND!
BUT
IF THERE'S ONE FOR DOGS...
NATURALLY THERE MUST BE A FESTIVAL FOR FUSSING OVER CATS TOO, RIGHT?!
KTAK
HECK, IN ANCIENT EGYPT CATS WERE REVERED AS GODS!
KTAK
K-TAK
FOUND ONE! A CAT FESTIVAL HELD IN WESTERN EUROPE ONCE EVERY THREE YEARS!!!
KATTENSTOET 1955 -
A PARADE HELD ONCE EVERY THREE YEARS, TYPICALLY ON MAY 10, AND BASED ON MEDIEVAL TRADITIONS
RAPT

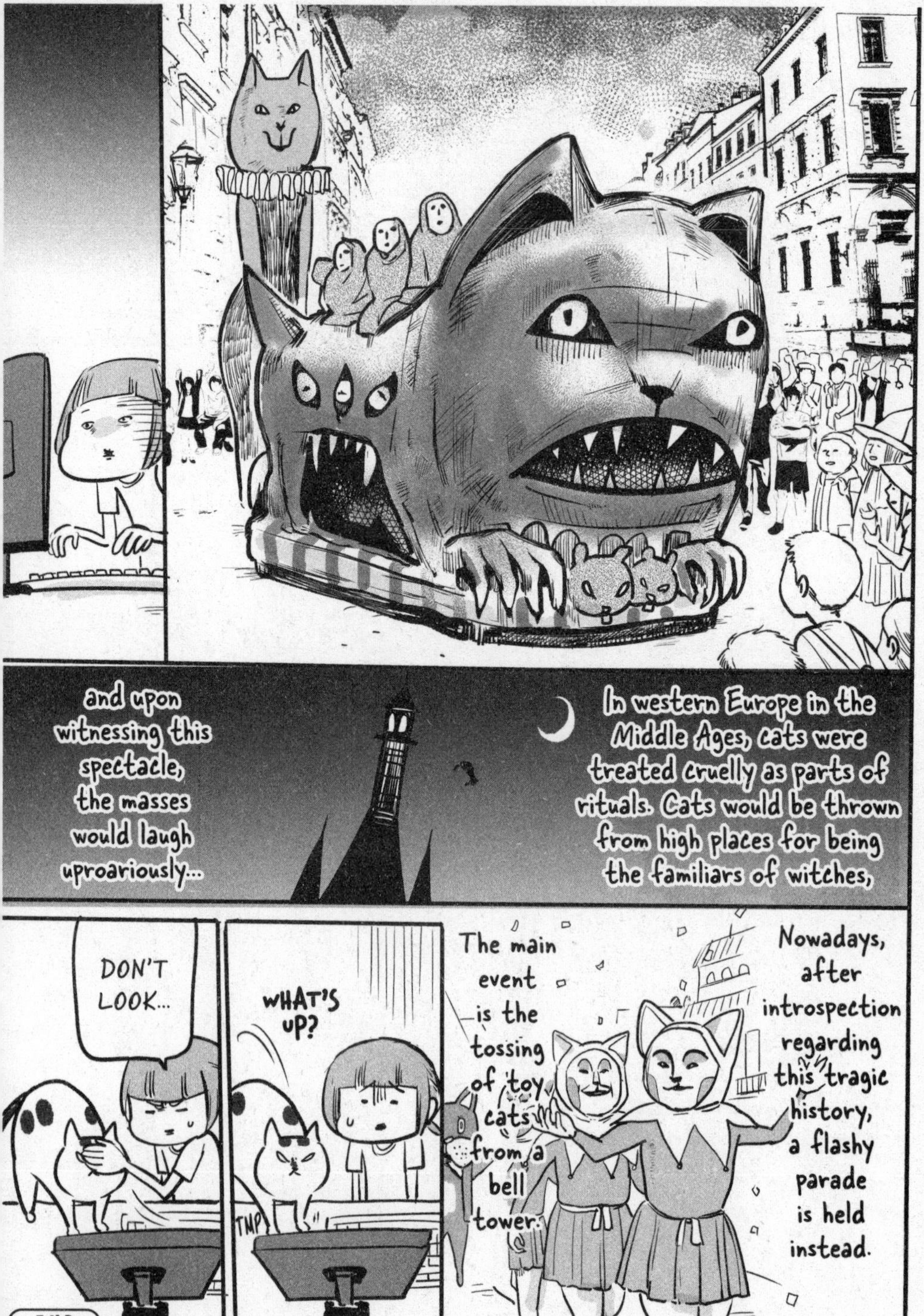
In western Europe in the Middle Ages, cats were treated cruelly as parts of rituals. Cats would be thrown from high places for being the familiars of witches,
and upon witnessing this spectacle, the masses would laugh uproariously...
Nowadays, after introspection regarding this tragic history, a flashy parade is held instead.
The main event is the tossing of toy cats from a bell tower.
WHAT'S UP?
TMP
DON'T LOOK...
END

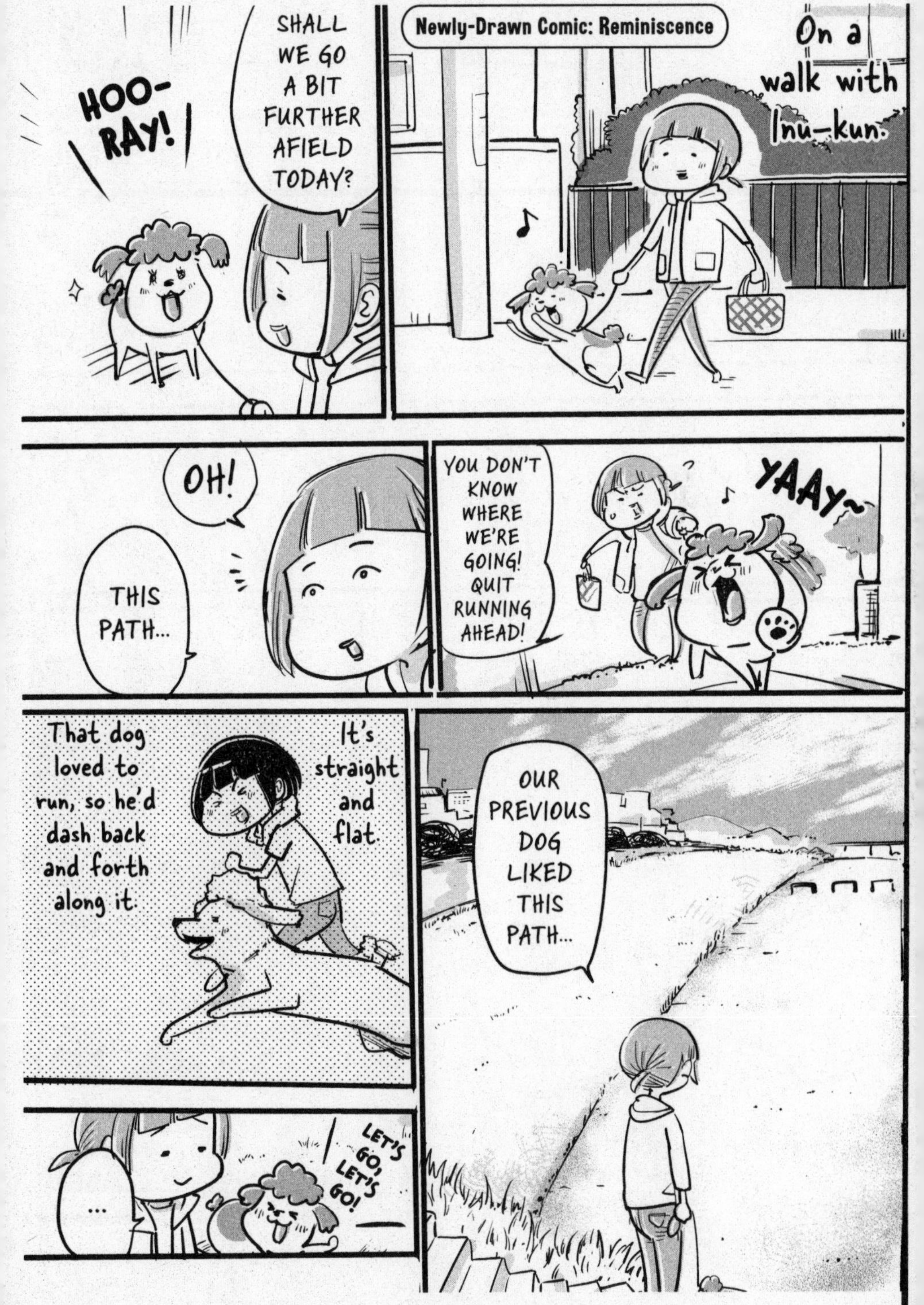
Newly-Drawn Comic: Reminiscence
On a walk with Inu-kun.
SHALL WE GO A BIT FURTHER AFIELD TODAY?
HOO-RAY!
YOU DON'T KNOW WHERE WE'RE GOING! QUIT RUNNING AHEAD!
YAAY~
OH!
THIS PATH...
OUR PREVIOUS DOG LIKED THIS PATH...
It's straight and flat.
That dog loved to run, so he'd dash back and forth along it.
LET'S GO, LET'S GO!
...

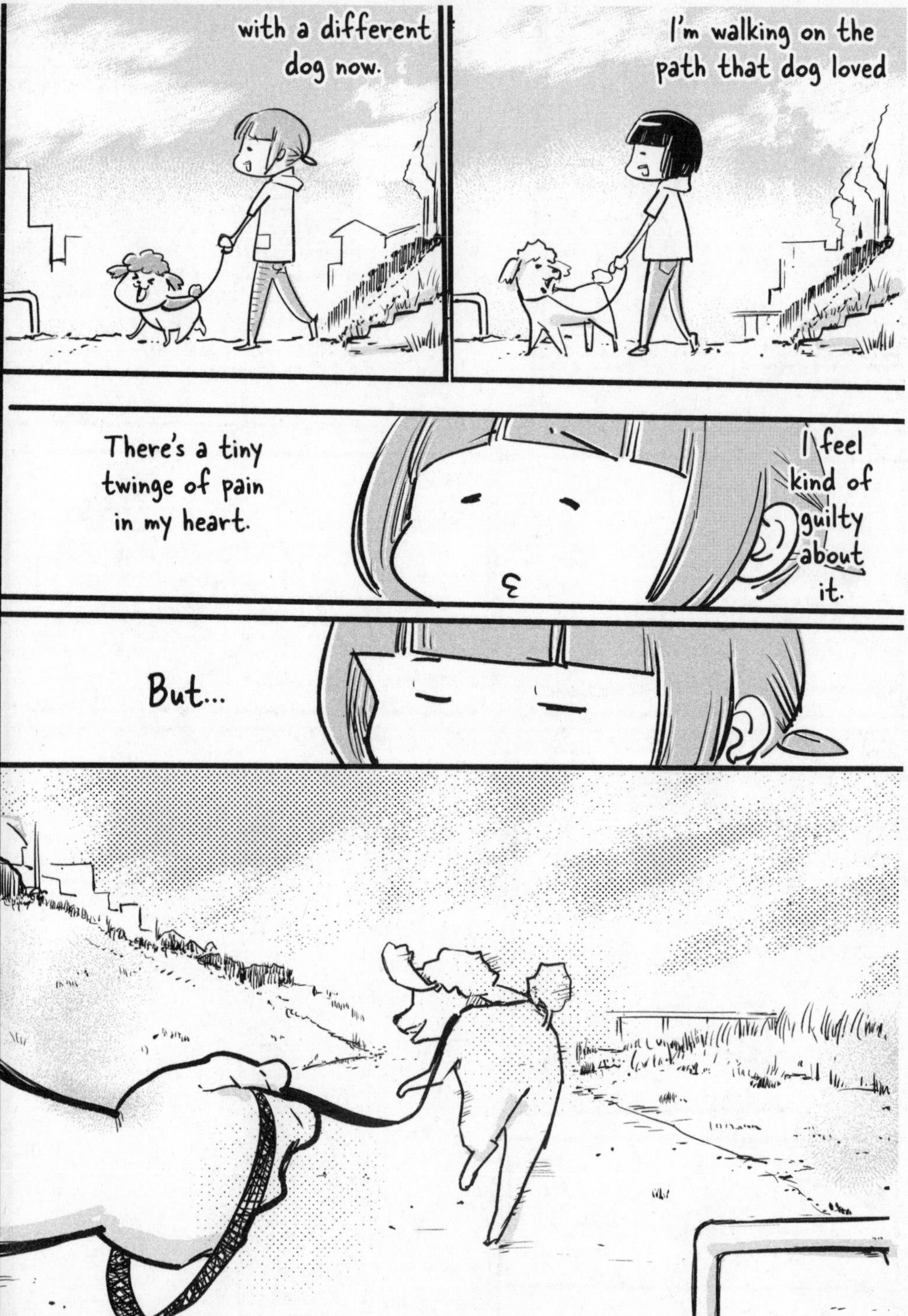
I'm walking on the path that dog loved
with a different dog now.
I feel kind of guilty about it.
There's a tiny twinge of pain in my heart.
But...

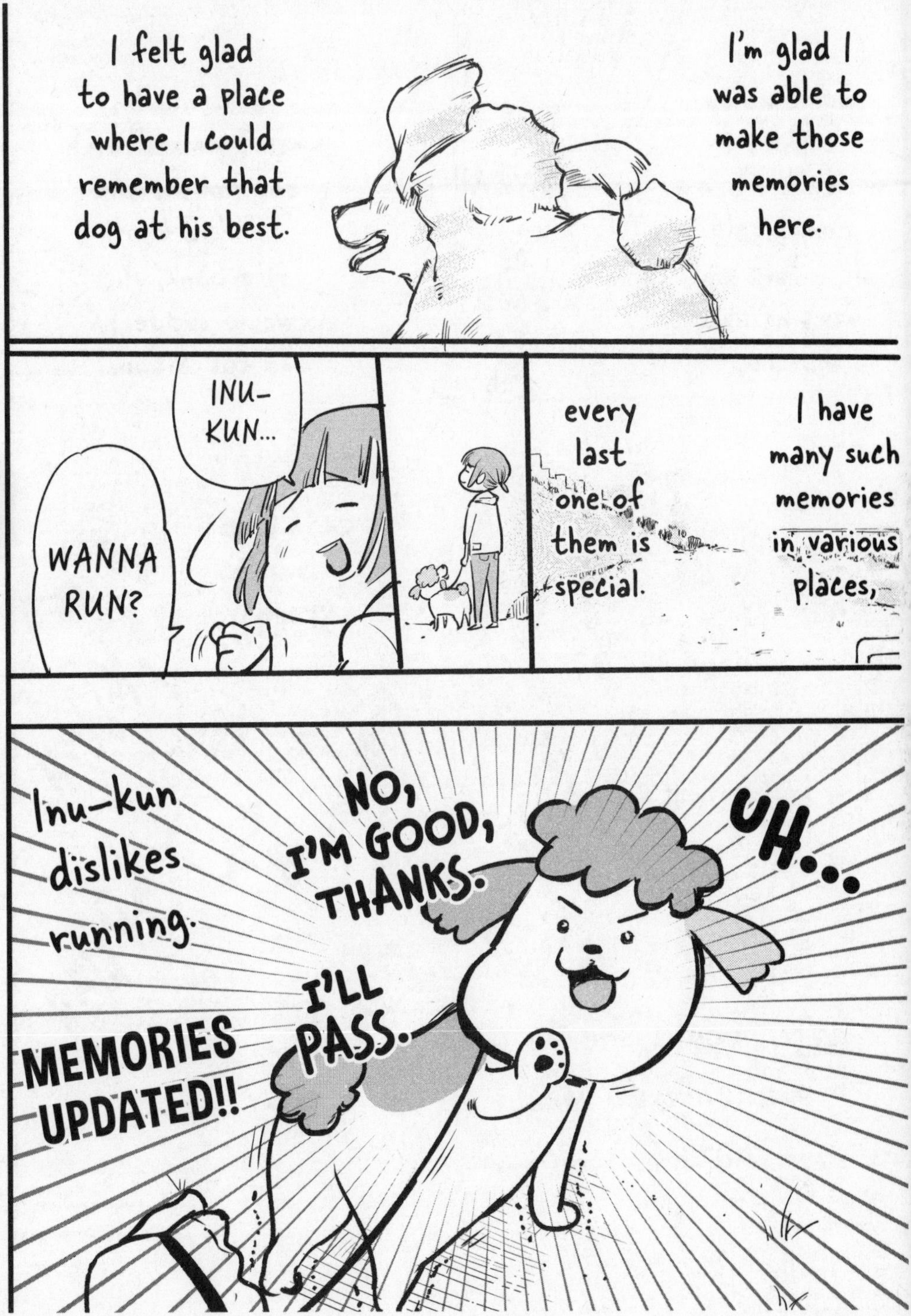
I'm glad I was able to make those memories here.
I felt glad to have a place where I could remember that dog at his best.
I have many such memories in various places,
every last one of them is special.
INU-KUN...
WANNA RUN?
UH...
NO, I'M GOOD, THANKS.
Inu-kun dislikes running.
I'LL PASS.
MEMORIES UPDATED!!

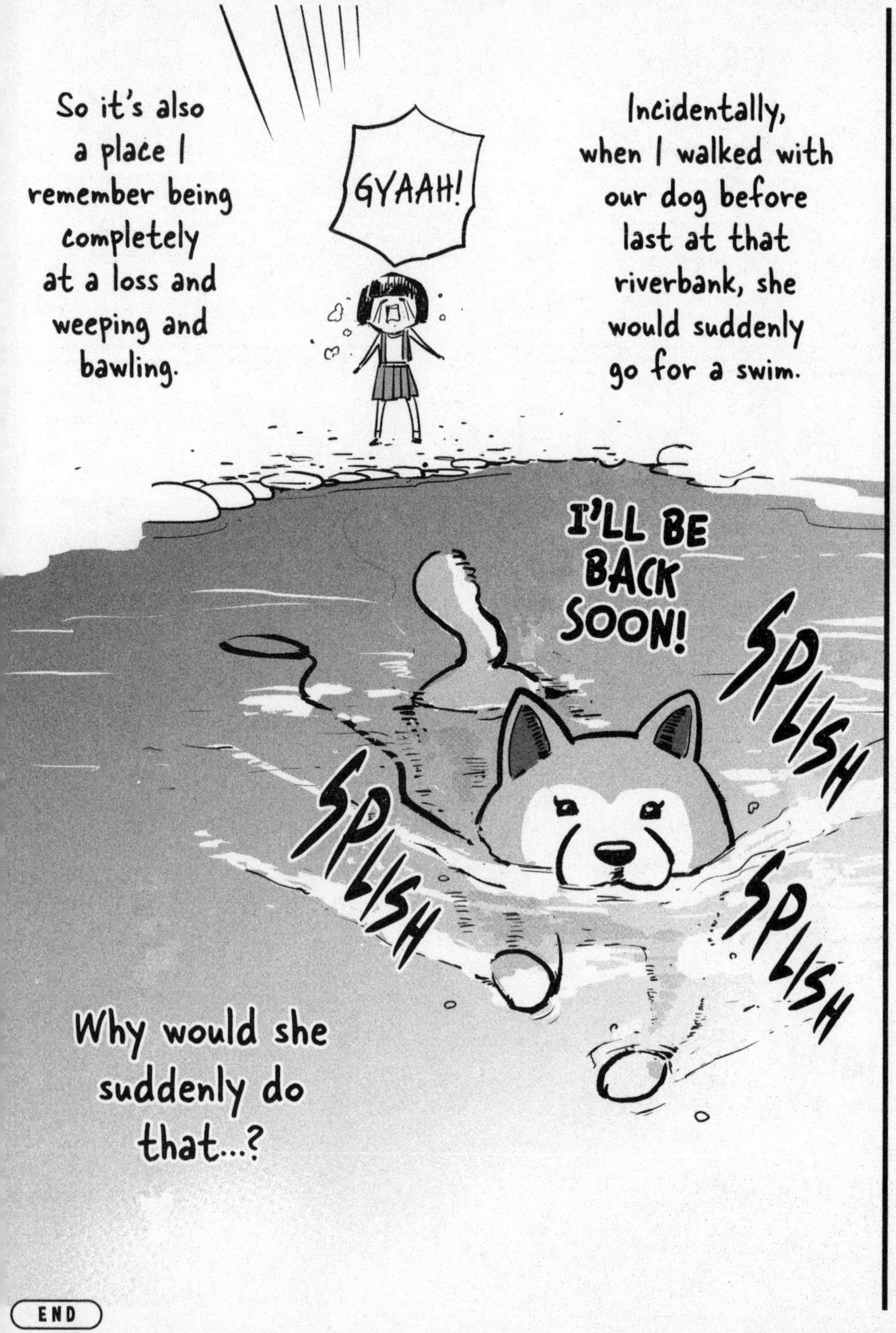
Incidentally, when I walked with our dog before last at that riverbank, she would suddenly go for a swim.
So it's also a place I remember being completely at a loss and weeping and bawling.
GYAAH!
I'LL BE BACK SOON!
SPLISH
SPLISH
SPLISH
SPLISH
Why would she suddenly do that...?
END

Afterword

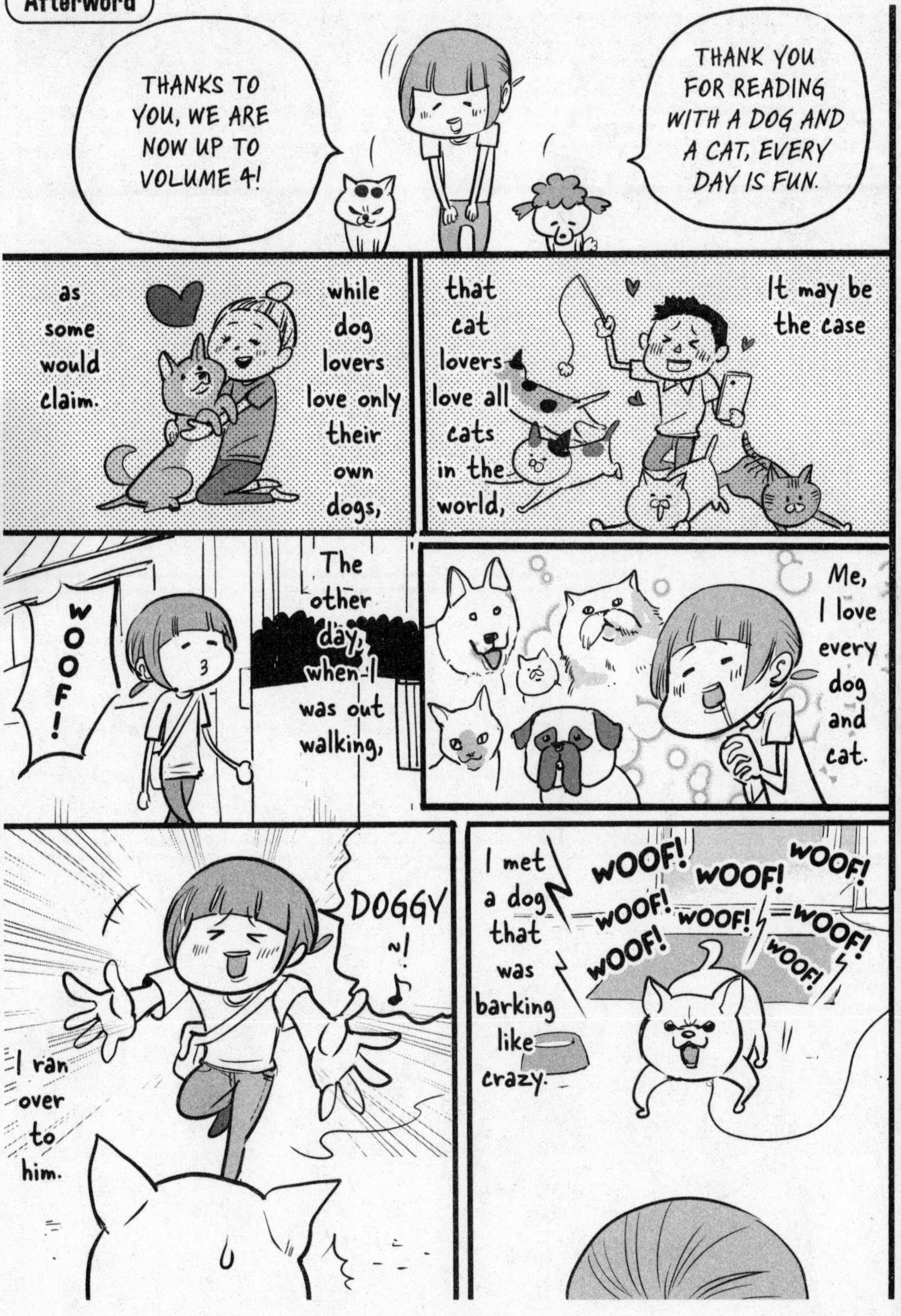
THANK YOU FOR READING WITH A DOG AND A CAT, EVERY DAY IS FUN.
THANKS TO YOU, WE ARE NOW UP TO VOLUME 4!
It may be the case
that cat lovers love all cats in the world,
while dog lovers love only their own dogs,
as some would claim.
Me, I love every dog and cat.
The other day, when I was out walking,
WOOF!
I met a dog that was barking like crazy.
WOOF! WOOF! WOOF! WOOF! WOOF! WOOF! WOOF! WOOF!
DOGGY~!
I ran over to him.

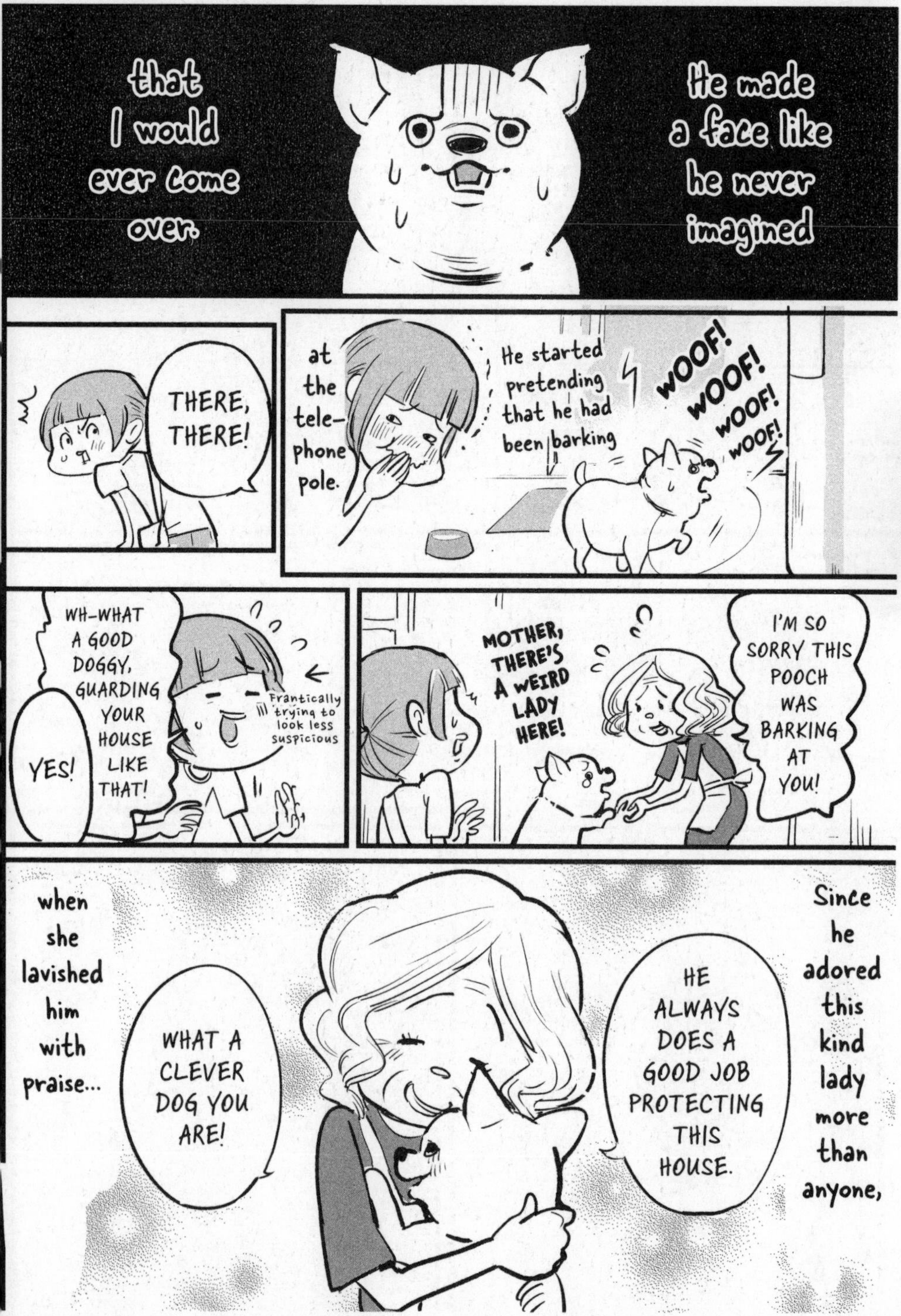
He made a face like he never imagined
that I would ever come over.
WOOF! WOOF! WOOF! WOOF!
He started pretending that he had been barking
at the tele-phone pole.
THERE, THERE!
I'M SO SORRY THIS POOCH WAS BARKING AT YOU!
MOTHER, THERE'S A WEIRD LADY HERE!
WH-WHAT A GOOD DOGGY, GUARDING YOUR HOUSE LIKE THAT!
Frantically trying to look less suspicious
YES!
Since he adored this kind lady more than anyone,
HE ALWAYS DOES A GOOD JOB PROTECTING THIS HOUSE.
WHAT A CLEVER DOG YOU ARE!
when she lavished him with praise...

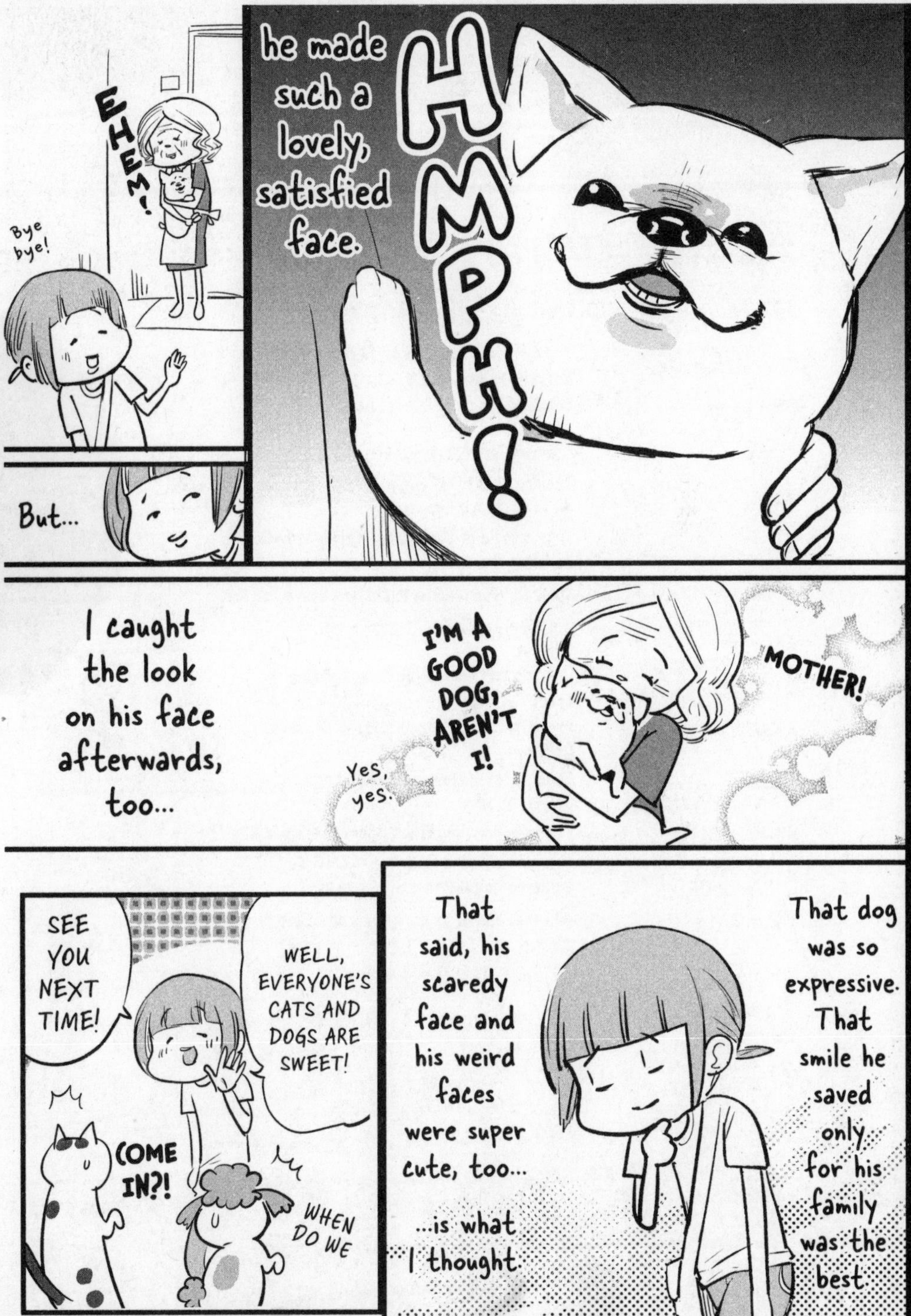
he made such a lovely, satisfied face.
HMPH!
EHEM!
Bye bye!
But...
MOTHER!
I'M A GOOD DOG, AREN'T I!
Yes, yes.
I caught the look on his face afterwards, too...
That dog was so expressive. That smile he saved only for his family was the best.
That said, his scaredy face and his weird faces were super cute, too...
...is what I thought.
WELL, EVERYONE'S CATS AND DOGS ARE SWEET!
SEE YOU NEXT TIME!
WHEN DO WE
COME IN?!

To be continued in Volume 5

IS BEING SERIALIZED ON TWITTER! Information

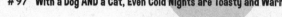

BDOOM

VOLUME 4 EPISODE TITLES WHEN SERIALIZED ON TWITTER

#97 With a Dog AND a Cat, Even Cold Nights are Toasty and Warm

#98 〃 You Suddenly Realize How Mature They Have Become or Not, So Every Day is Fun

#99 〃 Ear Cleaning is Intensely Fun

#100 〃 Training Them Makes Every Day Fun

#101 〃 They're Cute Whether You Praise Them or Scold Them, So Every Day is Fun

#102 〃 Trying to Be of Service to Them is Chaotic, So Every Day is Fun

#103 〃 Their Sudden Chattering Makes Every Day Fun

#104 〃 Anticipating Things Makes Every Day Fun

#105 〃 Lending and Borrowing Things Makes Every Day Fun

#106 〃 Even When You're Denied, It's Still Fun Of Course

#107 〃 Their Toilet Maturity Level Makes Every Day Fun

#108 〃 Their Desperation When Guests Arrive is Also Fun

#109 〃 There Are Places They Don't Like, So Every Day is Fun

#110 〃 Whether You're an Early Bird or a Late Riser, It's Fun

#111 〃 A Single Gate is This Much Fun

AND HE HASN'T STOLE IT!!!

WHO NEEDS THIS?
THWAK
THWAK
THWAK

ME, TOO!

SUNDAY ☆ (AND TRYING NOT TO TAKE ANY WEEKS OFF!)

"WITH A DOG AND A CAT, EVERY DAY IS FUN"

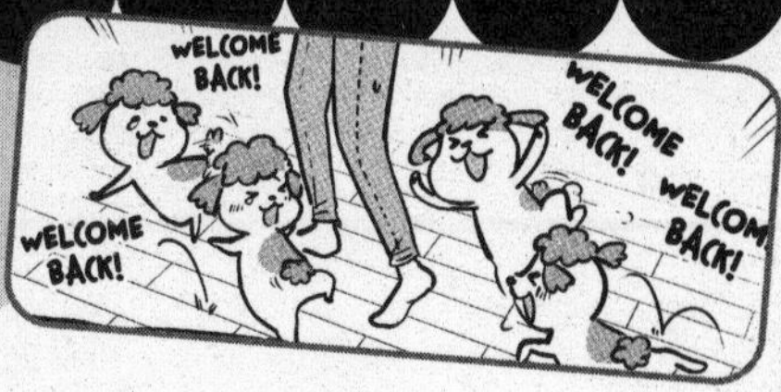
WELCOME BACK!
WELCOME BACK!
WELCOM BACK!
WELCOME BACK!

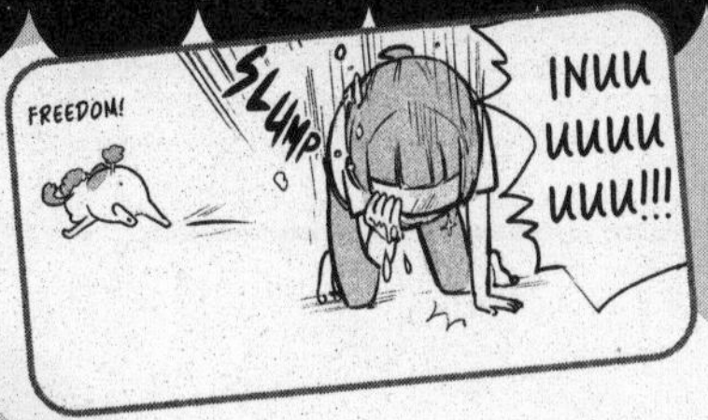
FREEDOM!
SLUMP
INUU UUUU UUU!!!

#112 〃 Pointless Discoveries Make Every Day Fun

#113 〃 Coming Back From a Trip is Very Fun

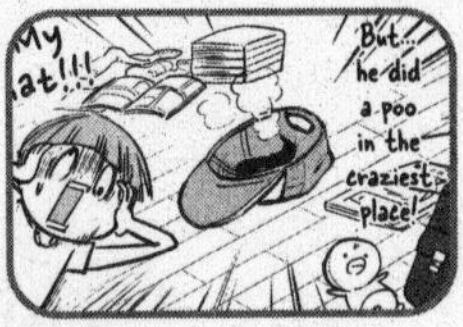
My
at!!!
But... he did a poo in the craziest place!

#114 〃 Their Occasional Combo Moves are Fun

#115 〃 The Way They Each Look at Their Failures Makes Every Day Fun

#116 〃 It's Fun When They Say "Welcome Home" Every Time

#117 Thinking that "Welcome Home" Might Start Way Earlier Makes Every Day Happy

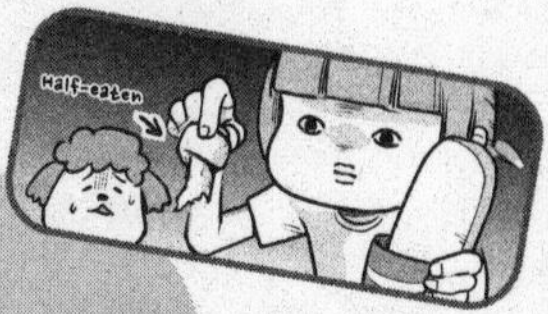
Half-eaten

#118 〃 Their Level of Trust in Their Owner Makes Every Day Fun

#119 〃 Making Them Stylish Makes Every Day Fun

#120 〃 The Way They Quietly and Stealthily Hide Things Makes Every Day Fun

#121 〃 Being Able to Play with New Toys Makes Every Day Fun

#122 〃 You Can See the Same Scenery in a Slightly Different Way, So Every Day is Fun

#123 〃 Mornings Off are Leisurely and Fun

#124 〃 Petting Them is Different, So Every Day is Fun

#125 〃 Brushing Them Makes Every Day Fun

#126 〃 The Form of Their Trust is So Different, It Makes Every Day Fun

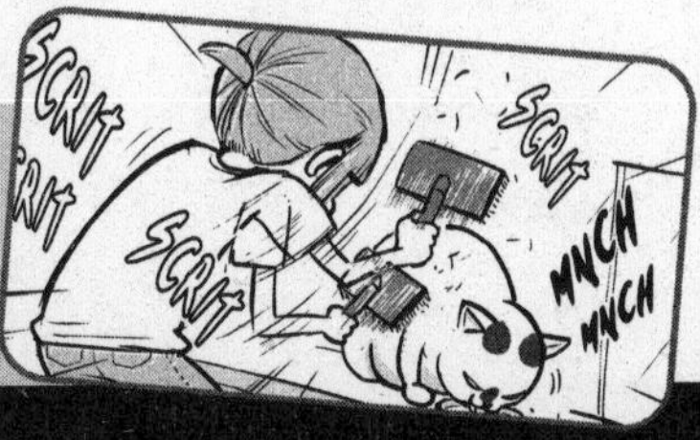
SCRIT
SCRIT
SCRIT
SCRIT
MNCH MNCH

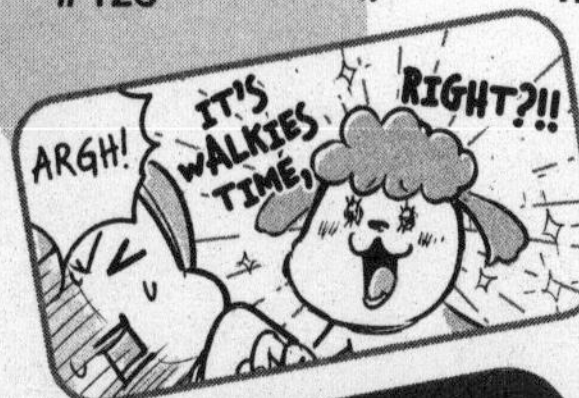
ARGH!
IT'S WALKIES TIME,
RIGHT?!!

Twitter @hidekiccan

APPEARING EVERY

With a Dog AND a Cat, Every Day is Fun 4

A Vertical Comics Edition

Translation: Kumar Sivasubramanian
Production: Risa Cho
Eve Grandt
Alexandra Swanson (SKY Japan Inc.)

© 2019 Hidekichi Matsumoto. All rights reserved.
First published in Japan in 2019 by Kodansha, Ltd., Tokyo
Publication rights for this English edition arranged through Kodansha, Ltd., Tokyo
English language version produced by Vertical Comics, an imprint of Kodansha USA Publishing, LLC

Translation provided by Vertical Comics, 2021
Published by Kodansha USA Publishing, LLC, New York

Originally published in Japanese as *Inu to Neko Docchimo Katteru to Mainichi Tanoshii 4* by Kodansha, Ltd., 2019

This is a work of fiction.

ISBN: 978-1-64729-043-6

Manufactured in the United States of America

First Edition

Kodansha USA Publishing, LLC
451 Park Avenue South
7th Floor
New York, NY 10016
www.kodansha.us

Vertical books are distributed through Penguin-Random House Publisher Services.

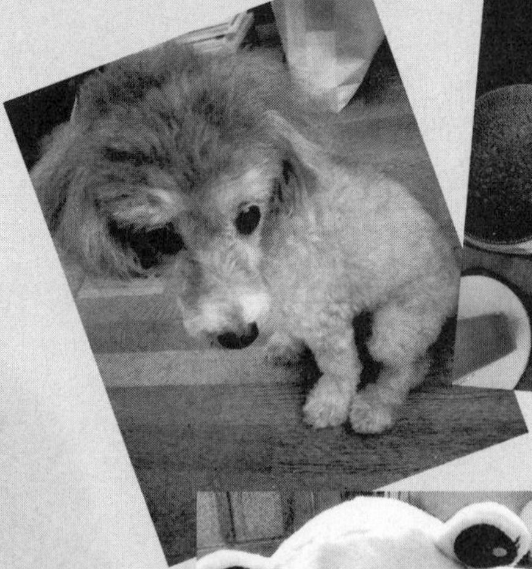
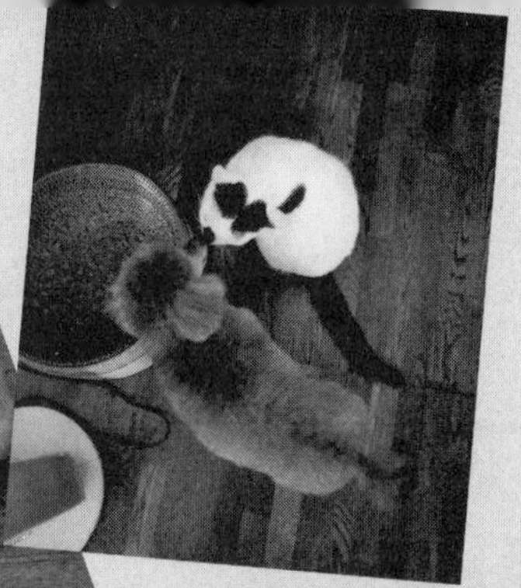
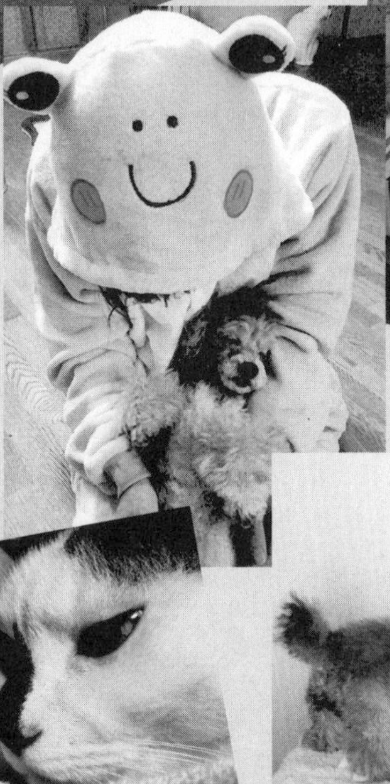
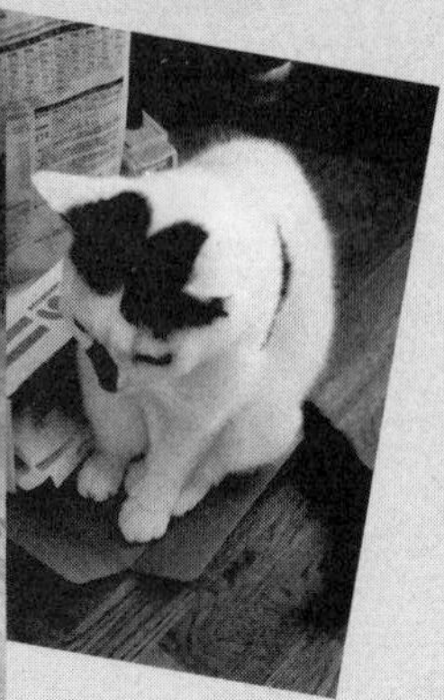
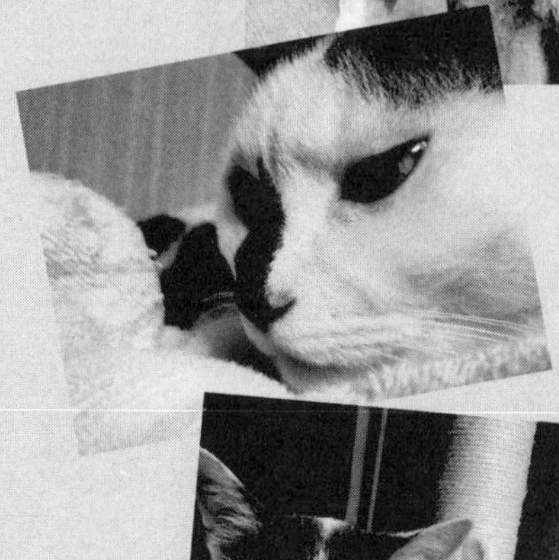
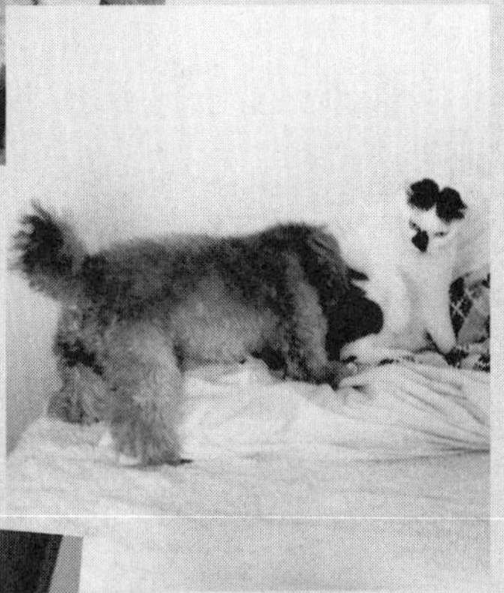
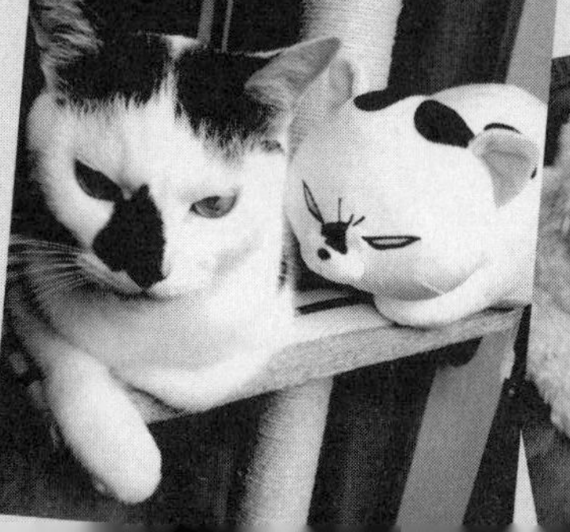
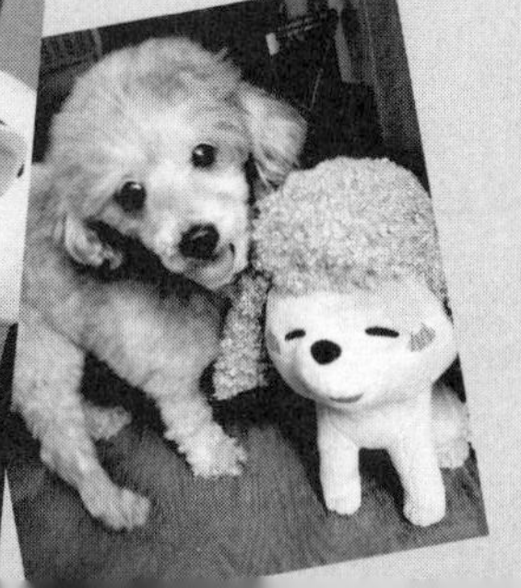

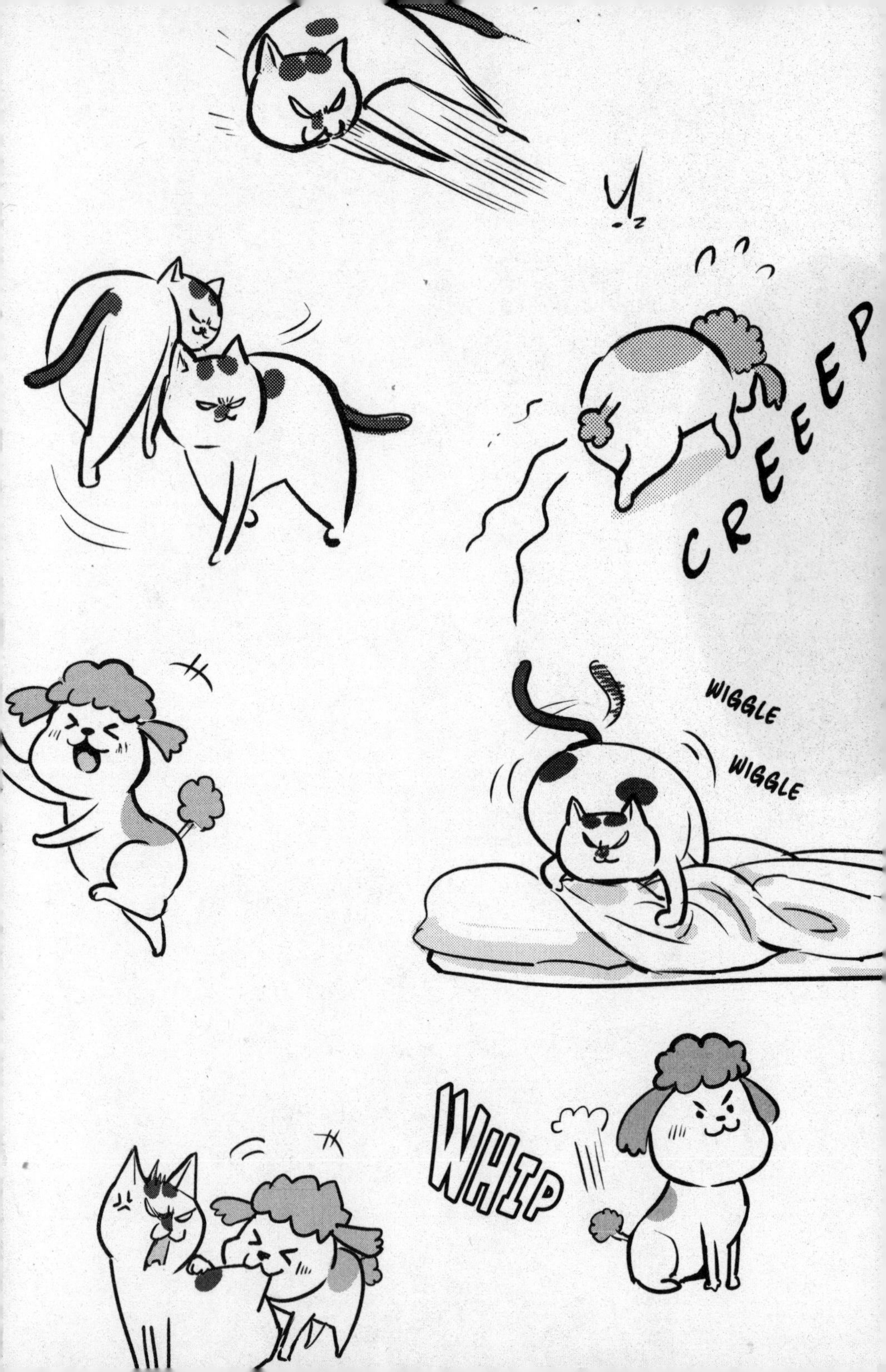
CREEEP
WIGGLE
WIGGLE
WHIP